S0-CFC-623

"If you're not interested in increasing sales, stay away from this book! Ron Finklestein has gathered numerous experts to share their marketing secrets for success. If you're looking for secrets (that actually WORK!!!), pick up 49 Marketing Secrets and be prepared to blow the doors off last year's numbers."

— Phil Gerbyshak, Relationship Geek and author of 10 Ways to Make It Great!

"As a company that is in the midst of a branding and marketing effort, Ron's book really made me take a hard look to make sure we were spending the money and time in all the right places. 49 Marketing Secrets is a great resource for any individual or company that is ready to hit the ground running and start seeing a positive return on their efforts."

— Rick Turner, Executive Director, The Forum Conference Center

You'll see a great ROI for the time you spend browsing "49 Marketing Secrets" and taking action on just a small portion of the information inside. Ron Finklestein masterfully assembled a treasure trove of techniques and strategies from a variety of savvy, seasoned, veteran consultants, lecturers, and practitioners... all of whom are in-the-trenches entrepreneurs. The contributors have distilled some of their best marketing ideas into bite-sized bundles of wisdom that -- when applied -- will work to grow sales and increase revenue…if you're interested in growing your sales, get this book. Read it. Pick and choose one, two or three ideas. Put them into action at your organization. You'll get results!

— Eric R. Voth, investor, author, entrepreneur

WARNING: 49 Secrets contains dozens of incredibly addictive and valuable Knowledge Nuggets for the Business Brain. Investing even ten minutes a day reading one or more of these nuggets will improve your potential for success. Be careful though: You may discover strategies for SUCCESS that will carry you far beyond those of your non-reading competitors.

— Alan L. Plastow, MAT, PMP, Author, Modern Pirates: The only resource for protecting your company from the software police & copyright cops. Founder, The Business Technology Consumer Network http://BizTechNet.org

I read many business, marketing, sales and leadership books, and most of them fall into one of three categories: 1) strategic (high level and/or planning focus); 2) tactical (in the trenches "how tos"); or 3) approach (different ways of thinking or approaching business topics). I was surprised and pleased to find that 49 Marketing Secrets (that work) to Grow Sales is the first book that I've ever read that addresses all three areas - planning, how tos and different approaches. 49 Marketing Secrets is a valuable mix of new ideas, new approaches and action steps that will help anyone grow and improve their business. Each hard hitting chapter is loaded with marketing and sales "secrets" that work, and I found myself taking lots of notes of ideas that I will implement to grow my business. Finally, a book that delivers what every business owner wants - ideas that work and that they can easily implement. Bottom Line - 49 Marketing Secrets will grow and improve your business . . . all you need to do is "listen," learn and take action. The results will be immediate and powerful!

— Jeff Nischwitz, Director of Member Opportunities, NEO\SO, author of Think Again! Innovative Approaches to the Business of Law, and a regular speaker and trainer on sales, business development, marketing, leadership and team building topics.

49
Marketing Secrets
(THAT WORK)
to Grow Sales

by
Ron Finklestein
© 2007. All Rights Reserved.

New York

49 Marketing Secrets (THAT WORK) to Grow Sales

by Ron Finklestein

© 2007. All Rights Reserved.

ISBN: 978-1-60037-248-3

Published by:

MORGAN · JAMES
THE ENTREPRENEURIAL PUBLISHER ™
www.morganjamespublishing.com

Morgan James Publishing, LLC
1225 Franklin Avenue, Suite 325
Garden City, New York 11530-1693
Toll Free 800-485-4943
www.MorganJamesPublishing.com

Cover Design by:
Daniel Stark

Interior Design by:
Rick Shaffer
rshaffer@shafferdesign.com

Habitat for Humanity®
Peninsula
Building Partner

AKRIS ™
LLC
Business Technology. Business Success.

Dedication

As always, I must thank my wife Sheila for her patience, love, and support. As a small business owner, my income is directly tied to how well I market my company and myself. At times I am more effective than others. Her support has been instrumental in my success.

I also dedicate this book to every small business owner. Life in the corporate world has changed so much, and many people have chosen business ownership as an alternative to corporate employment. I believe that there is an inherent need in all of us to create. Individuals who start a business are unique, and should be honored and praised for their courage, work ethic, and risk-taking tolerance. This book is for you. I honor and respect you for taking action.

Acknowledgements

Any project of this magnitude requires a team who sees what can be accomplished by a project of this nature. I would like to thank all the people who contributed to this book. Many I did not know when I started this project, but I now consider them friends.

To Dr. Tony Alessandra, Paige Stover Hague, Esq., Pete Johnson, David Garfinkel, and the others who provided me with guidance and direction.

To all the contributors to this anthology who freely shared their time, knowledge, and experience to help others grow their business. For many of you it was very difficult to document what works for you, not because you did not want to, but because you have been doing it for so long it became second nature to you and it required you to stop and think about it. It is a difficult process and I thank you for doing it.

To David Hancock, who provided me with my "Celebrating Success" publishing imprint that allowed this book to be published.

Thank you to the Ictus Initiative team: Elizabeth Nollner, Carolyn McKibbin, Cameron Van der Veer, Catherine Pappas, Amanda Scoville, and Elizabeth Hague, who did the book's editing. It is difficult to blend many different contributors into a book that provides a solid roadmap for those reading it.

To Rick Shaffer from Shaffer Design Works for formatting this book.

To Daniel Stark for the creation of the book cover.

Thank You!

Endorsements

"Wow. A wealth of info that only a fool would ignore."

— Robert Schepens, Champion Staffing

"49 Marketing Secrets makes what you learn in standard marketing textbooks look like child's play. Why would so many self-made millionaires give away their best marketing tactics? The best I can figure is they had an axe to grind and wanted to set some records straight. Whatever the reason, I am a better man for their teachings. These tactics really work."

— Ben Mack, #1 Amazon Best-Selling Author, Think Two Products Ahead

"Success in business requires a strong vision, a positive attitude and knowing what to do and when to do it. I'm astonished by how many answers this book has to the questions business owners ask all the time. Strong marketing paves the way to lasting success, and you'll find what you need in '49 Marketing Secrets' to get wherever you want to go."

— Joe Vitale, author "The Attractor Factor" and "Zero Limits"

"The heavy hitters, the shining stars, the bright lights — they're all here for you in this brilliant and enlightening book. It should be mandatory reading for anyone who loves marketing and profits."

— Jay Conrad Levinson, The Father of Guerrilla Marketing
Author, "Guerrilla Marketing" series of books
Over 14 million sold; now in 43 languages

When I read a business book, I look for a book that is practical, packed with examples, and easy to comprehend. I don't have time for anything less. In 49 Marketing Secrets (that work) to Grow Sales, Finklestein and the contributors present specific, actionable guidance based on real experience. The issues cover everything from modularized strategic planning to leveraging radio talk shows to grow your business. Best of all, the writing is conversational, such that the reader feels like s/he is actually speaking with the authors. The book makes for a quick, but very powerful read. If you are a small business looking to grow by standing on the shoulders of giants and implementing their practical suggestions, 49 Marketing Secrets is more than worth the time you'll invest to read it.

— David J. Akers, President & CEO of the Northeast Ohio Sourcing Office

Table of Contents

Introduction

Chapter 1
Thinking to Win – Planning at 50,000 Feet   2

Chapter 2
Branding and Corporate Image 64

Chapter 3
Media Strategies 114

Introduction

This book was written specifically for the small business owner. I define the small business owner as the entrepreneur who runs his own business (or plans to start one) up through the owner who runs a more established business of less than $50 million in revenue.

As a small business coach, consultant, and small business success expert, who has worked with hundreds of businesses, I kept seeing the same problems surfacing from the companies that engaged me to help them. As I peeled back the layers of each problem, I found that many of them could be solved if we could increase their sales. This was a problem because many small business owners did not know how to create measurable, repeatable, and predictable processes that would keep the sales pipeline full with qualified prospects. Much of the work I did was to bring the best practices from other companies to my existing clients. This was interesting, because each of the companies I worked with did some things right, but they did not know what that right thing was. They were too close and did not see the opportunity clearly.

In creating this book I wanted to provide small business owners with a safe and inexpensive way to learn about marketing from other business owners who have been there, done that. This experience is what makes this book different. Each chapter was written by a successful marketing expert, business owner, or consultant who used a specific technique to grow his or her own business and clients' businesses. These individuals freely shared their knowledge with the specific intent to help you grow your business. Since each of the contributors are small business owners who understand how challenging it can be to make the hard decisions, they also understand how difficult it can be to find qualified marketing experts that can be trusted to help grow a business.

I subscribe to Dan Kennedy's philosophy that the small business owner should not delegate out the responsibility for marketing, because it is the lifeblood of every business. If it is to be done well, the business owner must be actively involved.

That is why I included contact information for the contributors. As a business owner, if you find something that works for you and you want to learn more, you can contact the individual who wrote the article.

The book is structured to help you understand the entire process from why a marketing strategy is important to how to create a strategy to the tactics necessary to implement a successful marketing plan, and how to hold yourself accountable for the implementation of the plan.

One of the most important things you should do as you read the book is to create a marketing strategy. Don't wait until you have completely finished reading to begin building a strategy, nor to begin executing it, even though you may be afraid of making a mistake. Marketing is about testing and finding out what works. Then, select a few tactics from the options in the book that you think will work for you. Begin implementing each tactic one by one so you can measure the results. Remember that marketing is forever changing and requires that you document the results of each test. When you find what works for you, continue performing the same activities until the tactic ceases to be effective. Try to implement at least three marketing actions that you will do regularly so that when one loses effectiveness you will have other actions that continue to work. We made it easy for you to implement the ideas in this book by including action steps in some chapters to help you customize individual marketing tactics to your specific situation. The only thing that's left is for you to do is to take ownership and implement the ideas in this book.

To your success,

Ron Finklestein
The Small Business Success Expert
AKRIS LLC
330-990-0788
www.yourbusinesscoach.net
info@yourbusinesscoach.net

Thank you for purchasing this book. You made a good decision.

To receive your free white papers described on the front cover please go to **http://www.49marketingsecrets.com.**

There will be a register button.

Hit this button and register.

After you have registered you will be taken to the download page where you can download your free gifts.

Enjoy and may your business prosper.

Thinking to Win
By Ron Finklestein

The key to success lies in how well you create an "attitude of success." My studies have shown that there are seven behaviors that all successful people exhibit. When these behaviors are implemented in the highest levels of an organization and are combined with the correct attitude, they cascade down through the organization. Successful business owners understand that the organization they manage takes on the attitude of the top person in the organization, and they strive to ensure that their behaviors reflect this.

Selfishness

When I say successful companies are selfish, I am not referring to the childish behavior of everything is "mine, mine, mine." I am referring to a mature selfishness that allows them to make decisions based on the outcomes they want to experience.

Being selfish asks, "How do I protect my time, energy, and money so I am only spending them on those things that will take me closer to my goals?" This kind of selfishness allows you to make sure your precious resources are only being spent on activities that benefit your company. But, until you can define the types of customers you want to attract and the problems you can fix for them, it is very hard to be selfish.

Focus

It is very hard for a company to be focused if you don't know where you are going. The dictionary defines focus as "close or narrow attention; concentration." Without a clear perspective, you cannot focus on the desired outcome. It is too easy to become distracted, unorganized, and inconsistent. When you understand what it is you are to be selfish about, you generate a clear focus—a sense of purpose.

Discipline

Discipline is controlled behavior resulting from training and self-control. Your mind is made up. You have decided to achieve your marketing goals. Being disciplined means you will not abandon your goals. Discipline has taught you that business life is not smooth and that there will be rough spots. Experience has taught you that by being disciplined, you can get through the tough spots. Your eye is on the target, and you have the discipline of a laser-guided missile; you seek out your objectives, and your focus never falters.

Persistence

Webster's Dictionary defines "persistence" as the continuance of an effect after the cause is removed. Once you take the time to create a marketing strategy and implement a marketing plan, your goals will be clear. And when you are focused, disciplined, and selfish, your persistence allows you to see any unplanned obstacles not as problems, but as opportunities. After all, if it was easy, anyone could accomplish what you are accomplishing. But not everyone is on the field of battle with you. They see obstacles and stop. You see obstacles and see opportunities.

You keep your eyes clearly fixed on your objectives; you try different things to overcome these obstacles. You know where you are going; you know you can't be stopped. You know that your persistence is what drives you forward. You will find a way around any obstacle, and keep right on going.

Ownership

Ownership is the state of being an owner. It is taking the legal right to the possession of a thing. Not only tangible things, but also your dreams, your goals, your business, and your life; if you do not take ownership for achieving your dreams, who will? As Jesse Livermore said, "There are only two emotions in the market—hope and fear. The problem is you hope when you should fear, and you fear when you should hope."

But not you. Your fear is motivation to move you forward because you learned that when you take action, you get results. You always hope for the best and plan for the worst. You are ready for what life throws at you. You have to be. Taking ownership is about change—making change to move forward, changing behaviors that are not working, and dealing with the world as it is and not as you want it to be.

You own the outcome because you are clear about where you want to go, and you take ownership for it. With ownership, you know that if you are not getting your desired results, you can take action and change the outcome. Ownership is so very empowering. You know that if you do not have the skills, you can learn or hire someone to teach you.

Orientation toward Results

Results mean ending in a particular way. Once you define your goals—the outcomes you want to achieve¬—and how you want things to end, you can take ownership to create your desired outcomes. You can create the results.

When you don't get the results you want, you fall back on persistence, ownership, focus, and discipline, and know that you have the skills, the drive, the desire, the knowledge, and the road map that will take you where you want to go. Results are simply a way of measuring your success. You either get the job done, or you don't. If you don't, because of your ownership, you go back and try something different. No excuses. No remorse. Only results. You understand, as Yoda once said, that "there is no trying; only doing."

Focus on People

All successful people understand that their success comes with, and through, other people. Successful people recognize these individuals and appreciate them for their contribution to the results. They will also assume complete responsibility for things not working. They must because there is no other course of action when you are the owner and take ownership.

You will learn how to implement these behaviors in the next section. So take out your pencil and begin creating and developing your strategy, and changing you life.

Everything in this book is important, but to make the most of all the information contained within, you need to understand where you want to go and how you will get there. Then and only then can you implement the tools and techniques described in the later sections.

Planning for Growth:
The 3 Ways to Grow Your Business
By Damian Petrini

Ask any business owner, executive, or entrepreneur how many ways there are to grow a business, and most of them will tell you that there are dozens, hundreds, or even thousands of ways.

You may be relieved to know that there are only three ways to grow any business, in any industry, with any product or service. Those three ways are to increase the number of new clients, to get them to buy more, and to get them to buy more often.

I first learned this concept from master marketer, Jay Abraham, a concept which Jay refers to as the "Three ways to grow a business model." The beauty of this concept is that it can be applied to any business, in any industry, offering any type of product or service.

Increasing the Number of New Clients

The one area that every business spends time on is increasing the number of new clients that can use their products and services. The downside of this method is that of the three ways to grow a business, this is the most expensive, the least profitable, and the most time-consuming.

The more ways you can make available for prospective and current clients to do business with you, the more likely people will buy your products or services.

You can use websites to capture prospective client information, build email distribution lists, and encourage people to make contact with your company to learn more about your product or service. All of these will allow you to build up your client base.

Here are a few things that you can do to your business to get more clients:
• Create systematized referral programs.

- Build a network of strategic alliances and joint ventures to create joint marketing efforts and share the client acquisition cost.

- Implement a search engine optimization (SEO) and a search engine marketing (SEM) strategy to leverage the power of the Internet.

- Offer special first-time buyer discounts and incentives, and offer people additional bonuses when they make their first purchase.

- Identify what types of companies exist that are already marketing to your ideal prospect and offer to do a revenue share with those companies for any of their clients that purchase from you.

- Offer free samples, trial memberships, and money-back guarantees.

- Offer free informational reports on what to look for when buying your product or service.

Increasing the Size of Each Client Transaction

Just step inside any fast food restaurant and chances are that you will hear the clerk behind the counter ask you if you would like to super-size, up-size, or jumbo-size your order at the time of purchase. The same thing applies to the Internet.

Up-Selling, Cross-Selling, and Re-Selling

Whether you are buying a hamburger from McDonald's™, ordering a latte from Starbucks™, or getting a book online from Amazon.com™, you will be presented with a chance to add more to your order.

The amazing thing about the process of up-selling, cross-selling, or re-selling is that it is not hard to do; all you need to do is ask. Try it today in your own business. Every time one of your clients makes a purchase, ask them to buy a larger quantity, add-on an additional product or service, or pre-buy in advance more of the items they just bought.

Okay…so besides asking, what else can you do to get your clients to buy more? Bribe them! Offer them incentives that reward them for making a larger purchase, adding on additional products or services, or signing up for future purchases in advance.

The best time to ask someone to buy something is immediately after they make a commitment to a purchase.

Here are a few things that you can do to your business to get your clients to buy more:

- Make a list of products and services that people buy before, during, or after purchasing your product or service and contact them about offering their products and services to your client base.

- Create a list of every product and service that your business offers and then make a matrix of all of the possible cross-selling opportunities that can be offered with every purchase.

- Bundle products and services into packages.

- Offer bonuses when customers purchase larger quantities.

- Create pre-paid packages.

- Offer tiered-level service or warranty packages (e.g., gold, silver, bronze, etc...)

Increasing the Frequency of Each Client Transaction

The third way to grow your business is to increase the frequency of purchase transactions by getting your clients to buy more often. For example, if your clients typically buy from you once every six months, how can you get them to buy four times a year, or once a month?

The answer? Simply give them more reasons as to why they should. Offer incentives that encourage your clients to come back to your store or contact your business on a more frequent basis. Look at the success of frequent buyer programs that reward people for making additional purchases.

Here are a few things that you can do to get your clients to buy more often:

- Set up frequent buyer or reward programs for your clients.

- Offer bonuses when they make purchases on a regular basis.

- Create monthly membership programs.

- Make sure that you make offers to your clients on a consistent and regular basis.

The Power of Exponential Growth

If using one of the three methods to grow your business can increase the profits of your business, imagine what kind of explosive growth you could achieve if you worked on improving all three areas simultaneously!

Imagine that you have 1,000 clients, spending on average of $50 two times a year. That's $100,000 in revenue. If you increased just a 10 percent in all three areas, that would turn into 1,100 clients, spending on average of $55, 2.2 times a year—which makes $133,100 in revenue.

Do you see the power of exponential growth? Instead of a 10% increase in revenue, you end up with over a 33% increase in revenue!

Once you start to spend time proactively focusing on and implementing strategies that increase the number of new clients that use your products or services, get them to buy more, and get them to buy more often, you will be amazed at the amount of profits that your business can make and how quickly your business will grow.

The most important thing to remember about these methods is that they will never do you or your business any good at all if you never take any action to proactively implement as many items as you can in each area of business growth.

Action Items

1. Be Proactive: Spend a few days making a list of all of the possible ways that you might be able to use to increase your number of new clients, increase the size of each client transaction, and how you could increase the frequency of transactions.

2. Add More Value: Focus on how you can add more and more value to each of your product and service offerings to your clients and prospects.

3. Up-Sell and Cross-Sell Opportunities: Identify other products and services that you can bundle with, add, or offer to every single person that does business with you. Always ask everyone to buy more and by more often, and let the law of numbers work in your favor. If only three of every ten people said yes to an up-sell or cross-sell opportunity, how much more revenue and profits could your business gain?

4. Create a Systematized Referral Program: If you don't already have a systematized referral program in place in your business, invest the time to create and outline a process that you can use to consistently request referrals from your clients, prospective, vendors, business associates, joint ventures, or anyone else that might be able to refer people to your company.

5. Calculate the Life Time Value of Your Clients: Invest some time to calculate what the lifetime value of your clients is, so you know exactly how much money you can afford to invest in acquiring new clients.

6. Test and Measure: Always test and measure every aspect of your marketing and business growth efforts. Only through testing and measuring will you truly be able to know what is working well and thus should do more of, and what is not working you should do less of.

7. Think Geometrically: Don't let a day, week, month, or year go by without proactively focusing on increasing each of the three areas of growing your business. Challenge yourself to see how many more strategies, tactics, and methods that you can consistently add to your marketing and business growth efforts.

Damian Petrini is Director of Marketing for Tornado Technologies, Inc., a full service software and technology development company, based in

Cleveland, Ohio. This company specializes in developing custom software applications that allow businesses of all sizes to streamline, optimize, and maximize their business processes through the use of customized software solutions. Petrini may be contacted via email at dpetrini@tornadosoft.com; for more information, please visit http://www.tornadosoft.com.

Chapter 1

Strategic Planning
One Piece of Paper, Two Sides, Three Principles – You're Done!
By Dr. Pete Johnson

Many years ago there was a king who had a very small kingdom in a land very far away. As kings go, he was unusual—he was so very proud of his kingdom that he felt an obligation to his people to do everything in his power to continually make this kingdom a better place in which to live. And for this the people of his kingdom had tremendous respect for their king. As the king grew old, he felt the weight of the critical decision of naming a successor to his throne. Rather than automatically choosing his eldest son as successor, the king saw potential in each of his three sons, each one a year apart in age from the other and equally educated and trained by the best possible scholars and teachers his kingdom could provide.

The day finally came when he felt he could postpone his decision no longer. He summoned all three of his sons to walk with him to a large field at the end of the forest within eyesight of their castle. With them, the king took a bow, three arrows, and a brightly colored stuffed parrot. Positioning the stuffed parrot on the branch of a tree at the very edge of the forest he called his eldest son over to him, handed him the bow and one of the arrows, and faced him in the direction of the parrot. To his eldest son he then said, "Son, before you do anything, please tell me everything you see."

The eldest son replied, "Father, I see a brightly colored stuffed parrot perched on the limb of a large tree at the end of the forest. Between our position and the forest there is a field with low grass and a few rocks. The forest is very green with lots of leaves but I can see the parrot very clearly."

The king thanked his son, took the bow and arrow back from him, and asked him to go and stand with his two brothers. He then summoned the next oldest son, handed him the bow and an arrow, and faced him in the direction of the stuffed parrot. Again he said, "Son, before you do anything, please tell me everything you see."

The second eldest son replied, "Father, I see a red, green, and yellow stuffed parrot perched on the limb of a tree about four feet off the ground at the edge of the forest. I can see off to the left our castle in the distance. It is a very clear day and the sun is very bright."

Again the king thanked his son, took the bow and arrow back from him, and asked him to go and stand with his two brothers. He then summoned the youngest of his sons and repeated the process.

The youngest son replied to the king, "Father, I see a very brightly colored stuffed parrot."

The king again said, "Son, is that everything you see?"

The youngest son replied, "Father, I see a brightly colored stuffed parrot, I see only a brightly colored stuffed parrot, I see nothing but a brightly colored stuffed parrot."

The king then replied to his successor of the throne, "My son—shoot the parrot."

We, as busy business professionals, can very easily find ourselves in situations when it becomes almost impossible to maintain our focus regardless of how much we recognize the critical importance of Focus and Intensity. The purpose of the following article is to help you not only maintain your focus on the goals and objectives you have in business, in your career, and in your life...but to show you a way to help create the motivation to press on even when things may seem to be unraveling all around you. It truly all comes down to Focus and Intensity and how you apply it.

Strategy and Planning

There is probably not a success-driven professional in the business world today that does not recognize the proven value and importance of planning and preparation. Perhaps even more important, some business professionals have learned to elevate their planning efforts to an even more sophisticated level... that of strategy in action. However, while the idea of strategy is currently enjoying a resurgence of popularity in the business world, the concept itself is not new, but rather has been around for several thousand years. Perhaps one of the first known published works on the subject of strategy dates back to about 500 years BC, when in the land now known as China a highly accomplished warrior named Sun Tzu published his concepts and guidelines for conducting war under the title The Art of War. This one book has become one of the single most quoted books of the past several decades. Its direct application to marketing and business makes it well worth reviewing as we consider what it takes to achieve and maintain a serious "Competitive Advantage" in the marketing arena today.

A successful strategy—be it marketing, sales, or business—tends to follow several key principles.

Principle #1: A strategy should be Simple. The more complicated we make it the more difficult it may be to implement or to adapt to our ever-changing market environment.

Principle #2: A strategy should be Quick. It should not take an exhausting amount of time to develop, let alone execute. Perhaps one of the greatest improvements of strategy in the past decade is the emphasis on modularity and adaptability. Everyone can use this incredibly powerful strategy system and apply it to their own current situation regardless of whether they are company leaders, achievement-oriented sales professionals, or people who are just not satisfied with the speed that their current strategy and planning approach is providing them.

Which brings us to **Principle #3:** A strategy should be capable of producing very immediate, visible, measurable results. The watch-words here are…How Soon, How Much.

Four Phases of Strategy

Unlike the more traditional or academic approaches to strategic planning— which tend to begin with a SWOT Analysis (Strengths, Weaknesses, Opportunities, Threats) or perhaps in some instances the even more exhausting Environmental Scan—we think strategy should be done using a four-phased approach, starting with the Focus Phase.

Phase One: Focus – Although this does incorporate several of the same elements as a traditional approach, such as a mission statement or statement of purpose, it tends to avoid the frustrations of getting bogged down in some of the arduous tasks such as the wordsmithing of the perfect "Vision Statement of the Future"... unless that is of interest to its developer. As we said earlier, this should be flexible and can include or incorporate whatever its developers choose, so long as there is a strategic reason for it. The focus phase is also where measurements, goals, and objectives are defined. More on this later.

Phase Two: Analysis – Again, this differs from traditional strategic planning in that the emphasis here is concentrated on identifying all of the critical questions and information that will be essential in keeping your strategy on track versus conducting extensive research. The reason is that strategy, being a more dynamic system, tends to demonstrate that the answers to these key questions seem to keep changing. Instead, it uses the timeliness of snapshots of information to continually adapt its planning. Analysis can take on a broad spectrum of categories, including:

Current Customers
Target Markets
Key Decision-Makers
Direct Competitors
Industry Leaders
Promotional Material
Marketing Channels
Internal Issues, etc.
(Samples of this information will be made available in greater detail at the conclusion of this chapter.)

Phase Three: Planning – Taking place simultaneously with the analysis phase is the Planning Phase, which outlines or lists every critical element that can help influence your targeted success. A key point is that this should be done as though there were no limits to your financial budget and you had all of the necessary resources you could possibly need. A common error here is that we may tend to "filter" our thinking based on what we "know" we can or cannot actually afford. Of course the reality is that everyone has some limits to their resources—Money, People, Technology, Expertise, Time. But it may also be very possible to be able to beg, borrow, and steal to make up for what you lack—you never know which opportunities may present themselves later, so don't limit yourself now. This is the time for out-of-the-box thinking. We can reel ourselves back to reality on the final phase of our strategy.

Phase Four: Intensity – Phase Four is Intensity, which is the point where the mission is to execute the planning of the previous stages as precisely and rapidly as possible. This system uses a spreadsheet tracking form that helps coordinate the implementation of all follow-up actions. A copy of this format is available free of charge upon your request. There are obviously other options such as PERT Charts, Microsoft Project, GANT Charts, and a long list of other alternatives... but remember Principle #1: Simplicity!

So what does this all mean to you? If you have not yet taken the initiative to develop or write your own Personal Strategic Plan, Marketing Strategy, Sales Strategy, Business Strategy, or what ever you prefer to call it—do it now! It will, without question, become one of the most leveragable activities you may ever do. It will give you an immediate benefit of unprecedented control over the outcome of your goals and objectives than you ever thought possible. And even more importantly, there is now a method by which it can be done using only two sides of a single sheet of paper! As we keep reminding you... simple, quick, immediate results! So why not invest a couple of hours and experience the dramatic difference?

How to Form Your Personal Strategic Plan

Outline of Side-A (The Focus Phase): Name, Date, Business Name, Industry, Products/Services, Mission Statement, Top 5 Performance Measurements, Last Year's Numbers, This Year's Numbers, Next Year's Numbers, Top 5 Major Objectives (or Targeted Accomplishments), Role-Model for Each Objective, Target Date, Top 4 Key Strategies, Role-Model for Each, Key Target Date for Each, Top 3 Current Critical Issues (Problems or Challenges), Critical Dates for Each, Top 5 Immediate Strategic Priorities, Lead, Target Date, Current Status, Next Action for Each.

Again, what you are creating is a snapshot of the means to develop and proactively pursue strategic goals and objectives far more concisely than what tends to traditionally be done. One of the important keys issues is that even if you are unable to complete your plan in a timely manner it has been designed to be modular and be developed and fine-tuned as you go. Just by starting to develop your initial draft you will be putting yourself in the top 10 percent of the most highly motivated and organized people in your industry.

Keep in mind that strategy and planning, when done properly, anticipates that adjustments and changes are an essential element of life. The fact is, the concept of strategy is perhaps the only process that not only embraces change but relies on it as a competitive advantage. If it were not for the elements of challenge and change that impact everyone's planning efforts then literally everyone with minimal effort would be millionaires. It is these challenges and changes that do in fact help make us strong.

Outline of Side-B (Analysis, Planning and Intensity Phases): Top 5 Biggest Current Customers, Our Point of Contact, Their Key Contacts, Last Year's Business Volume, This Year's Business Volume, Next Year's Business Volume, Our #1 Direct Competitor for Each, Top 5 Biggest New Sales Opportunities, Our Point of Contact, Their Key Contacts, This Year's Potential Business Volume, Key Issues, Our #1 Direct Competitor for Each, Our Overall Top 3 Direct Competitors, Their Comparative Annual Business Volume, Their Strengths, Our Competitive Advantages, Key Professionals on Each of Their Teams, Our Strategic Plan Wish List (Critical Elements for Improving Our Success), Tracking Process for Our Top 5 Performance Goals, Key Lead for Each, Next Performance Review Date, Current Status, Next Critical Actions, Our Strategic Planning Team, Targeted Quarterly Performance Review Dates, Review Meeting Location and Time, Coordinator or Lead for each Quarterly Meeting.

This approach very effectively crystallizes the process of strategy and planning down to a single sheet. But as you can see we've undoubtedly focused on expanding far "outside the box" in our thinking and definition…which is precisely what every truly smart strategic thinker will always do. As you fill in the key information for each item or question feel free to modify the various items to more effectively suit your specific needs or situation. This approach can also be very effective using your computer to print the information and data on a series of 3x5 cards so that they can be carried in your shirt pocket or purse for easy review and updating. Again this is intended to be a guide and not just a template.

The Process of Progress-On-Plan: All too often we start out with tremendous intentions only to find that at the first sign of resistance our plans and goals quickly become compromised in light of urgent circumstances and changes in priorities. Yet in most cases deep down inside we realize we've just lost focus on our goals and mission. In response to this dilemma there is a mechanism that has proven invaluable in not only maintaining our focus but helping to remind us of the actual progress we are making in spite of the chaotic state we sometimes find ourselves in. The key principle here is to focus on the positive results we've been able to achieve and push ourselves to continually expand upon that which seems positive.

For this consider a Weekly Action Plan which helps you focus on listing everything you've successfully accomplished during the course of the past week. The template that is provided also focuses on identifying your Top 5 Business or Company Priorities as well as your Top 3 Personal Priorities. The last item in the template suggests that you list the best new idea you learned during the past week that will help make you smarter and become more effective than you were the week before. The issue is to focus on "progressive" learning or learning from your experiences every week. Imagine what it could mean if you invested in yourself to do this Weekly Action Plan for just four consecutive weeks. Save your past "Plans" to refer back to and demonstrate to yourself and others the measurable progress you've accomplished in just a single month. If you work for a company, think how far this might go to communicate the bottom-line value that you contribute to your job and your company.

Can you achieve and sustain success without any planning or strategy? Of course! However, if your current approach is not producing the level of success you desire, perhaps you may want to consider a very streamlined approach to strategy and planning that can make a measurable difference in as quickly as four to six weeks. The choice is yours—continue to get what you currently have or expand your possibilities. And we're here to help. Best wishes for your continued success.

Pete Johnson, or Dr. Strategy, is www.StrategicPlanning.com. He has spent the last twenty-five years researching, analyzing, and advising some of the world's top performing organizations on how to improve their bottom-line performance. As a result of this extensive ongoing research he's pioneered a unique, fluid approach to strategic planning that makes it possible for you to adapt immediately on demand to the critical issues you might encounter in competing for success in today's constantly changing global marketplace. His Strategic Planning website provides visitors with extensive strategy, planning and implementation support systems to help dramatically simplify and streamline the entire process.

Qigong for Business
5 Rules for Business Health and Success
By Jack R. Howe

The ancient Chinese "life energy practice and exercise" known as Qigong was used to enhance and benefit the health of its users, to increase the effectiveness of natural body rhythms, and clear up any blockages, be they physical or mental. But why restrict so many benefits to just our bodies? What business doesn't need help clearing up blockages and increasing the effectiveness of its systems? So use the following Qigong for Business as an exercise for increasing the success of your business by keeping it healthy. Qigong for Business involves five parts, each addressing a different aspect of businesses:

Rule #1 Everything you do counts! – Leadership

Rule #2 Exhaustive Examination of the Facts

Rule #3 Expansive Expressions of Faith – Big Plans

Rule #4 Execution and Commitment

Rule #5 Engrossing Engagements.

No matter if you're self-employed and starving to make ends meet or a mega-corporation paying out dividends, each of these rules will provide your business with an ROI higher than its cost of implementation. Each of these Qigong for Business exercises, when practiced and applied, will result in a more successful business.

"You can exhort all you want about excellent execution; you're not going to get it unless you have disciplined strategic choices, a structure that supports the strategy, systems that enable organizations to work and execute together, a winning culture, and leadership that's inspirational. If you have all that, you will get excellent execution."

– Alan G. Lafley, CEO P&G

Rule #1: Everything you do counts! – Leadership

This sums up the challenge of leadership. So many books and classes have been written and taken to explain leadership. Because everything you do has some kind of effect, it is almost impossible to define the characteristics of good leadership that are essential to Qigong for Business, the life force that will ensure your business success.

A boss of mine reminded me of this leadership rule in his own way when he said, "You're the big cheese now—don't smell up the works." In his own way he was reminding me that everything I did or did not do would be observed— and it would count. It wouldn't be so much what I said, it would be what I did or did not do that would most impact my ability to lead my division to success.

So if everything we do counts towards our leadership quotient, then how are we to make the right decision when faced with a difficult choice? For me and many others it is a simple choice between **Conscience** and **Convenience** (to learn more about this subject, read *The Language of Conscience* by Tieman H. Dipple. Jr.). Another perspective is offered in a short book by Eric Harvey and Alexander Lucia, *Walk the Talk*. Chapter Three is titled "The Conflict of Contradictions." The phrase "unconscious do anothers" begins to lead one to understand that we have to step back and examine our actions, not just our intentions. Are we living our values and walking our talk? Actions like paying bonuses to management while asking another worker to take pay cuts or go without raises or similar bonuses sends the signal so clearly illuminated recently when American Airlines tried to convince its rank and file that management bonuses were necessary to save the company while pay cuts by rank and file we also necessary.

Have you ever said, "Our employees are our most important asset?" If you were you to survey them, would they agree? In most 360-degree reviews, more than 80 percent of managers are surprised to learn the level of disconnect between their intention and their actions. So I urge you to take caution before you jump to any conclusions about your style and its results.

ROI

Is there a return on investment for the business rule **Everything You Do Counts**?

What is the contribution margin needed to justify this effort? I will turn to the numerous surveys done to define the best places to work. Among the evidence in these survey results we find integrity listed high on the list and often mentioned by employees as a reason to justify claiming their employer a best place to work. So what? Additional reports suggest that the cost of replacement of a typical office worker is between 150 and 250 percent of their annual salary. Move up the income chain to sales and mid-management and the numbers become staggeringly high. One professional services firm has estimated that it costs almost $9 million to hire the wrong worker or to have to replace a worker that was productive when they left. Imagine—your costs are not that high, but they're higher than you think. And if we add the cost of replacing a customer, we have once again hit a staggeringly high cost.

The fair question is: Can one action or mis-action really have that big an impact? Yes! The examples are numerous; let me share one from my personal experience. In an attempt to manage budget expenses, a Fortune 2000 company passed a rule that any sales person who did not spend their expense budget by the end of each quarter would be penalized in their bonus payouts due quarterly. Can you imagine the consequence of this simple action, where someone's business acumen failed them completely? The driving objective of this sales force became spending expense money, not closing more business or making greater profits. This is but one of hundreds of examples where a lack of business acumen (not thinking though the consequence of the decision) has negatively impacted business results (actually driving an opposite result from the intent).

Everything you do Counts – The challenge of leadership is rule number one in Qigong for Business. The ROI for keeping this rule and making your choices from Conscience rather than Convenience is more than enough to put it as number one among our rules.

Rule #2: Exhaustive Examination of the Facts

Our research supported a clear understanding of the facts that surround the business as essential to Qigong for Business. Business Acumen again plays a major role in 1) Understanding what the facts tell us (insight), and 2) What facts to examine (information). We suggest that there are two series of metrics that should be examined and they are different for small business, mid-cap, and large cap firms. The two series are A) Financial and B) Non-Financial.

Recent reports from CPA and CFO organizations suggest that eight out of ten CEOs can not properly interpret their own financial statements. This is not a reflection of the intelligence of the CEOs, but rather the result of years of rulings and GAAP (general accepted accounting practices) making it confusing for those not trained in the *language of money*.

Use the following trick to help you: READ-only.
Responsive
Efficient
Appreciated
Decisive

The metrics you watch should be ones that are **responsive** — if you do something positive or negatively, what you are watching should be responsive to the action. The metric should be **efficient**. If it takes longer to gather the information than it does to make use of it, should it be done? The metric should be **appreciated** by those who are dependent upon it. There is a famous story in business schools about an Admiral at Pearl Harbor. When asked by a subordinate why he was not doing a specific report, he replied, "Son, no one was reading it." Finally, if you are watching a metric, you should be able to make a **decisive** decision as a result of the report.

A couple of highly-recommended metrics for small business would include the following:

SGR (sustainable growth rate) – tells you when you will run out of cash.

ROAI (return on asset invested) – tells you the earning power of the business.

LIQUIDITY – we recommend NBP (net balance position); ratios that effect your NBP and suggest ways to improve it.

(You can obtain the formulas for these metrics by writing to us, by purchasing our eWorkbook, or by check with your local CPA.)

The facts don't have to be all about numbers. In the book *The Churchill War Papers*, vol. 2, Martin Gilbert reports that Churchill never failed to confront the most brutal facts. Early in the war, he created an entirely separate department outside the normal chain of command, called the Statistical Office, with the principal function of feeding him the most brutal facts of reality, continuously updated and completely unfiltered. "Facts are better than dreams," wrote Churchill in *The Gathering Storm.*

Imagine being in the ocean with no compass, no sexton, no stars, and no landmarks to guide you. How will you find land and dock your ship? Without some benchmark to go by, we are hard-pressed to navigate these waters; even still waters can be difficult under these circumstances. Imagine how much more difficult it would be in troubled waters: "The dirty little secret about entrepreneurial life in America is that the overwhelming majority of small business owners create zero equity for themselves. You spend a lifetime building a company only to discover, when it is time to sell, that it is worthless" (George Gendron, Former Editor and Chief of Inc. Magazine™).

Knowing where you want to go is important – Knowing where you are – critical!

ROI

The most important return on investment for an *exhaustive examination of the facts* (both financial and non-financial) is that you get to keep the company. Failing to pay attention, failing to follow the right metrics, failing to learn how to focus on values rather than just numbers can result in failure. You think it can't happen to you? It happens to 80 percent of all companies that are less than two years old; of those left another 70 percent fail before year four. The upside is that companies that face those facts, pay attention, and manage by the right metrics can grow at a rate 17 to 28 percent faster than their peers. Those companies that face the facts find their profitability is over 40 percent greater than their peers who do not link their actions so closely to the value of metrics.

The odds are working against the most ambitious entrepreneur regardless of experience. An **Exhaustive Examination of the Facts** is a critical factor in making the business a success that will provide a profitable exit strategy for the stakeholders.

Rule #3: Expansive Expressions of Faith – Big Plans
Three years of research indicated that making big plans and including everyone at your company in them was the ultimate expression of faith. Everyone wants to know that their work is important. When everyone in the organization knows how their work fits into the big picture they find their work more satisfying. Companies that are acknowledged as great places to work ensure that every employee knows how their team effort contributes to the success of the customer.

An expansive expression of faith means you have faith in the partners you choose. When you share your goals and objectives with your partners it's easier to accomplish them together. These partners include your vendors, your employees, and your customers. When your intent is to assist your customers in solving their problems you have a winning value proposition.

To have an expansive expression of faith, plan big. You must play to win, not just to avoid losing. You need big goals, clear steps, planned reviews and adjustments, and focus on a shared specific vision.

A friend of mine runs a successful technology company. As technology often does, it began to creep up on his business and a tipping point (*The Tipping Point: How Little Things Can Make a Big Difference*, by Malcolm Gladwell) was about to occur. His choices were to re-trench, continue to support the existing technology, and employ a planned but limited growth while continuing servicing his existing customers. This plan offered an excellent five-year exit strategy.

Alternatively, a choice to burn the bridges, abandon the old, embrace new technology, and become the front runner of the new technology that presented itself. He chose the bold, audacious, risky, challenging path by making big plans. Two years into the plan the company has more revenue and profitability than ever before. The strategy is paying off—the steps he took to make this happen are beyond the scope of this article but worthy of in-depth reporting for all who face similar challenges. He engaged everyone with an expansive expression of faith. Faith in their ability to be a part of making this happen, faith in his market research, faith in his team to deliver, and faith in the big plans.

Don't wait until your business is failing to implement big plans as part of your daily business strategy. Start now and don't stop, ever.

Failing to plan is planning to fail.

Driving your business with integrity is the first step toward working a plan to succeed. It is my contention that in the books I've read about management and leadership, and my own experience as well suggests that when you help other people get what they want, you get what you want.

ROI

In keeping with our formula, rules are great but only when they deliver measurable results to the bottom line. The Qigong for Business must deliver the same healthy business results regardless of the size, industry, or age of the company. This is also true for Qigong for health. The practice and exercise must deliver better health to the individual regardless of age or position. An Expansive Expression of Faith—Plan Big is a rule that returns bottom line profitability.

Rule #4: Execution and Commitment

Nike™ created the tag line, "Just do it!" The particular sport doesn't matter, it is the involvement, activity, and the execution that counts.

From their popular book, Execution: *The Discipline of Getting Things Done*, Larry Bossidy and Ram Charan offer the following definition of execution: Ex-e-cu-tion (ek si kyoo shun), n. 1. the missing link. 2. The main reason companies fall short of their promises. 3. The gap between what a company's leaders want to achieve and the ability of their organizations to deliver it. From 2000 till 2002, 20 percent of America's top companies fired their CEO. Why? Failure to execute the plan.

If **Execution** is the rule, how do we implement the rules to avoid the failure of these aforementioned CEOs? Again, from Bossidy and Charan's *Execution*:

"Know your people and your business
Insist on realism
Set clear goals and priorities
Follow through
Reward doers
Expand People's capabilities
Know yourself."

You never get what you expect – only what you inspect.
If you don't or won't follow through, why would you expect anyone else to do so? Perhaps the most frustrating aspect of being a consultant is to see a client adopt a strategy, do all the right things and for some inexplicable reason stop doing what worked. If you don't change your habits, you will not change the outcome. Habits, good or bad, drive us daily.

The second half of the rule is **Commitment**. Hand-in-hand, **Execution** and **Commitment** must arrive together to survive. Without commitment, execution will become like an attitude adjustment—quite temporary. Without commitment, execution is a false hope.

Hope is not a strategy.
Commitment is our promise to us to do something. **Commitment** is our promise to others to ensure that we keep our promise. We cannot expect anyone to take our commitment seriously until we demonstrate our willingness to follow up and *inspect what you expect.*

I am sure that each of you has stories where a lack of commitment, a failure to follow through and an unwillingness to inspect resulted in tragedy. I will share one example here to make the point.

At an international trade show in Hong Kong, I had taken a break on the balcony overlooking Victoria Harbor. I was quickly joined by another fellow who had come out for a cigarette. We began a conversation; he complained that his warehouse in a nearby island nation had been looted completely of all its valuable electronic content. The prime suspects were the caretakers of the warehouse. I asked how often he inspected the warehouse or had it inspected. It had gone unattended by outside sources for over nine months. With not so much as an inspection log or report of any kind on the status of the material in the warehouse, my acquaintance was shocked at the outcome. A bit more dialogue revealed the local authority from his company was barred from this facility and the rent had gone in arrears. But he continued, "We are a huge American Company—someone should have told us."

I will leave the placing of blame to you, my reader. I'm only suggesting that in no way did my storyteller ever accept any of the responsibility. You only get what you inspect not what you expect.

ROI

Is there an ROI for execution? Can there be an ROI for any idea unless it is executed? My premise is that without action, without a change in habit, without a commitment to inspect what you expect – nothing changes. No change equals a zero ROI. Conversely, positive results from actions taken produce returns on investments.

Implied in every good rule is the need to do something different. History and human nature work against us with this. In order to enjoy the new results we seek, we must change our habits. We must execute. We commend you to commitment. Without commitment, there is no assurance that even the execution will prevail.

Our best advice: Inspect what you expect!

Rule #5 Engrossing Engagements
We have reached the last of the five rules: Engrossing Engagements. To have a business that will grow and outperform its competitors, careful attention must be paid to insuring we build jobs that are engaging. Today's employee is not the same employee we hired twenty years ago or even ten years ago. Today's employee has grown up with more information flow daily than many of us have had in a lifetime

My recommended starting place is to hire tough. The rule at Motorola™ when I started there was to only "hire people you want to work for"—an interesting approach that insured high quality, well-qualified hires throughout a multimillion dollar enterprise.

The message here is that by hiring tough you are tough on yourself first. Know what your values are—clearly state and live them. Don't allow the employee perspective of what you say to be different from what you do. The history books of US companies are littered with examples of how this contradiction can kill a company. You want to grow strong companies. You want to have employees that understand their role in the business and how it impacts the business.

When everyone is pulling together for a common idea the results are rewarding for everyone. In the book, *GUNG HO!*, Ken Blanchard and Sheldon Bowles remind us of the importance in allowing everyone the dignity of work. One of the three important values to learn is what they termed the Spirit of the Squirrel— Worthwhile Work:
1. Knowing we make the world a better place.
2. Everyone works toward a shared goal.
3. Values guide all plans, decisions and actions.
As you recognize the dignity of work you again employ business acumen. Engrossing Engagements are essential elements for the companies voted best places to work. Best places to work typically outperform their peers and competitors 17 to 28 percent when all other things are equal.

ROI

Regardless of the size of your organization, having committed, driven, enthusiastic employees are a benefit. It is the dignity of work and allowing everyone to know how their contribution counts that drives companies to greatness. There can be a seat on the bus for everyone. A recent award-winning entrepreneur says he hires anyone that can and is willing to do the job. Anyone! This entrepreneur took his company from four employees and one customer on the verge of bankruptcy to $150 million a year in revenue with 150 employees and sold the business for six times his investment to a larger firm. He made both investors and employees millionaires along on the way.

The ability to build camaraderie, a sense of belonging, of insuring Engrossing Engagements is a sure winner and deserves to be included in the five E's for leadership and corporate growth.

I started out asking the question "Is there a common, universal set of rules that have been repeated and will work to insure business success and growth?" Conditionally, I added that any such set of rules should be universally applicable to businesses of every size in every industry. Such a set of rules would be more principals than just rules because of their universal applicability. I engaged in a survey of the literature from the *Art of War*—to Execution. Along the way I have gathered an extensive library of books on the subject, conversed and consulted with such leaders in the field as Dr. J. Lee Whittington, Dean of the Graduate School of Business Management, University of Dallas.

I have offered examples from my own reading and business practices of over thirty years. I have shared the work with scholars and foot soldiers in the battle for ethical business standards and successful businesses and they all agree: these principals, when applied to any business, will result in success.

Is it easy? No. Why? Because the drive behind every decision must be conscience or convenience. Everything we do, do not do, leave unsaid, or unaddressed communicates our values as clearly and often more succinctly than even the most eloquent prose or speech you might write.

It is no wonder that the odds are against small business startups making it beyond year four. And yet, every year more and more try. Why? Are they just lemmings in the great wave of free enterprise, or are they actually the power behind, underneath, and throughout free enterprise?

You are free enterprise!

Small businesses are the engine of free enterprise. You create more new jobs every year than the F1000 companies create in five years. You create and bring to market new ideas faster and more efficiently than big business. You are nimble, agile and work in cross functional teams because you have little choice, while big business struggles to emulate your success at innovation.

Jack R. Howe has over 30 years' experience in business management, sales, and sales management in complex operational environments. His background includes experience in industry, a major accounting/consulting firm, and in private practice. Clients have included multi-billion dollar firms and aggressively growing start-ups. In private practice, he has developed innovative business tools and solutions to remodel business enterprises for greater profitability. Howe is public speaker, mentor, coach and the author of *Please Don't Tell My Mother I'm a Salesman*, *30 Minutes to Prepare for the C-Suite Meeting*, **and is about to release** *The Tao of Customers for Life*. **Visit www.30minsto.com or www.ceotoolbelt.com for more information, or email Howe at jack@ceotoolbelt.com.**

Landing the Big One!
A Catalyst for Innovation and a Lesson for Future Growth
By Randy Geller

Whether in business or sport fishing, the biggest thrill comes from "landing the big one." Aside from the thrill, garnering a market leader as a client often catapults a business to a new level of success. Our company, AutoLotManager. com, has certainly seen that benefit.

The first time I went deep-sea fishing, I had little knowledge about landing the big one. Luckily, in sport fishing, it's easy to hire well-equipped experts at a reasonable price. For a small fee, I rented a capable boat equipped with the right tools and an experienced crew. We caught our chum (small fish used as bait) and headed out to the deep waters, where the big fish were. With the right conditions, a lot of patience, and a little luck, just maybe...

AutoLotManager.com had that bit of luck landing our first "big fish." AutoLotManager.com provides an online tool to help auto dealers better utilize their resources—particularly their used car inventory, advertising dollars, client base, and time. Specifically, we help dealers market used cars on Internet websites and through traditional media, track and manage advertising, and automate and monitor the follow-up with prospects and customers through our CRM application.

We had the good fortune of calling on an 18-store dealer group in our area that was very unhappy with their current supplier of one of our services. But they wanted more than we had previously offered. Closing the sale would be the easy part; dramatically rearranging our business model would be the challenge. Partly through ambition, and partly through naiveté, we undertook the challenge. I consider that step the biggest key to our future success. Ironically, that account itself has never been profitable.

So how did rearranging our whole business to accommodate an unprofitable account end up being so helpful? In short, we acquired the expertise and credibility necessary to quickly win over a significant market share—profitably. The first time utilizing that strategy was purely accidental. Now it is an integral part of our marketing plan.

Up until signing that first major client, AutoLotmanager.com had strictly been a software company. We developed and marketed an online service application to allow car dealers to create and print window stickers for used vehicles, and upload data and photos to websites such as AutoTrader.com and Cars.com. Our "Complete Version" software tied that "Inventory Module" to website products as well as a comprehensive CRM tool. Since most dealers already had websites and CRM systems, and those products were difficult to switch over, we emphasized our "Inventory Module" as our gateway product. That is the product we sold our new major client.

Being a used-car dealer myself, our products were naturally biased toward smaller dealerships. I simply understood that business better than that of mega dealer groups. Also, the smaller mom-and-pop stores were underserved, and access to decision makers was easier. We knew the cost savings would be more significant to those dealers, and the owners would take the "hands-on" approach our software thrived under. As a small local business competing against multinational public companies, we also surmised that large dealers and chains would resist changing to a brand new, tiny company.

Our original product was designed to help dealers bring certain services in-house; dealers could create their own used car window stickers and upload inventory data and photos to websites, saving money and increasing control. Our strategy worked; we quickly signed up about 20 small dealers, and even a couple larger ones who wanted to do that work themselves rather than contract it out.

But most large dealers objected to doing the work themselves. We recognized the missed opportunity, but accommodating those dealers would require an enormous shift in our business model that couldn't be justified for a small number of dealers. At that time, our 18-dealer chain fortuitously "flopped into our boat." They offered to sign a one-year contract with us if we would enter the data and photos for them. We weighed the pros and cons. We would need to hire, train, and manage personnel, select and purchase equipment, and modify the software for field entry of data and photos. On the positive side, about 75 percent of dealers wanted that service and would become legitimate prospects. It was an opportunity to grow rapidly with a guaranteed client base. As I said, partly through ambition and partly through naiveté, we decided to go for it!

In hindsight, we were ill-equipped, undermanned, and undercapitalized for the tasks at hand. Though we suffered through some major bumps and bruises, we were able to rise to the challenge.

There were several important factors to that success. Proper planning became essential. Just as I had hired the right deep-sea fishing expert, I knew AutoLotManager.com would benefit from similar business expertise. We hired an outside business coach to help us solidify a vision for our company, and then organize our goals, strategies, and business processes. We created user manuals, training materials, and position descriptions for team members. Creating a cooperative approach with the client was also extremely helpful. We catered our product to their specific needs. We even modified the software to accommodate their relationship with a third party who needed the data and photos. We cultivated a partnership mentality—we were "in it together." They understood we were sacrificing profit in return for the opportunity to gain valuable experience and an important reference. They also saw that we were willing to do whatever it took to make the situation positive for everyone. One of my partners and I even volunteered to personally take photos whenever necessary. Another very important influence to our success was managing customer expectations. We explained upfront that technological hurdles might create temporary glitches, but that ultimately, cost savings and superior service would be worthwhile.

Through tremendous effort by our entire team, we were able to overcome our lack of experience and resources to retain the 18-store chain as a client. We used that opportunity to hone our skills and obtain an influential positive reference. Soon thereafter, we were able to earn the business of most other large dealers in our local market, as well as many smaller ones.

When we entered our second geographic market, we were much better prepared. We utilized a similar strategy of going after the "big fish." We first signed up some small dealerships that could provide credible local references (in addition to our previous "big fish" references from our home market). Next, we customized our software to accomplish certain characteristics that larger dealers wanted. We offered an introductory pricing special, which created a sense of urgency and fostered a "teamwork" atmosphere. After signing the contract, we even provided extra services at no cost to ensure a positive reference for other dealers in that market. Again, my partners and I were very visible in the sales and implementation processes. We went to great lengths to provide incredible value, excellent service, and truly create a long-term partnership with the client. I've no doubt that many other dealers in that market will take note and switch to our service.

AutoLotManager.com has been able to acquire market-leading clients by aggressively seeking them out and confidently proposing a unique relationship. We tailor our products to their specific needs and therefore foster a "partnership" mentality. We offer enticing introductory pricing, and use our small size as an advantage by displaying personalized service. Attaining those clients has virtually forced us to innovate, systematize, and excel beyond our original expectations. As a result, we have become technological pioneers, superior service providers, and customer satisfaction leaders in our industry. We are growing very rapidly, retaining existing clients, and succeeding financially.

My first deep-sea fishing expedition ended in sea-sickness. Hopefully, the lessons of AutoLotManager.com can serve as the motion sickness remedy for other businesses to "land the big one."

Action Items
1) **Identify Potential "Big Fish"**—Open-minded, influential, and ideally, dissatisfied potential customers

2) **Create Unique Partnerships**—Offer customized products at special introductory pricing in return for feedback, patience, and a positive reference

3) **Manage Expectations**—Be honest about challenges upfront; foster "teamwork" mentality, remind client of long term benefits

4) Make it Personal—Get and stay personally involved, from presenting the offer (be blatant about wanting the business and why) to handling follow-up

5) Sacrifice—Spend more and/or work harder to ensure success and satisfaction

6) Ask for Referrals—Reward current clients for referring new business

Born and raised in Akron, Ohio, Randy Geller graduated from the University Of Michigan School Of Business with a Bachelor of Business Degree in 1988 with High Distinction. Geller then started his professional career as a salesperson at Geller Toyota-Mercedes Benz in Akron, Ohio, earning Mercedes' coveted "Star Salesman" recognition his first seven years there, and moving up into management as VP. Upon the sale of the dealership in 1995, Geller started Geller Leasing, Inc., an independent leasing company, and DotCom Marketing, an Internet marketing company for car dealers. In 1999, Geller opened a small upscale used car dealership in Medina, Ohio, which he subsequently moved to Wadsworth in 2005 and operates today as Jeff's Motorcars of Wadsworth.

In 2004, Geller co-founded MPG Interactive, Inc, owner of AutoLotManager.com, along with his three partners: Dale Malick, Doug Malick, and Michael Peterson. AutoLotManager.com currently serves almost 200 car dealers, mostly in Ohio.

Turbo-Charge your Business
Grow your People
By Ken Wright

Developing your people is an extremely effective way to continually market your business. It is much more difficult to bring in new clients through advertising and other marketing techniques than it is to continue a relationship with an existing customer through selling additional products or services, up-selling, and cross-selling.

Consequently, client retention and gaining new business through referrals can be a mainstay for building a successful and stable business. I have found that the best way to build a business foundation that revolves around excellent customer service and client retention is to create a business culture that revolves around developing productive, happy employees.

When you develop your people, you inadvertently enhance your marketing and advertising campaigns. Fulfilled employees are more likely to be engaged, and they will pass that motivation and passion for work onto their customers. When your customers are pleased, they will be more likely to continue to use your services or buy your products. But perhaps more importantly, a happy customer will sing your praises to everyone they know, and there are few advertising tools as effective as word-of-mouth promotions.

The following seven steps will help you to develop a more involved, satisfied, and dependable work force at your business to help increase customer retention and satisfaction:

1. **Listen**. Encourage open and honest feedback between yourself and each of your employees. Determine what they want to get out of their job. What are their goals? What do they need? What obstacles are they facing? Approach each topic or concern by really listening with your heart, without judgment.

2. **Have Empathy**. It is imperative to truly connect with your people. Spend time with each of them and find out what is happening, not only in their professional lives but in their personal lives as well. By taking a true interest in your staff,

you will relay to them that your company not only cares about its bottom line but also for each individual that is working there as well.

3.**Be Authentic.** Have a genuine desire to develop each of your employees for their own personal growth and achievement. Understand that people need to feel challenged and believe that what they do for a living adds value. Create an office environment that utilizes everyone's strengths and listen when people say that they enjoy, or don't enjoy, doing specific projects. By respecting your employees as people (and not simply the means to an increase in revenue), they will respect you and genuinely work harder because they believe in what they do.

4. **Train Them.** After determining the skills and expertise each of your employees currently have and comparing it to the skills and attributes needed to excel in their position at your business, provide specifically tailored training programs for your employees to help them move towards maximizing their capability in the office. When someone is great at what they do, they are more likely to enjoy it and be actively engaged. This will have a direct effect on the productivity of your employee, the customer service your business provides, and ultimately your bottom line.

5.**Give Honest Feedback.** Be fair, honest, and polite when giving feedback to your employees. Be sure that all of your comments are constructive. If employees are falling short, talk with them about how they can change their behavior while still moving forward. Don't concentrate on where they are falling short. Show them what they are doing well, and give some suggestions about how they can improve. Then follow up. Commend them for taking your advice. If they are still falling short, point out the problem and ask them to come up with a solution on their own. By putting the ball in their court, they will realize that you trust them and value their opinion, and consequently they will work harder to maintain that trust. Additionally, by helping your people improve, you will create momentum for your company.

6.**Share your Vision.** Help your people understand the overall strategic goal for your company and how each of their individual roles helps to achieve this vision. Be sure that your people understand your industry, and educate them on issues, changes, and advances that are taking place. Not only will your people appreciate you taking the time to educate them, they will also have a better understanding of why and when you have to make difficult decisions.

7. **Plan.** In addition to having a vision for your company, you need to have a plan for the future. While you may have a plan for the business, do you have a personal development plan for each of your employees? You should. And they need to know where you see them going in the future. Let them know how you want to expand, what new markets you want to tap, and how you see them growing with you. They will work harder when they see potential for both their own growth and the growth of the company.

When creating a business culture that revolves around people development, begin with those employees who directly report to you—presumably your managers. Once your development relationship is established with these employees, have them develop the same liaison with those who directly report to them. The people development culture will cascade down through your business until every employee is part of the system.

Keep in mind that this is not an easy task. You will need to be persistent, determined, and involved in a hands-on way. The effort to create a people development culture at your business is considerable; however, the results are remarkable. Your people will feel better about themselves, their jobs, and your company, thus boosting morale, motivation, staff retention, and results. Your customers will be pleased with your excellent customer service, consequently increasing customer loyalty, and they will become advocates for your business by providing warm referrals. By developing your people through the above seven steps, you can turn your work force into an outstanding marketing tool.

Ken Wright is Founder and President of The WrightCoach, a business coaching and leadership development firm specializing in individual and team development. Wright's business experience includes 32 years in the financial services industry and eight years as a CEO of a major financial group. With a long history of realizing his potential both in the business world and in his personal life, Wright attributes his success to being an approachable and understanding leader with very high expectations

concentrating on developing and inspiring people, and focusing on strategic implementation of key business objectives. For more information, please visit www.TheWrightCoaching.com, and to contact Wright, please email Ken@TheWrightCoaching.com.

Making People Your Business
4 Marketing Tactics for Your Small Business
By Bryon Palitto

Small businesses are the fabrics that weave together our American economy. Small businesses support the large businesses as vendors, supply our households with the basic services of life, make it possible to live in rural areas, and provide the seedbed for ingenious innovation. I believe that small businesses deserve competent, timely, and cost-effective help in the areas of business in which they are weak.

From my observations there are three broad categories of people who start small businesses. Entrepreneurs in the first category are technicians that excel in the production work. Owners in the second category focus on selling; they find (or create) a product or service their company takes to market. People in the third category are financially motivated and interested in money. Each of these three broad categories of business owners has their distinct strengths and specific areas of weakness.

I believe that this bit of understanding is important because it serves as a foundation for the following four marketing tactics.

One: Relationships and Serving

One of the most important marketing tactics is the great value of having a very sincere, passionate desire to make a difference in the lives of people.

Why do I conclude this? An overview of my history provides insight.

I grew up in a home where my father, Ron Palitto, worked in a very large, multi-national business. As a child I loved to listen to his stories about his work. Through these stories, he shared with me what he was learning and being challenged with, and the outcomes of problems solved. He has always been my personal mentor, and he is now a business mentor, coach, and consultant to me and everyone in my company.

Servitude, discipline, and perseverance were also a part of my youth. At nine years old, I began my first job as a paperboy with the Cuyahoga Falls City Press. At 10 years old I graduated to delivering the Akron Beacon Journal, 7 days per week, rain or shine, 365 days per year—no exceptions! I had a three-mile route that I walked every day delivering papers door-to-door. I did this for six years. I first discovered that life was not only about me at this point. Delivering papers at 6:00 a.m. on Sunday morning in -10° temperatures taught me that life is about serving people.

Beginning at the age of fifteen, I had an opportunity to work for a local dairy farming entrepreneur for five years. This farmer started several creative farm-related businesses that I helped operate as a teenager. Again, I further discovered that it is not all about me. Working outside all day in temperatures over 100° to provide feed for the animals continued to teach me about doing the right things for the right reasons at the right time.

During my full-time college career, I worked 60 hours a week for a local entrepreneurial team that owned and operated numerous recruiting and staffing organizations. I was their information technology resource who also ended up supporting all the remote users and supervising the data entry crew. The owners shared much with me about the beauty of operating and serving small businesses.

As time progressed, I joined a big, national consulting company. My role was as technical account manager to Cleveland and Akron based Fortune 500 companies. I was very successful in helping to grow the Cleveland branch. I was disappointed, however, that I could not help the small businesses from within this big business.

I am thankful that during the very formative years of my youth I was fortunate to have good instruction and counsel that enabled me to focus on what I could do for others, not what they could do for me. In early adulthood, I was clearly shown the value of having a sincere and passionate desire to make a difference in other people's lives. I did not invent these concepts or anything else that I understand. I learned from others and from my personal experiences.

TWO: Touching People

I discovered early on in the history of my own business that recruiting is very important – no one can do it alone and all teams must grow. Last year

I interviewed over fifty people. Some years I have interviewed over one hundred individuals. But what does this have to do with marketing, you ask?

The answer is a little complex. First, when I do most of the initial interviews, I have three items on my agenda:

1) Is this person a candidate for our team?

2) Who does this person know and where have they been?

3) Can they become an apostle of our company?

The second and third items are all about marketing. By the time I am finished with the hour and a half interview, this person knows all about who we are, what we do, why we do it, where we are going, what kind of team members we are looking for, what kind of customers we are looking for, and how they may or may not fit into my team. Often these interviewees tell me about potential customers.

My first interview agenda item also relates to marketing in a roundabout way. It leads to the third tactic I would like to share with you.

THREE: The Team

The team is everything. I know that popular business thinking is pretty convinced that the customer is everything. The good news is that customers are everywhere! How do you find them? With a team. Once you find a customer, what do you do? You have to perform. How do you perform? With a team. After you have performed, how do you continue to do business with that customer? With a team. The team is everything!

Who is this team, you ask? The answer to this question is the secret to my tactic number three. The team is made up of people that I and the other existing team members have recruited, qualified, tested, tried, approved, and developed. It is also made up of all the other alliance partners who have team members that are useful in fully serving the customer. It is the team of teams concept being promoted by the Business Technology HUB. I could go on and on about this concept. I believe it is the secret to success in our new economy!

FOUR: Personal Development

The fourth tactic is personal growth. I know that I am a lid that limits the potential of the teams I lead. I realize that everyone on the team or in the team of teams can be a lid at one time or another. We all need to grow. My experience is that in developing myself and others in leadership, strategic thinking, discipline in character, understanding people and their character and behaviors, project management, and all the while still truly caring about them and their success, we are better able to effectively serve the market. The market responds by providing opportunities to help others.

Action Items
One: Relationships and Serving

Understanding personality characteristics has been very valuable to me and to our team. Our methodology for training and implementation has been developed over years of study and observation. We learn and grow (change in a positive direction) every day.

The commitment starts with me. I believe in the value and thus strongly promote it. The interviewing process weeds out prospective team members who do not care about others and discovers prospective team members who do care about others. The interviewing process also discovers who wants to grow and who thinks they are done growing. After hiring a new team member, we wait a couple of months to give them an opportunity to naturally observe the team philosophies and methodologies in real action. After six to nine months we send the new team member to an intense one and a half day interpersonal styles workshop. This workshop is put on by our partner, Great Lakes Resource Center. After the seminar, we require the newly inspired team member to give us feedback on how well we, as a team, are following the principals. This process has been going on without their direct inclusion all during their tenure, however, now they are included in the discussions and actually given the focus. Hopefully we are able to send two of our team members through this training together so there is not as much pressure on a single individual. As time progresses, we encourage each other to read books like Dr. Tony Alessandra's Platinum Rule® series books.

Tip: Begin learning personality styles and incorporate them into your life. Get help to get started.

Two: Touching People

Who have you touched today? What do they remember about the interaction? What do you remember about the interaction? Did you have an agenda? Who was the beneficiary of your agenda?

My belief is that I was created to serve God who commands me to serve people with the tools He has given to me. I also believe that this same God has given every person a set of tools that He wants them to use in serving Him by serving people. With these two foundational beliefs, I attempt to make every interaction with another person a positive experience.

The experience I related above, about the interview process, can be one example of the implementation of these beliefs. Another example is in dealing with so-called competitors. My strong desire is to up-build these other service providers because the more people who are focused on truly serving the market place the better our economy will be.

Tip: Develop an understanding of yourself by writing out why you deserve to be alive, your eight to ten core values with definitions, your short term, mid term and long term goals and the fifty things you want to do before you die.

Three: The Team

I described much about the team already. Why care so much about the team? Without them, my impact is limited. With them, the impact can be multiplied. Even better is that most people function better in a group than they do alone. We actually end up with a compounding effect.

Tip: Tell one of your team members what you appreciate about them each day. Promote thankfulness. Promote respect. Promote growth.

Four: Personal Development

Teachers, coaches, and then mentors are required for success. I was fortunate to have had some very patient and dedicated teachers in my life. After a foundation was laid, some of these teachers became coaches. As I continued to learn and grow and make experiences, I recognized the need for mentors. I began to truly value and draw on mentors around the age of 24. As time has progressed their value to me and to those I influence has become more and more clear.

I have several mentors. They each have a different approach to mentoring and a different impact on me. Several I meet with irregularly. One I meet with weekly. I prepare questions and carefully note their responses. Often, I am able to try out my ideas, theories, or philosophies on them. Their feedback has been invaluable.

I recognize that I can be a limitation to someone else. This makes me very motivated to continue to grow.

I recognize that I will never be perfect. I try to send people around me if I sense that I am in their way.

Tip: Fill in your annual calendar with a regular time for training, coaching, and mentoring before filling in other appointments. A good coach will make you uncomfortable, like the feeling you have after doing fifty stomach crunches. A good mentor will help you understand how to apply what you are learning into your life. This often feels like a light turning on.

Much could be written on any of these four tactics. It is my firm conviction that relationships are everything in business. Also, please realize that marketing is only one of seven core competencies required to be successful in business. If you want to learn about the other six, please contact me.

Wishing you the very best!

Bryon Palitto is an entrepreneur and consultant. He is currently President and CEO of four businesses which are all focused on serving the small business community. He is also partner in several other businesses which

serve the small business community. He can be reached by e-mail at bryonp@thebusinesstechnologyhub.com. Learn more about his businesses by visiting www.thebusinesstechnologyhub.com.

Become a Never-Give-Up Marketing Machine

By Brian Stark

Did you ever wonder how some people achieve the seemingly impossible every day, when you can't get a thousand dollar raise, or close a single deal, without terrific hassle and effort? Have you ever wondered how some people seem to live stress-free lives—they have a perpetual smile on their face, everything seems to go their way, and opportunities just "fall into their laps" over and over? Do these people have something you don't? Do you constantly try to convince yourself that they're no more special than you, that they have no special gifts that you don't have, and that they possess no unusual or rare talent that you do not? But—do they have some special gift or edge? The answer is—quite obviously—*yes they do*!

Well then, what do these winners have that you lack? One quality that sets winners apart is a cultivated instinct to never give up.

These people are convinced that their mission is right and will be completed. They simply *will not quit* until they reach their goal. But that's only half of the story. You may be thinking this is simple persistence. It is not at all. In fact, what really distinguishes the winners in this field is that they possess the habit of never giving up. It's simple. There is no discussion. No analyzing to do, no program, coaching, or special workshop. Winners do not give up. Period.

Is it always good to be brutally persistent? Yes and no. Sometimes the mission is wrong, and never giving up means taking a project, business concept, or staff member's shortcoming as a challenge and pushing like hell¬—only to eventually be forced to concede. At least you have the choice to concede on your terms. Like all things, business is a numbers game. With experience, calculation, and careful planning, good choices far outweigh poor choices, and the learned practice of never giving up ends up being applied mostly to excellent opportunities.

Being in the habit of never giving up creates "stealth" opportunities. When you become known as one who never gives up, your adversaries rarely choose to challenge you. When competitors find out that it is you in a competitive situation, you often will win before even showing up. Others know not to waste their time trying to compete against you. Instead they'd rather choose a situation with a weaker opponent.

Possessing the habit of never giving up gives you a sense of confidence that elevates your personal presentation. When you do something the first time, whether it's baking cookies or fixing a flat tire, running a marathon or presenting a business proposition to other people… your hands get sweaty, you force things, things go wrong that you never expected, and although you get through the experience you don't know quite how you did sometimes! But once you have done it successfully 100 times, what was once terrifying and difficult becomes very easy and natural to do! When you go into a situation in which you have already seen, felt, smelled, and tasted success, then you are not scared or even phased by the prospect that "this is going to be a tough account to close" or "this vice president doesn't want me to get any further up the company ladder," because you already know how it feels to never give up—*you do it automatically*. It's easy and natural for you—it's what you do. You never give up. Period. You are a Never-Giving-Up Machine.

What does this have to do with small business marketing? Marketing is the activity of taking your goods or services to the market, moving them efficiently to a space where the largest quantity of the most ideal consumers will have an opportunity to view your offerings as part of *all* the offerings in the marketplace and, hopefully, select yours.

But to whom are you marketing? What are you offering? To what marketplace, exactly, are you moving these offerings? Aren't you offering your services or products to consumers, but also, your job opportunities to potential employees, your partnership to potential partners, your place in the business community to the community at large, your reason for continuing to your family and friends, and so on? Marketing a business—especially a small business, which by nature has to work overtime to define itself in its various market spaces—is an evolving, never-ending process, a war really, made up of various campaigns, battles, engagements, and skirmishes, being waged on several fronts at all times. It is this war in which I propose you must never give up. There are no winners or losers in the marketing war, only survivors! No one entity stands alone after everything is over and the smoke clears—because it is never over and there are always many players. In order to survive and thrive, you must keep pitching each little fight with vigor, enthusiasm, and fresh dedication.

You must become a Never-Giving-Up marketing machine. Every act, every discussion, every business move you make must be made with the consideration that it is a marketing activity—no matter how seemingly insignificant. Little things mean a lot, and attending to them gets you into a host of beneficial habits. When you go the bank to make a deposit, is the deposit well organized? Will the teller be glad to see you coming because you are a pleasure to deal with? What if, one day, that teller has a brother or sister looking for employment in *exactly* your field? Wouldn't you want them to suggest their sibling to you first? Will they? While you're in line to make your deposit, you just might meet a new customer in line. How did you dress today? Are you smiling? Do you radiate confidence and positivity? When you mail letters—even to the gas or electric company—do the envelopes market your business? Have you considered the people who will see that envelope? The mail carriers? The mail sorters? The people at the mail room at the utility company? How would *your staff* feel to send out a great looking piece of mail that trumpets the high quality of your business? You are then marketing to your own staff.

How is the phone answered at your company? Is your car clean and shiny every day? What if, as you are driving down the street, a key client happens to drive up beside you, and before you notice them, they notice you? Will you be making a positive impression on them at that very moment? How does your office look, feel, smell, and sound? Do your staff members love being there? Does it feel like the kind of place where only the best people would work? If so, you are effectively marketing the opportunity of working for you to your staff. If not—you are effectively marketing, to your staff, the idea of leaving your company for a better work environment—elsewhere!

And so it goes. In every single moment of every single day, you have thousands of opportunities to market yourself and your company to potential persons of importance to you—even if you don't know it at the time. You must be a Never-Giving-Up Marketing Machine, because your competitors—current and future—already are!

How to Acquire the Habit of Never-Giving-Up

As you transform yourself from simply understanding the idea of Never-Giving-Up to actually making it a part of your being, a way of life, it is important to remember that this is not about being rigid, inflexible, unemotional, or uncaring. This is not about crushing others, leaving others behind, or being mean-spirited, it is about having strong enough convictions that you move forward, regardless of obstacles, on an ongoing basis, in every endeavor where good sense dictates Never Giving Up! Winston Churchill said it best:

"Never give in. Never give in. Never, never, never, never—in nothing, great or small, large or petty— never give in, except to convictions of honor and good sense. Never yield to force. Never yield to the apparently overwhelming might of the enemy."

How to Become a Never-Giving-Up Machine in Five Easy Steps:

1. Learn to "pick your battles." You cannot do everything, and you cannot do everything you are doing well.

2. Carefully evaluate each situation—learn to evaluate quickly and privately.

3. Begin in advance by making a commitment to yourself that this thing is going to get done, whatever it takes. "I am going to become a pilot." "I will sell a million dollar order." "I will double the size of my business in 3 years."

4. Review daily the several significant commitments you've made to yourself. Make them the last thing you think about when you go to sleep and they will be the first thing that pops into your head when you awaken.

5. Think about *everything* you do. This is focused brainwork. Consider the implications of every action. Consider how every action affects others, and

how those actions market you and your business—either positively or negatively, now and in the future—and do something about it.

Why is Never Giving Up Important?

It isn't important—it is essential. It is essential because success in all endeavors, but business in particular, often goes to those who are left standing after everyone else has fallen: To the last players in a tight market; to the salesman who makes just one more call and eventually lands the account no one has cracked; to the manager who tries one more time to find a way to help a brilliant but difficult team member see the company's vision as his own before firing him; to the owner who has pitched her vision to dozens of financiers, but just hasn't found the right one.

So you thought nobody liked your idea. Actually, lots of people might have loved your idea—just not the people you found. Or you couldn't get the financing you thought you deserved. There are hundreds of reasons no one financed your project—most of them having nothing to do with your project! Yes, your boss promoted someone else over you. Etc. Etc. Blah Blah Blah. Are these reasons to give up? Stop trying? Decide it really is impossible? **Never!**

It is your job and yours alone to make your vision a reality. Henry Ford said, "What is desirable and right is never impossible."

Consider this: You are simply the carrier of the ball, but the ball was here before the game started, and it will be here long after it's over. The challenges you face are as old as history itself. These challenges are a regular—even boring—part of the human condition. Your experience with them today is normal! The stories of overcoming great obstacles and unbearable odds go back to the beginning of time. That is because it is the stories of those who never gave in to unbearable odds that we remember today. Jesus Christ, Mohandas K. Ghandi, Martin Luther King Jr., George Washington, Thomas Edison—the list is endless. Will you place yourself on that kind of a list?

Become a Never-Giving-Up Machine, and everything you desire in life will be given up—to you!

Brian Stark is a real estate investor, lender, and financier with offices in Cleveland and New York. He and his brother, Paul Stark, host a weekly radio talk show filled with motivational and inspirational ideas which they share with their nationwide audience. The Stark brothers also offer business success and motivational coaching. They can be reached through their website at www.starkworld.com, or by calling 216-426-8400, X14.

Employee Evangelism
Let Your Workforce Create the Buzz
By Ron McDaniel

An advocate is someone that tells others about the benefits of using a certain product and, through their enthusiasm, encourages others to look into and often promote the said product to someone else.

Wouldn't it be great if you had just ten people out there strongly advocating what you are offering?

If you are looking for advocates among people you do not know well, then you have a lot of hard work in front of you. However, there is another group that many small and mid-sized businesses utilize—*their own employees.*

If your current work culture says employees work should a set amount of time on a set of tasks, and this amount does not take into consideration the extended network of people each employee knows, you are missing out on a huge opportunity.

Employees in the right environment and with the right encouragement will create buzz and word-of-mouth marketing for their organization. They need to understand that buzz is everyone's responsibility and they should have success stories and good information that will help them create buzz more easily. It's an efficient and cost effective strategy that not only motivates and excites your employees, but also gathers additional momentum for your buzz. This phenomenon is called "Employee Evangelism."

Some key strategies that can help you begin an Employee Evangelism movement in your organization are:

• Let people know how and why you want to do something, and how it will benefit them.

• Create a Buzz Guide that spells out the do's and don'ts of creating buzz.

- Publish and distribute success stories, company information, and interesting trivia to employees and customers. Encourage them to share it.

- Publicly recognize employees that create buzz.

- Encourage reporting of buzz efforts.

- Set a goal of a minimum number of buzz attempts each week.

- Encourage employees to become experts in a given field.

If you do those things, and also give your advocates clear examples and instructions on buzz tools, you will find your business growing quickly. Some examples of buzz tools are:

- Blogging

- Podcasts

- News sites where you can post news, such as www.digg.com

- Email follow-ups with stale connections

- Build a Squidoo lens

- Bookmark company pages with social bookmark tools like del.icio.us

- Hand out coupons to people they know

There are hundreds of variations of this kind of buzz creating opportunity. The most important thing to remember is that doing one or two of these things occasionally is not going to make an impact. If you successfully build a culture of buzz where every employee feels like they are responsible for the success of the organization, then you will be able to sustain the buzz effort and eventually hit a crucial mass where you have customers lining up for what you have to offer.

The best part of this whole idea is that this technique costs less than traditional marketing and advertising, and word-of-mouth is shown to be one of the most effective and influential mediums to get your message out to potential customers. It is well worth the extra effort, and in a relatively short period of time it will be paying off.

Ron McDaniel is a long-time entrepreneur, technology specialist, Internet marketer, buzz marketer, and word-of-mouth marketing specialist. He is also a teacher, professional speaker, and author. His mission is to get the world talking about his clients. His book, Buzzoodle Buzz Marketing - 57 Word of Mouth Marketing Challenges, shows how to create buzz for yourself and your organization in just a few minutes a day and is available for purchase on Amazon.com. McDaniel is available for speaking, training and limited buzz consulting. Please visit www.buzzoodle.com for more information.

Building Your Business on Innovation

By Dennis D. Laughlin

Everyone starts their business with a winning idea, that one core competency which distinguishes their service or product apart from everyone else. Wouldn't you like to install a system in your business which perpetuates that winning idea and makes growth and profitability easier to achieve? When we start a business we have an energy that is generated from this advantage we have developed; our innovation fuel tank is on full. As time goes by, however, it is very easy to find yourself unable to sustain the rate of growth and match the energy levels you experienced in those fertile days of the launch. Often business owners chalk this up to "maturity" and sometimes falsely celebrate the "normalcy" that sets in. My experience has been that such feelings are the first warning sign of a business plan going bad.

Innovation is often misunderstood; many times it is mistaken for invention. The two are actually quite different concepts. I think of invention as taking a green field and developing a totally new concept in the world. I am involved in a high-tech electronics firm devoted to medical products. This company developed a new implantable cochlear device, a permanent hearing aid. This was an invention. There was a huge amount of human and physical capital, not to mention research dollars, invested before a single device is even designed, let alone produced and tested. Innovation is looking around you for the unrealized potential of ideas, products and methods, which, when applied, have the appearance and many of the characteristics of an invention. Of course, much of the development time and hard work are already performed and all you are left with is the task of making relevant changes to apply to your business. I don't mean to underestimate the hard work innovation can require. There are a whole new set of skills which need to be developed to become an *innovation opportunist*. An innovation opportunist embraces the mission of setting new directions for their operations and their market segment. The job, however, is much different than the corporate think tank or a structure of an engineering firm dedicated to product development. To the opportunist, the entire world is fair game; he/she is in a giant scavenger hunt for useful tools.

Opportunists are made, not born. In other words, opportunism is a learned behavior. They survive in a culture that recognizes that in the competitive markets we all serve there is no such thing as an insignificant advantage. The first step to creating a culture for innovation is learning to communicate to everyone in the organization just what business you are in and what advantages your core competency delivers. It is important to have a strong statement understood by all in your organization concerning your current advantages. Along the way many innovations may present themselves, but one of the keys to successfully developing them is to make certain they are concentric with your core business.

My current company is a manufacturer of control products for the HVAC industry. Our focus is on making certain that homeowners are able to be comfortable in their homes while also keeping fuel costs to a minimum. Our company has moved the HVAC industry to develop products for retrofit applications. Over the past three years we have launched a new product on average of every 72 days. Some of these products are very innovative and have allowed us to seek patents and design protections, others have been products which assist our contractors in installation and are "borrowed" from other industries and applied to our needs. The result is that something is always new at Arzel® Zoning. Along the way we have consistently stayed away from products that do not fit our stated market. Interestingly, limiting the scope actually increases the pace of innovation. Why? Because with a well identified target it is much easier to look for applicable improvements. The sort process is shorter.

The next step toward creating an innovative culture is to share the tasks. Diversity rules once you have your focus statement, a varied background, and the viewpoint for your search team is essential. After all, you are looking for varied input. Don't be so presumptive as to think you can pick who out will have a good idea. In our company, we have developed many innovative damper solutions. These are ideas that often times come from comments in the field. Some come as complaints, others as a result of a failed product autopsy, and still others as a result of an assembly technician in our plant having an idea to increase quality or ease of manufacture. Our latest patent applications list nine co-inventors on the application; they span sales, tech support, and administration and assembly employees (by the way, there is not a single degreed engineer in the bunch).

You must find methods to increase input. I remember the movie, *Short Circuit*, where "Johnny 5" (the little robot character) came to life. His great line is, "Input ... I need input." That is just what you want for your company. Input comes from every imaginable direction. In today's "Googlefied" environment, no search term is too off the wall. It is amazing the speed with which new ideas can appear. I also routinely go to trade show events outside my core industry. When I want to improve my marketing skills, I go to the *The Motivation Show* in Chicago and see how professional marketing companies advertise themselves. Last year, we started working through distribution, and we needed to develop point of sale displays. So I went to the INEXPO event for retail display professionals. If imitation is the most sincere form of flattery, than I intend to flatter my way to successful marketing programs. I routinely go to the *Electronic Home Expo* to find out the state of home automation control design. When I go I don't just look at the product, I also look at display design and pick up literature for review. Input knows no boundaries.

I am addicted to classified ads. Why? There are many new technologies that don't have the capital for ads in the editorial section of a magazine and don't have a publicist to write articles for submission and are trying to get the word out wherever they can. Classifieds are often times a real source of new technologies. I know we are all busy and have no time for spam. But if you can bring yourself to waste five minutes a day, some of the newest ideas in marketing and e-business appear routinely in your spam folder. Trust your virus protection a little more and once in a while open a few of these—you will see e-marketing techniques to copy in your own business.

Create a group within your company to manage innovation projects. I called ours the Product Evaluation Action Team (PEAT). It is PEAT's job to discuss the potential impact of ideas and then to put some structure around the development process. Once an innovative idea has surfaced it needs to be treated with respect and have a process which allows for evaluation. This is no time to be unfocused. Even if the idea came in a most casual manner, the way you execute its development says everything about the importance you place on innovation. Again, I favor a cross-section of disciplines to be involved in your review group.

A few years ago, I was approached to create a mentoring group. We have a contractor, a wholesaler, a trainer, and a media person, and a manufacturer (myself) as the basis of our group. We rotate meeting at each others' businesses, and we set one topic (set by the host) for an hour-long discussion. All other discussion is free-form and topical to the day. The result: four friends who are now a part of your innovation team. Pick them wisely and you have the best focus group money can buy and a tremendous resource in gathering intelligence for your business. One piece of advice: Don't use your professionals, accountant, attorney, or consultant for this group. Money clouds their advice and your perception of its value. This group is different from an advisory board or a Board of Directors—those are a one-way street. You will need to give advice in a mentoring group, which is perhaps one of its most valuable attributes. There is nothing like having to express yourself to others to clear your thinking.

I am also a big fan of creating alliances with industry peers. Arzel® has done this effectively on several levels. We partner for training with several other companies. The net result is, of course, a broadened customer base, but also you begin to share your message with industry allies and the second generation of referrals is very worthwhile. As a practice we seek out new companies whom we might help. In our early years, Arzel® was forced to sell direct to contractors. As such we developed a good model on how to speak to contractors and where you needed to be to gain some traction in the HVAC Contractor world. We have let these companies share costly booth space, offered space in our contractor newsletter and held mutual events from time to time. The result was a progressive atmosphere for our customers and a real boost to our innovation index as a company. I was spending the money for all of these items, cost sharing was not nearly as important as benefit maximization. Our alliances have been geographically driven, vertically driven, horizontally planned and some we helped just because they were friends. My point is don't be driven by convention, be a passenger of opportunity.

The benefits of an innovative organization are numerous.

- I find it to be an incredibly fuel-efficient engine for corporate growth. Certainly there are many other ways to organize and grow businesses. Most of these models however require larger up-front investment of capital and manpower. Truly innovative companies almost exist best on fewer resources.

- I have many larger competitors today who cannot begin to approach our development schedule strictly because their required conventions regarding product development slow the process to a crawl. I love to create separation from my competitors; once you achieve it you have that agile reputation forever.

- You become less predictable to your competitors. Every minute they spend analyzing why you are acting as you are is one more minute you have to close the gap.

- You are going to win the Buzz War. Activity breeds discussion and anyone who does not understand the value of word-of-mouth advertising is about to enter into the realm of the dodo.

- It creates a sense of optimism for employees. My experience is that optimistic employees are more productive, have less absenteeism, and the sense of ac complishment is a strong reward. Participating in an innovative company is empowering for employees. I do think it is imperative to recognize innovative employees at times other than an annual review. Find reasons to celebrate their innovative contributions.

- Delegating innovation in the organization is a great way to develop leadership and perpetuate your management team. People build on successful projects and learn cooperation.

I appreciate technological advances as much as the next guy. I am a product of the era of the golden age of space flight and grew up in awe of the accomplishments of NASA engineers. I have just come to realize, however, that not all of us are going to be able to pull off the NASA breakthrough kind of invention. I also realize that while Velcro was a terrific development for space suits, it makes a great way to hang sales posters on the wall, and that helps me earn a living. If it wasn't for duct tape, Apollo 13 would have been a tragedy instead of a testament to innovation and borrowing pieces of technology for new important applications. Innovation is all about being in touch with your business at a level which allows you to continually expand your horizons. You need to enlist as many people as you can in the fight. You need to be committed to sharing the recognition. You need to be passionate in your promotion. You need to be open to change. You don't need big budgets, a dedicated R&D department, or lots of letters after your name (MBA, EE, ME, CEO).

History is filled with failed companies who did not embrace innovation because they tried to hang onto the product line that brought them into being. When the world converted from the vacuum tube to the transistor not a single vacuum tube manufacturer made the switch—not because it happened overnight but because they did not embrace innovation and failed to find a way to adapt. Look at fully utilizing all of your team and your resources; no matter how limited you may perceive them to be. I have learned that there is nothing common about common sense and that common sense applied to product enhancement and delivery is a powerful tool. Innovation is like solving a child's connect-the-dots puzzle. You just have to have some imagination where to look for the next dot. It is there that you just have to make the connection.

Dennis D. Laughlin began his working career in the banking industry in 1974, rising to the position of Senior Vice President and Regional Manager for Bank One in Cleveland, Ohio. In 1987 he formed Dennis D. Laughlin Associates, an investment banking company that focused on small and middle market businesses in need of capital and marketing expertise. Since 1987 Mr. Laughlin has served as a consultant to over 400 companies and has extensive experience in the process of product design and launch.

In 1997 Laughlin signed on with Arzel to help develop the Arzel name in the HVAC community and to increase market share. Since 1997 Arzel Sales have grown 3500 percent. Laughlin was Co-Founder of the Zoning Marketing alliance and currently is an ARI Board member and is Chairman of the Zone Controls Product Section. He has been a speaker at several national and regional ACCA, RSES, PHCC and events, and has been a frequent writer and contributor to Contracting Business Magazine, The News and the RSES Journal. He currently serves as President of Arzel® Zoning Technology, Inc.

Branding and Corporate Image
By Ron Finklestein

Many business owners, especially those just starting, do not have a good understanding of just what a brand is and how to create one in their business. And even if they know what a brand is, they may not know how to utilize a brand to their best advantage.

The best definition of a brand comes from Wikipedia: "a brand is a symbolic embodiment of all the information connected to a company, product, or service. A brand serves to create associations and expectations among products made by a producer. A brand often includes an explicit logo, fonts, color schemes, symbols, and sound, all of which may be developed to represent implicit values, ideas, and even personality."

To use a brand effectively, you must create a brand that reflects you and your company in the best possible light. You must also be consistent in its use throughout all forms of your marketing: visual marketing, direct marketing, creating a message, hiring the people to support your brand, and the display and use of your brand. For example, I am careful to brand myself in a very specific way. I recently received a call from a company that wanted to advertise on my website. It was from a reputable company and they wanted to pay well for advertising on my website, but what they wanted to advertise was not consistent with what I do (nor did I want to be associated with this brand). Advertising this brand on my website would not allow me to attract the kinds of people I wanted to meet and do business with. So I turned them down, my decision based on much more than money.

In this section you will hear from people who are experts in the use of creating and utilizing a brand. You will better understand that a brand stands for everything you and your company represents. A brand should be thought out and designed to reflect your business in a way that leaves no confusion. At a very personal level, you are your brand; It is the way you dress, how you act, and how you treat others, just to name a few. Everyone has heard the saying, "people do business with people they know, like, and trust." Your brand tells your audience what is important to you and why it should be important to them. Your brand should tell your audience why they should "know, like, and trust you."

Most small business owners pay little attention to their brand. This is a mistake. Your brand does not need to be expensive, but it does need to be well thought out. It needs to reflect your image in the market; how you want others to perceive you and your business. You don't need to spend millions to create a brand, but you do need to be consistent in the use of your brand so you do not confuse your audience. Like your business, your brand should grow over time.

It is very difficult to change your brand. Even if you are not active in promoting a specific brand, others may have already branded you in their minds. This happens because you have not told them how to think about you and your business. You should make this brand what you want it to be – not what others assume it is. And you should hire others that embody what your brand represents.

As you read this section, take notes on what you are doing right and build on those behaviors in your business. It is always easier to build on what you are doing right than to change what you are not doing. But do also take notes on what you are not doing that you should be doing so you can take corrective actions. Building a business takes time, and so does building a brand. When done right, you can use branding to attract others (customers and employees) who see value in your product and services. In order to do this, your marketing plan should have a section on company branding. After reading this section, update your marketing plan with a section on branding.

The Visual Components of Your Brand

By Rick Shaffer

Direct economic value of a powerful brand is obvious. We pay a premium to wear labels on the *outside* of our clothing. Evidently, the fundamental elements of brand marketing have been appropriated by global brand marketers. Yet those fundamentals remain, as a matter of simple marketing common sense, accessible to all. How we approach them is a matter of perspective that implies our own vision.

Visual Marketing

Humans are a visual species. Individually, pattern recognition is one of the most primal means by which we differentiate and learn the nature of everything around us. As you read this, the phrase "How do I look?" is being thought or said somewhere. These expressions began with our visual art and images. The visual expressions of societies throughout history—from the cave paintings of Lascaux, to illuminated manuscripts, to the art of the renaissance and later movements, to the invention and social dominance of television—have shaped our society. The computer now dominates the field. And that which indicates visual expression also defines, qualifies, and impacts every level of your business, regardless of product or service.

Visual marketing encompasses everything from which customers view a brand identity. Examples of these are logo, identity system, printed collateral, sales tools including PowerPoint presentations, web presence, media advertising, sales promotion vehicles or delivery vehicles, and anything that bears your company's symbols. These are all brand attributes. These attributes should carry forward a consistent design defined by typography, color, and layout. It is no coincidence that brand category leaders are invariably the ones at their visual best they present simple, memorable, appropriate, and consistent visual images across every conceivable communication channel. Visual cues differentiate them from the mediocre. Think about it if attention to visual brand imaging did not support sales, improve competitiveness, and deliver substantial return on investments, those brand leaders would not keep spending the money, would they? Why, then, do so many businesses underestimate the power of their appearance? Perhaps they forget tangible visuals are what the customer actually sees.

Elaborate strategy statements, committee approvals, and budget spreadsheets do not interest the consumer.

To stay current, focus on powerful visuals that speak to the core business customer. For example, if your business produces sprockets, your company's visual marketing efforts should be centered around the demographic/psychographic of those who are likely to purchase a sprocket, distribute sprockets, etc. Core visual messaging, reinforced by positive customer experiences, will ultimately drive brand awareness, loyalty, and repeat sales. Regardless of the size of your business, focus on the four key areas of visual marketing outlined below. These key areas can help give your marketing strategy visual impact.

1. Logo and Corporate Identity

Who are you? What can you do for me? Why should I care? Those fundamental questions are answered first by your corporate identity. Logos and symbols are far more than a visualization of the mission statement. They imply a customer experience so critical to 21st century marketing. If a customer views your logo and it doesn't visually compel him to look further, you have lost your sale.

Think of business cards as your professional attire. They might be a first and only impression. The choices of color, design, paper, and print leave a profound statement as to the currency, quality, and appropriateness of your brand. The same applies to your stationery, which may include, but is certainly not limited to, letterhead, envelopes, and shipping labels. Carefully think through how you will use them. Cards with tiny type, or letterhead with a format that restricts content, will prove impractical. Be certain to consider both digital and printed formats of your logo and letterhead. This will conserve time, energy, and your marketing budget whether you are a startup or an established company.

One of the most important attributes in developing a successful corporate identity is the consideration of color. Color is one of the keys to visual marketing. It can set tone or spirit, evoke emotional response, help create a lasting impression, and ultimately win a sale. Color theory as an element of design is just one consideration of the visual marketing that should be at the heart of your efforts. Your brand is the most valuable commodity of all. Just like everything else in business you get what you pay for, so choose wisely when enlisting a creative firm to help with these tasks. Now extend this line of thinking to other elements of your company's identity. These might include signage, uniforms, menus, interior design, and event marketing. Be relentless in your pursuit of a consistent and memorable brand image that differentiates you from your competition.

2. Collateral and Sales Materials

Whether appearing in printed or digital formation, these are direct representations of your business offerings. Large or small brochures, sell sheets, catalogs, and other literature are essential to making a great impression. Running a business without a strong visual emphasis on collateral is like having a party without guests. No one can envision how inviting your products can be, or how relevant and necessary your services are. Good collateral, designed in synergy with your brand identity, will support your brand image. It will provide your company with a polished appearance even as it provides vital information to potential customers and clients. Powerful, memorable, and informative collateral can be created in all shapes and sizes. Many enterprises today conserve vital marketing dollars by investing in powerful collateral, then limiting printing costs by delivering via digital download from corporate website, affinity sites, and blogs. This saves valuable printed copies for specific direct sales efforts.

3. Web Presence

Only a few years ago, the Internet was referred to as "New Media." It is now the 800-pound gorilla in the marketing conference room. Yet for all its specific niche marketing opportunities and literal differences, every web strategy should begin with an eye to integration within your visual brand image. A website is a far-reaching visual it takes your company around the world. When *you* travel, you prepare yourself with a proper wardrobe. It is the same for your website – it should be a clear, neat, concise layout with simple navigation encompassed with a Search Engine Optimization (SEO) strategy. Like a good map on a trip, this will enable your site to reach many customers.

A good web strategy should include:
• Appropriate visual integration with your brand image

• Page design creativity `and navigation that respects the viewer's needs and objectives

- Programming that takes into account both current and future site requirements

- Cross-platform, cross-browser compatibility

- Search Engine Optimization strategy

A site that ignores any of these considerations simply wastes valuable marketing dollars and opportunities to increase your company's brand equity. To achieve them all, make sure your web development process seeks out web partners with the requisite skills to do the *whole* job. Few individuals can claim total savvy in brand management, graphic design, programming languages, and SEO. It is critical to demand and evaluate web developers' previous work. Make certain the web house you select can illustrate relevant, effective sites that reflect various brands, audiences, and solutions. Assure yourself that they can provide cost-efficient on-line database management, e-commerce, and other specialized applications that your site may require. Be certain your site can change as your needs evolve. With the ever-growing popularity and necessity of Search Engine Optimization strategies, it is critical to ask for a track record of success in those areas, especially given the rapidly growing expense of a good SEO program.

Many clients are best served by combining the talents of several resources working together. These resources include a design firm or ad agency for the brand integration and visual marketing aspect of web strategy, and a technically savvy web house to execute the site. Remember, it is only one mouse-click from your site to the next one. Make sure your site maintains visual impact and use it to capture your customer's attention long enough to achieve your objectives.

4. Advertising and Direct Mail

Every advertising effort should be part of an integrated campaign that visualizes your brand's relevant attributes in a way that hits the audience simultaneously in the mind and heart. Utilize various media, such as TV, radio, newspaper, magazine, web banners, and direct mail, or better yet, the most cost-effective combination of all them within your budget. While a unique differentiating message relentlessly told must be at the center of your brand strategy, the visual execution of that strategy is the key to getting your story told. Quite simply, how you say it is just as important as what you say.

A consistent visual style—appropriate to your brand, your key message, and your audience—is vital. Style should include original and consistent photography or illustration. Only original imagery can honestly speak the unique brand image you want to convey. This will contribute to the visual differentiation you are after. Too many times, the advertising budget fails to account for the critical visual element. The result is ads appearing ordinary, dated, or stale. It doesn't have to be expensive. It just has to be well thought-out. Original art can be amortized across all media – including print, broadcast, Internet, collateral, and sales promotion. In this area, small investments can reap large dividends.

In truth, the power of branding really is in the eye of the beholder. Visual marketing will help you put your brand there and keep your company looking its best. The computer is the latest and most important tool for brand identity. Powerful logos need to be integrated to attract attention. Your organization's marketing materials are best executed by employing outside creative resources. Choose visuals that have a fresh, novel, and strong impact to make your business stand out and succeed.

Here are a few action items to get your started:

Logo and Corporate Identity
Bring meaning to your company by utilizing ideas of symbolism.

Collateral and Sales Materials
To help develop collateral create an outline of your companies offerings and services.

Web Presence
A flow chart or sketch will assist in organizing the pages you want to appear in your Website.

Advertising and Direct Mail
Put together a well branded advertising and/or direct response/mail campaign by thinking about photography, illustration or other creative graphics.

Rick Shaffer, founder and creative director of Shaffer Design Works, LLC and Winner of the Pianko Award for design, Magnum Opus Award, and the Premiere Print Award has grown his company from a small boutique design studio to a major player in the Ohio and National Marketing arena. With over twelve years of graphic design and marketing experience behind them, Shaffer Design Works specializes in advertising and marketing design for business and professional organizations. Shaffer Design Works' clients range from some of the most well-respected fortune five-hundred companies to smaller firms desiring a "personal touch". While most design and marketing companies are caught up in bureaucracy and red-tape Shaffer Design Works prides itself on their ability to exceed even the highest expectations, "Your Brand is our Passion" says Rick Shaffer. Rick takes an active role in the community by serving as a board member on the local Chamber of Commerce, Sales and Marketing Executives, along with networking and helping many businesses and colleagues in the Cleveland-Akron area. Shaffer resides in Streetsboro, Ohio with his wife and two sons. For more information on how Shaffer Design Works can help your business grow Email rshaffer@shafferdesign. com or call 216.536.8376.

Direct Response Branding

By David Garfinkel

The Tug Fork River is no stranger to blood. It cuts through the Appalachian Mountains and, for much of its course, separates West Virginia from Kentucky. In the late 1800's, one family, the Hatfields, lived on the West Virginia side of the Tug Fork. Another, the McCoys, made the Kentucky side of the river their home.

The Hatfields and the McCoys got into a famous feud that lasted 11 years. It led to more than two dozen violent deaths, seven life prison sentences, and one hanging. Eventually, the violence ran its course. Both sides decided enough was enough, and they found a way to get along.

In business, we have our own version of the Hatfields and the McCoys; the Branding and Direct Marketing "families" have gotten into a nasty feud of their own.

Branders condescendingly refer to direct marketers as "sleazy" and "the black sheep of the family." Direct Marketers accuse branders of being "frauds," "bureaucrats," and "mental midgets." Though the conflict is primarily verbal and emotional, rather than physical and lethal, it has still been quite ugly. And the results have been just as deadly for the businesses served by marketers. Why? Because only a tiny percentage of new businesses make it to their fifth birthday. And of those that do, only a small portion of those businesses make enough profit to make staying in business worthwhile.

This sad state of affairs is as much a failure of the marketing business owners have paid for as it is a failure of the individual business owners. It is because neither the Branders nor the Direct Marketers have ever provided an acceptable, reliable, and complete enough solution to keep most businesses in good financial health.

What's The Difference Between Traditional Branding and Direct Response Marketing?

Branders believe familiarity breeds success in the marketplace. Branders say, in effect: If they know you, they will buy from you. Advertise to get your "brand" known in the marketplace; that's all you have to do. Branders talk about recognition scores and other measures of consumer awareness, as if those metrics indicated the health of a particular business.

Direct Marketers believe that sales are everything. Plus, they insist that sales can only occur at a specific time—and that time is called "now." The idea of banking on sales that might occur sometime, somewhere in the future? That's a losing bet. Merely building familiarity without asking for the order—right away—is a pointless exercise and a waste of money, say the Direct Response Marketers.

You can see why the two camps don't get along.

For many years, I was a hard-line direct marketer. I never met a definition of Branding I liked, and I really hated most advertising I saw. But I was always uncomfortable with the exclusion of Branding from the direct marketer's toolkit, because I knew that there was some truth to the Branders' claim that people buy from businesses they know about.

In 2006 I came across a new definition of Branding that appealed to me and made sense from a Direct Marketing perspective. That wasn't nearly as surprising as the source of the new definition: A former executive of some of the world's largest advertising agencies, including J. Walter Thompson and BBDO—a man who had orchestrated national mass media Branding campaigns that had increased sales by hundreds of millions of dollars.

His name was Ben Mack. He said Branding was not a logo, a color palette, a jingle, a slogan, or a company name. His definition of Branding was: *the relationship a company has with its customers that determines how likely it is that the customers will buy from the company again.*

That definition was revolutionary to me. And refreshing. Finally, a definition of Branding that made sense, which could work side-by-side with Direct Marketing.

The Birth of Direct Reponses Branding: The Market Institute

One of my clients, The Market Institute, hired Ben Mack. He used his Branding method to describe and sculpt the corporate personality that represented this company's values and offered the kind of relationship it wanted to have with its customers.

Ben's Branding work also turned out to be the perfect launch pad for me to write direct-response copy. I found that having the Branding work done as a foundation made the take-action-now sales copy richer, more textured, and more effective.

Company executives used our work as the basis of a complete marketing plan for their service—education in stock and options trading. By using the Direct Response Branding, they are able to set themselves apart very favorably in a crowded and competitive field. They report it paved the way for selling new customers into their program.

Who would have thought that Branding and Direct Marketing could work together?

I never would have imagined it, and still couldn't, based on the old vague and cryptic definitions of Branding. Ben's definition is a breath of fresh air.

How Your Business Can Profit From Direct Response Branding

If your advertising and other marketing initiatives are giving you all the business you can handle at an acceptable cost per new customer, then what I'm about to tell you will be an interesting but optional addition to your marketing arsenal.

However, if you are like most businesses, you fall into one of three categories:

• Either… Hard-Core Branding, where you don't count on your advertising specifically to bring you any business,

• Or… Hard-core Direct Marketing, where you believe that while Branding may work for some businesses, it's irrelevant to yours,

• Or… Not wedded to any particular business philosophies about advertising, marketing, or getting new customers.

Any of those ring a bell? You would benefit considerably from Direct Response Branding if you fall into any of those three categories. Most business owners I have worked with fall into the third one. Yes, they want new customers! But no, they don't have a deliberate strategy or philosophy about how to get them.

The good news about Direct Response Branding is that, for the first time, you have a ready-made, proven strategy that doesn't force you to make an either/or choice (either Branding, or Direct Response). You can have the best of both worlds, and your business will prosper in the process.

The key to making this work is to understand that *every marketing message you send out to prospects or customers needs to strive towards two goals.*

The first goal is to *bring your prospect closer to making a purchase*—or, if the person is already your customer, then the first goal is to bring that person closer to making *another* purchase.

Not indirectly, not timidly, not by a hint—but by a clear and appealing invitation.

This, of course, is the Direct Marketing portion.

The second goal is to insist that every marketing communication *directly and overtly communicate the uniqueness of your business to your prospects and customers* in a way that makes you more appealing than your competitors and indeed preferable to anyone else in your marketplace.

And that's the Branding portion.

How do you build this kind of overpowering marketplace advantage into your business? You start with six marketing components.

The Six Major Pieces of the Direct Response Branding Puzzle

1. **Inner Essence** – You could almost call this the soul of your company. What's inside the hearts and minds of your leaders? This is what represents your most important values, along with what you're willing to promise to your customers.

2. **Marketplace Identity** – How you are perceived by your current and future customers, so that they want to do business with you and also so that what they see is consistent with who you really are.

3. **Unique, Compelling Benefits** – What your customers get from you, or can expect to get from you, that they can't exactly find anywhere else.

4. **Statements of Promise** – What you tell your current and future customers in your marketing messages about what they can expect when they do business with you.

5. **Proof of Promises** – Evidence that you really do deliver on your promises.

6. **Invitation to Take Action** – Where you spell out a specific next step for your current and future customers to take.

Each of these pieces plays a vital role in weaving a web of irresistible appeal throughout your marketing.

Your Inner Essence is something no one can knock off, because it is unique to your business. The key to making this work is coming up with a tightly-worded promise that threads through all of your marketing. Then, the second puzzle-piece, your Marketplace Identity, encapsulates that Inner Essence in a series of statements people can grab onto and understand the value of your uniqueness.

As we go down the list, we move from the broader brush strokes to the finer details; from the intangible and visionary to the practical and concrete.

Unique and Compelling Benefits should be tangible enough for your prospects and customers to visualize. Your Statements of Promise positively predict high-quality future experiences and outcomes for your customers.

Proof of Promises? That's where you'll really set yourself apart in the marketplace. Very few companies take the time to think through the rich chain of events from Inner Essence through convincing Proof of Promises. When you do, suddenly you have ruled out many or all of your competitors, and prospects who were shopping around, now choose you.

Finally, the Invitation to Take Action is really where the rubber meets the road. By making a compelling and appealing invitation, you are guiding new business your way on a regular and profitable basis.

Three Questions to Maximize All of Your Marketing

Direct Response Branding is a new idea, but it's also a very deft combination of proven techniques from two warring camps in the marketing industry. Not everyone will be able to cash in on all the advantages of this new approach right away. However, here are three questions that can help you get the best benefits of Direct Marketing Branding from any marketing message:

1. Does it communicate a core-identity that fairly represents you – and that your customers find magnetically appealing?

2. Are the unique, compelling benefits of your business evident to your customers?

3. Does each marketing message make a simple, obvious invitation to your current and future customers to take action that will lead to doing business with you?

Many people in marketing have a vested interest to keep the Hatfield and McCoy feud going between Branding and Direct Marketing. That is, to make you believe that one precludes the other, and it would be disastrous to combine them into one marketing strategy.

If someone tells you that, do yourself a favor and don't believe them! Because if you do, you'll not only be depriving yourself and the rest of the people in your company, but you'd be cutting off a lot of potential customers from doing business with you.

Remember that Branding and Direct Marketing are the two missing pieces of the puzzle to create a comprehensive and far more reliable marketing approach for businesses that want to thrive and last.

David Garfinkel is founder of the World Copywriting Institute in San Francisco. He's author of Advertising Headlines That Make Your Rich and co-author of Guerrilla Copywriting. His groundbreaking multimedia product Copywriting Templates has revolutionized the teaching and practice of writing effective advertising. To get more information about Copywriting Templates, visit: http://davidgarfinkel.com/profitable. Sign up for his World Copywriting Newsletter by visiting www.copynewsletter.com.

Serving Up the PIE
A Crucial Piece of Your Brand
By Kurt A. Minson

In the marketing game, the biggest key to success is the ability of your message to generate, expand, and accelerate favorable and compelling perceptions of what your product or service will do for a client. These perceptions, which are really mental pictures, need to differentiate your offerings from those of your competition in the minds of the prospects you want to acquire. The idea of the perceptual power of your message working its magic in the market mind is crucial. It's important because the human brain is essentially a pattern recognition device, much like that super-charged checkout scanner next to the National Inquirer at your local grocery store. As a species we tend to capture data and link it to the current pictures/patterns and associations that we already have mentally on file. This means that we base many of our buying decisions primarily on the nature of the emotions that are elicited from the patterns that our brains recognize.

Sure, I know what you're thinking, some folks (that would be our friendly neighborhood accountants, engineers, actuaries, architects, and physicians) use only hard data to make these type of buying choices. The truth is, while more objective data may go into the decision-making process in these particular individuals, visceral, emotional responses to both the object and the data surrounding it is still key to the decision itself. All that accumulated information often serves as the justification for an emotional choice already made. In short, in order for your good message to penetrate and support the rise of a real brand inside the market mind, it must target the human brain and emotional network first and often, to move consumers to desired action.

Pattern recognition machine…one concept to a single slot in the mind.
On top of these cool "scanning mechanics" lies the fact that, just like in the grocery, building and keeping a good set of recognition protocols requires that the brain build the vast majority of its relationships in a defined, one-to-one format. The fact that humans track a single idea back to its source in this fashion generates a message-to-perception-to-behavior code that can be tougher to crack than many marketing approaches would lead business owners to believe.

This means that whatever your marketing message is, if you want it to be preeminently effective, you must "own" it in the minds of the markets you want to capture. Essentially, your business must be the only one that leverages that concept in that specific way. When marketing attempts to be all things to all people (think Ford or GM), the buying tendencies of the market mind tend to dismiss that undefined "pseudo-brand" out of hand. But what does all this biopsychology have to do with how to play in your prime?

Pundits talk a great deal about the necessity of developing a particular market focus, a "sustainable advantage" or Unique Selling Proposition (USP). Each of these concepts stress that a business should represent its approach by a limited phrase or, better yet, a single word that captures an important idea. This word or phrase is that one powerful notion that a business can lay claim to and call its own. Think "driving" for BMW, "the network" for Verizon, "cold refreshment" for Coors or "cheap chic" for Target. This idea ownership implies a level of power to recognize and crack the message-to-perception-to-behavior code specific to engaging with customers/clients to effectively sell products. It also speaks to the ability of your company to leverage that power to cut through the gazillions of other competing messages that clutter the market. Ultimately, the goal of great marketing is to get nicely situated in a highly desirable courtside seat in the hotly contested mental arena of potential buyers and to stay there 24/7.

The challenge is that, while most companies spend their time and effort working closely with their products and/or services, very few take the time to look deeply inside their own business cultures. Only by knowing themselves well enough to fine tune and deploy key cultural concepts can a business take an idea and elevate its performance to a level above a garden variety USP. In my firm, The M Group, we call such a high performance idea—correctly framed, culturally balanced, and executed—the Prime Idea for Engagement, or PIE. The elements that are most important to make the Prime Idea effective are primacy, size, singularity, boldness, significance, divisibility, and sustainability.

You need to be first or pretty darn close!
Often in business, a company will wait until they have their new product perfected before they take it to market. Make no mistake, having a product or

service that doesn't function well can be a death knell, but so can being second in the pool. For example, most Americans are pretty sure of the first president of the United States, but surprisingly, very few can name the second or third guys to sit in that big chair, though both John Adams and Thomas Jefferson were exceedingly formidable men in their own right. Whether you happen to be a fan of energy drinks or not, Red Bull made a formidable claim early in the game for the designation of the drink "that gives you wings." As a counter to the primacy argument, "if you can't be first, be darn close and be noticeable" can also be a great strategy. Bill Gates didn't invent the idea of software or even the DOS code that much of Microsoft's Windows is based on. But once he got control of the early code, he made sure that he made a splash in the marketplace – and the rest is history.

A Prime Idea is Usually Big!

A common business mistake is to adopt a small idea or litany of them (think price, customer service, good people, or company integrity) as the foundation for core marketing. Wal-Mart has demonstrated that any idea, including something like price, can be expanded to become really big, however, this is the exception to the rule. Common company references like the ones mentioned above are tough because they are deployed by far too many organizations and just get lost in the clutter. Also, while these concepts have merit, they often would be considered to be just part of the price of admission and not of exceptional stand-alone value. On the other hand, a company like Nordstrom's, well-known for its customer service, shows the power of going big with a common idea. The retailer is rumored to have taken a return on a set of used snow tires from a dissatisfied customer. Not a big deal, until you consider that Nordstrom's doesn't sell tires of any type and never has. Big ideas go beyond that first round of consideration and tap into something more vital and yes, emotional, to fuel a set of deeper perceptions in the market mind. These patterns of good or great pictures build linkage directly into the human emotion centers and, through this route, access buying behavior and the sales momentum that naturally increases revenues and profits. Another company's founder, Fred Smith, didn't get that great grade "A" on the project paper that introduced the idea for the company that became FedEx. However, he took control of one of the most powerful PIEs in recent memory when the business proclaimed, "When it absolutely, positively has to be there overnight" and then built the infrastructure and technology to make it possible.

You have to own it.

Singularity in a Prime Idea means that your idea "belongs" to you and barriers exist to stop anyone else from laying claim to your concept or its spot in the market mind. Additionally, your PIE must be the one concept you ride early and often and when the game is on the line. Volvo owns one idea: safety. One of the biggest challenges for Detroit's Big Two, Plus One (GM, Ford, and Daimler-Chrysler) is that they refuse to choose a single concept to ride. This muddies the message waters, even within their own companies, and their huge losses underscore this point. For many businesses, coming up with an original idea, let alone a Prime Idea, in a mature sector feels all but impossible. This might be true if one didn't consider that you can create a new sector from scratch and own it, instead of fighting an entrenched competitor. Pierre Omidyar applied this approach nicely when he mused that an online auction business might be a nice sideline as an alternative to conventional tag or garage sales. That was before he founded eBay and started a firestorm instead. One small caveat of singularity is that it also works in reverse. While the company owns the concept it promotes, the concept also owns the company when executed well. Volkswagen's attempt to build a big, luxurious German sedan fell as flat as a potato pancake when its Phaeton debuted, even though the car had a very cool and unique power plant and was based on the highly successful Audi A8 platform. The young hip urban professionals who made the Golf, Passat, and New Beetle popular "baby" German performance cars couldn't stomach the notion of going establishment and driving their father's big cruiser, and all the players couldn't see spending upwards of $65,000 for a big VW. Fahrvergnugen indeed!

Boldness

Creating a new sector certainly can be revolutionary, but the equation that leads to this outcome doesn't take a nuclear physicist to pull off. Human beings get most of their information through the five senses of sight, hearing, touch, smell, and taste...psychics and gypsies need not apply. These sensory inputs lead to the mental patterns and recognition dynamics previously discussed. Does your singular idea not only belong to you, but also thrill the senses in a fresh and, yes, powerful way? Scott's hit on two senses at once when they said that their Turfbuilder products would produce a thicker, greener lawn. Memorex suggested crystal clear fidelity when they asked, "Is it live or is it Memorex?" Burger King's Charbroiled Whopper hits hard with the sensory impacts on taste, smell, and the popping of broiling beef. The better your PIE appeals to the senses, the bolder it will be in the marketplace.

Significant

Sure your company now owns a big idea that also impacts the senses, but is that enough? To really be Prime, your idea must also be significant. This element is so important that it has two separate facets to it. Internal significance means that the idea is well-grounded in your corporate culture. Remember Kodak copiers? I thought not. As arguably the greatest American camera film company and a tearjerker extraordinaire with those Kodak Moment spots, the company certainly knew traditional photographic reproduction. That knowledge, however, did not equip them internally, to translate their market power into business copier reproduction success.

The other significance must take place outside your business, in the markets where you do business. New economy companies, like Yahoo!, Dell, AOL, and YouTube depend almost exclusively on this type of timely external significance to build momentum and profitability. Who would have ever thought that a complex set of computer algorithms (Google) that helped folks play online sleuth to find all kinds of information on the internet would become one of the juggernauts of the American economic landscape, a Dow Jones Industrial Average company and be translated into a verb to boot...have you "Googled" me yet?

Divisible

Market observations have shown that line extensions of popular products often dilute the power of the core brand, by pulling buyers from the core product and not competitor's brands. Companies, however, are still obsessed with using an established concept to build momentum for something new. Certainly, Johnny Depp has to be feeling pretty good to see the record receipts for the 2006 megahit *Pirates of the Caribbean 2: Dead Man's Chest*, the granddaddy of all sequels. Soda makers are having a tougher time, however, as Vanilla Coke, Vanilla Pepsi, Coke Blak, and Lime Pepsi will probably give way to licorice, liver and

Brussels sprouts flavors if the current trend of propagation continues unabated. In moves belying its relatively small size, Apple has done a tremendous job bringing its "cool technology" PIE, in the form of iPods of all sizes and sleek white computers, into the national mix without any cumbersome 15-character alpha numeric model numbers to speak of.

Sustainable

Your business can talk the talk when making claim to a strong concept, but can it walk the walk by carrying it forward for the long term and against strong competition? Ad campaigns are built to titillate in the moment, but Prime Ideas must be built to endure as the central focus of marketing activity for years. Like them, love them, or hate them, DeBeers still owns the concept of diamonds in the U.S. and most of the rest of the Western world. This is so, even though that position is constantly under attack from companies like Leo Schachter, who proclaim the power of their specific diamond designs. Predatory business practices, slow product introductions and Bill Gates riding off into the public sector sunset notwithstanding, when most Americans think of software, that little Washington State-based company, Microsoft still has significant chops in the segment they helped create. Even with the advent and early success of Frontier, Jet Blue and other low-cost carriers, Southwest still holds the market mind title as the nation's low-cost carrier. Built specifically to eliminate the waste of traditional carriers and reduce ticket prices, the airline's culture is designed to promote savings at every turn. From their economical Chicago hub (Midway, not O'Hare), khakied and polo shirted flight attendants and lack of significant extras keeps overhead controlled and the company profitable. Even the introduction of their online savings notice service, Ding!, brings low cost squarely to rest within the market mind.

Most companies have a good idea about the nature and internal dynamics of their products and services. The challenge is that too many businesses spend most of their time looking only at these elements, but not at their internal culture or how the market place perceives their company and what they make or promote. Many ad agencies or marketing firms talk at length about branding, positioning, and mind share. But it must be noted that none of those things can happen successfully without a big, primary, and robust fundamental concept; a

Prime Idea that can serve as both the fuel and foundation for the central brand inside the mind of a consumer.

Kurt A. Minson, Chief Engagement Officer of The M Group Consultants is the originator of the "Full Engagement" and "Prime Idea for Engagement" concepts. He has an extensive social science background, with degrees in psychology, sociology, philosophy and economics, as well as concentrations in French, German and the classics. He brings a deep insight into human thought, behavior, motivations and decision making into the process of marketing, sales and customer service. Since 1994 his firm has integrated a cultural backbone into the exposure, engagement and client experience work that they do for professional service firms and other businesses in the Midwest. In addition to the conventional weapons of the trade; advertising, design, events, PR and web, Minson uses personality profiles, appreciative inquiry, structured interviews and other tools to tap the cultural essence of client organizations. These investigations uncover the "diamonds in the rough" that can be developed into Prime Ideas and provide the roadmap that allows his firm to effectively deploy engagement and experience training. Minson's other service offerings include image and wardrobe, personal promotions, ideation, diversity, franchise development, branding-positioning and recruitment for engagement. All of these elements are focused on building performance business cultures that understand how to take what they have to acquire, expand relations with and keep more clients to build revenues and profits.

For more information, please visit www.mgroupconsultants.com or contact him at (330) 762-4441.

Make Your Brand Irresistible
Overpromise and Overdeliver
By Rick Barrera

Hard times create amazing successes. Despite all the talk today of an oversupply of goods and services, industry consolidation, menacing imports, stalled prices, and shrinking margins, a few remarkable businesses have discovered how to make their brands irresistible to more and more customers. And they have done it in remarkably speedy fashion, seemingly coming out of nowhere to virtually own their markets.

Consider, for example, Google, which went from being a nonsense word to a global verb and supernova of the Internet in only three years, which then led to its becoming a publicly traded company with an $80 billion market cap. Or what about the gizmo named TiVo, which changed television viewing forever for millions of American families by creating buzz outside the typical sales and marketing channels? Dozens of similarly surprising brands—names like American Girl, Best Buy, Chico's, Hardiplank, and Washington Mutual—are thriving in all sorts of sectors, from manufacturing to wholesale to retail, and they have been built far more quickly and inexpensively than brands that rely solely on traditional approaches, most notably advertising.

How do these luminaries do it? They overpromise and they overdeliver. It's a new, faster, and less-expensive approach to beating the competition that I call TouchPoint Branding. Simply put, they have made big promises to their customers, and they are delivering on them in big ways at three important points of interaction.

TouchPoint Branding begins with a unique, attention-grabbing brand promise that radically differentiates a company from its competitors. Google, for instance, vows to lead you to virtually anything you want to know, in 0.2 seconds. TiVo's pledge is TV— your way! American Girl promises dolls that enchant girls and teach them how to live a life of substance. In a glutted business environment in which everyone seems to be shouting the same message simultaneously and at peak volume, exciting breakthrough brand promises are the best ways to stand out from the crowd.

New companies must develop unique brand promises just to battle their way into the marketplace. Established businesses, faced with fighting off upstarts and differentiating themselves from their rivals, have to periodically overhaul their brand promises to adjust to changes in their environments, their competitors, and their customers.

But simply coming up with a unique brand promise, or Overpromise, isn't enough. When you Overpromise, you will be saying that you are confident your brand will perform. You will be putting your whole reputation for honesty on the line, making a solemn contract with hundreds, thousands, maybe even millions of customers. And, as wise managers know, trust is the hard currency of business success. The price for squandering it—sabotaging a brand's promise—is always too high to pay, because, at the end of the day, the priceless intangible called integrity is the richest asset on any company's balance sheet.

So after a brand promise has been clearly established, you must also Overdeliver by keeping your promises in imaginative, dynamic, and unique ways. And to do that, managers will need to get their entire organizations aligned to execute that big promise flawlessly and, above all, consistently, every day with every sale or interaction. You must give your customers more than they ever expected from you at each of three critical moments of interaction—the Product TouchPoint, the Human TouchPoint, and the System TouchPoint. That's where your advantage over competitors will emerge.

Product TouchPoints occur where customers interact with the product or service your company is selling. These are contacts in which the customer actually experiences, handles, buys, uses, and disposes of a product or service. They are the primary factors in most buying decisions. For Google, a Product TouchPoint occurs every time a visitor types in a query and gets a search result.

The second key contact point, the Human TouchPoint, occurs when the customer directly interacts with an organization's people. While I believe that most companies rely far too heavily on human interactions, I am not in favor of eliminating them. They make it possible to deliver on your brand promise in ways that only fellow humans are capable of—for instance, by empathizing with customers, clearing up misunderstandings, and tailoring solutions to a customer's particular circumstances. It is at the Human TouchPoint that frontline people can bend, and sometimes break, the rules in a customer-friendly fashion. Organizations like the Ritz-Carlton hotel chain, for example, have built their brands on the shoulders of Overpromising, Overdelivering frontline employees. The Ritz brand promises to deliver the gold standard of human service.

The third key area of interaction, System TouchPoints, include all other points of contact between a company and its customers. They occur when customers encounter processes (paper invoices, for example, and frequent buyer programs) or systems (technological tools like ATMs and websites) that facilitate transactions and interactions. Seattle-based Amazon.com is a prime example of a business whose online retailing systems and processes are so intuitive and so helpful that its customers seldom have any need for traditional customer service. They find what they need and order it, get progress reports by e-mail, pay online with their credit or debit cards, and get their goods by express shipment. It is here, by the way, in the promise of technology, that companies can make their biggest gains by Overdelivering to reduce the variables that hinder consistently excellent service.

All three TouchPoints are vital to an organization's success, though to differing degrees. All three require a substantial and continuing investment of funds and managerial energy if they are to do their job properly—although I should point out that you don't have to be a billion-dollar corporation or have access to vast sums of venture capital to build a terrific brand. Small and medium-sized organizations can do it as easily as large ones—and sometimes even better. A real estate broker in my hometown of San Diego differentiated himself by using TouchPoint Branding. The broker's TouchPoints include a high-value brochure mailed to potential buyers, accurate floor plans done by an architect, aerial photography, inspections and reports completed before a home is listed, and an interior designer who "stages" sellers' homes. It paid off in more properties sold much quicker and at a higher percentage of the list price than his competitors.

When properly executed, TouchPoint Branding enables managers at every level to inspire their employees to over-deliver on the company's brand promise. This is the breakthrough that can revitalize your company, just as it has propelled the trailblazers I've written about here.

Action Items:
1. Create a clearly articulated Overpromise for your brand that tells customers and potential customers how your brand is different and why they should buy it.

2. Draw a Customer Experience Map that shows the customer journey from initial need through purchase, use and disposal.

3. Identify the three Critical TouchPoints from the customer's point of view.

4. Build unique brand experiences around each of these TouchPoints that Overdeliver on your Overpromise.

5. Execute flawlessly!

Rick Barrera is president of Overpromise, Inc., a customer experience consulting firm that designs and executes differentiating marketing strategies for companies of all sizes. An influential business lecturer for many Fortune 500 companies, he is also co-author of Non-Manipulative Selling and Collaborative Selling. "Overpromise and Overdeliver" is published by Portfolio and China Machine Press. An excerpt is available at www.overpromise.com. Barrera lives in Rancho Santa Fe, Calif. and can be reached at (858) 759-2559.

Hiring to Your Brand
Why Your Recruiting Methods Should Be As Unique As Your Brand
By Rick Barrera

When Hollywood directors cast a superstar they count on two things: box office draw and the professional actor's ability to *act*, by which I mean the ability to stop being Philip Seymour Hoffman, Charlize Theron, or Jim Carey and instead become the three-dimensional living embodiment of someone else. Watch *Capote, Monster*, or *Lemony Snicket's A Series of Unfortunate Events*, and you will see the incredible transformations these actors make in their own personalities to literally become the character, sometimes even adjusting their own physical makeup, such as by gaining or losing huge amounts of weight, to ensure a complete and congruent representation.

Now think about your own employees, especially those who spend the most time interacting with customers. How willing (or capable) are they of completely transforming their bodies, minds, souls, and personalities into the ideal personification of your brand?

I'm sure you would agree that most are not capable of these radical transformations and that even if they were, they would be unwilling to spend huge parts of their lives pretending to be someone they are not. Radical transformation requires enormous energy, rare talent, and is highly stressful. Counting on radical transformation in each of your people is not the formula for creating consistent, positive, scalable customer experiences.

Instead let me suggest that you use a technique well-known to the directors of high school musicals and local theatre companies—type casting. Type casting means that you put someone into the role who is *already* the character! There will be little acting required because they live and breathe the character everyday just by being themselves. Their thoughts are the character's thoughts. Their beliefs are the character's beliefs. Their actions are the character's actions.

In the high school musical, for example, the prom queen is cast as the damsel in distress who mesmerizes all of the men, the school jerk is cast as the antagonist, and the captain of the sports team is cast as the hero who will save the beauty.

The result? A very successful play! Why? Because very little acting is required to ensure a consistent, predicable, and believable outcome.

Type casting is a simple and proven method that ensures your people will behave as the natural extension of your brand at every touch point. To be sure, hiring to your brand requires that you are already clear about your brand's positioning and have defined the brand personality you want to project in the marketplace. Let's look at how some great brand builders have used type casting to extend their brand to the frontline.

Southwest Airlines: People Who Love People!

Southwest Airline's mission is to be *the* low cost airline. That means no frills of any kind that might get in the way of keeping costs down. But flight attendants are required to be on every flight, so Southwest uses their flight attendants as brand differentiators in the highly competitive airline market.

Interviewees for positions at Southwest are given a card deck on which are written several in-flight announcements that they might be required to make as part of their flight attendant role. They are then told that they will be given time to practice before their actual interview and are lead into a room where they are told other applicants are also practicing while waiting for their own interviews.

The interviewees' actions in this room are in fact the actual interview. Do they hide in the corner and try to go it alone? Or do they actively engage the group or other individuals in the task? Do they suggest the other person go first or do they selfishly insist on going first? Do they try to inject humor into the situation and into the announcements or do they rigidly stick to the script? Are they creative and improvisational? Are they personable and easily likable? Do others gravitate toward them or away from them?

Southwest doesn't try to train these core attributes into their people nor do they expect them to act in order to display them. They screen for people who are natural "connectors," those who really love interacting with strangers. Whether their supervisors are watching or not, these people will behave in exactly the same way because this is who they already are. The connector's personality already matches Southwest's brand personality.

The results of this strategy have been stellar for Southwest both in terms of customer experience and financial gains. Southwest has posted 32 consecutive years of profitability in an industry that is rarely profitable.

On a recent Southwest flight our flight attendant made a big deal of congratulating a 94-year-old man who was taking his first flight ever. Despite his fear, failing health, and near blindness he had completed the flight without a problem. All of the passengers cheered and clapped and a few even had tears in their eyes. She concluded the announcement with, "He appreciates your allowing him be your pilot." The passengers roared with laughter. What a great way to end a flight and what a great story to tell the friends and family who have come to greet you. Southwest's brand came to life, courtesy of the flight attendant's natural sense of humor.

Microsoft: Super Smart Problem Solvers

Microsoft, the world's largest software company, also takes great pains to hire to the brand. Microsoft believes that the best software is created by the smartest people who are the best problem solvers. During their interviews, Microsoft poses exceptionally difficult problems to potential employees and then assesses the applicant's attitude toward the problem, their approach the problem, and the quality of their logic. Microsoft looks for people who do not shut down when faced with seemingly impossible tasks but rather are challenged and inspired by them.

Typical questions in a Microsoft interview might include:

"How would you move Mount Fuji?"

"How many piano tuners are there in the world?"

"How would you design a spice rack for a blind person?"

"Why are man hole covers round?"

"Blindfolded and sitting in front of a bowl containing three different colors of jelly beans, how many jelly beans would you have to take out to be certain of getting two of the same color?"

The answers to these questions routinely run to 100 pages or more. This is not a recruiting process for the faint of heart. If you want to work with the best and brightest minds in the world on Herculean software tasks, you'll have to prove yourself worthy.

While Microsoft is currently challenged on many fronts, there is no doubt that the firm has changed the world with its software and made its founder one of the richest men in the world.

Patagonia: Going Easy on the Rock

Patagonia is an outdoor clothing and accessories company with a deep commitment to the environment. Its founder started the company to design and sell environmentally-friendly mountain climbing pitons. So where does Patagonia do most of its recruiting? Outdoors, of course. Patagonia leaders and employees, whether on or off-duty, are always on the lookout for other sports enthusiasts who share their deep concern for the wilderness and its preservation. Neither the smartest engineer nor the most talented designer would last long in the company if their environmental values did not match those of Patagonia.

The result of this recruiting strategy is that Patagonia is a global leader in environmentally-friendly manufacturing. They use 100 percent organically grown cotton even though it means their clothing will cost more. All of Patagonia's facilities recycle, compost, grow gardens, have edible landscapes, minimize their use of energy and water, and purchase electricity only from renewable sources. Patagonia encourages its employees to carpool and use only recycled paper.

Can you imagine managers and supervisors trying to impose these kinds of restrictions on a culture without Patagonia's shared beliefs? No amount of policing could ever make it happen. Yet, because of Patagonia's deeply-held collective beliefs, awareness equals action. While continuing to grow the company's revenues and profits, every Patagonian is on a constant search for better ways to lessen Patagonia's impact on the environment—which also tend to be better for the company's profits, especially reducing production costs, by for instance reducing monthly utility bills through energy-usage reduction.

The results have been astounding. Customers who share Patagonia's passion for both outdoor sports and environmental conservation have flocked to the company, driving the privately held company's sales past the $200 million mark.

Washington Mutual: Regular Folks with a Flair for Retail

Washington Mutual is on a quest to be "The Premier Retailer of Financial Services" in the United States. They want their brand to be "exclusively for everyone." Their focus on "everyone" is a marked contrast to the trend of financial institutions' focusing increasingly on the "merely affluent," "the mass affluent," and the "super affluent." Washington Mutual, affectionately called "Wamu" by their customers, has created a financial institution for "the rest of us."

Wamu recruits not bankers nor financial superstars, but rather regular folks with retail backgrounds who have not lost "the common touch." There is no banking jargon spoken at Wamu. There are no deposits and withdrawals, just people putting money in and taking money out. Even their ATMs speak in the vernacular. At the end of the interaction the ATM screen asks "Would you like to do something else?" and the choices are "Sure" and "No Thanks."

Wamu values "plain talk" and recruits those who can use plain language to communicate even the most complex financial transaction. Wamu has no place for those who are sophisticated, haughty, or pretentious and screens them out as part of their recruiting process. Their benchmark is that a potential applicant should never use any language that would not be used by a neighbor talking to a neighbor over the back fence. Wamulians, as they call each other, also dress casually to let customers know that you don't need to dress up to go to the bank or to apply for a mortgage. Their Simply Free Checking is… simply free. No fine print. No explanations needed.

Washington Mutual's share price has skyrocketed from $0.02 per share in 1990 to more than $45.00 per share today. They are #1 in brand awareness in the top 20 markets in the U.S. and are one of the top three mortgage companies in the U.S. Clearly, they have reached their goal of being "exclusively for everyone."

Starbucks: Passionate Coffee Lovers Who Live the Coffee Culture
Starbucks, or "fourbucks" as they are sometimes called in reference to the price of their coffee, has become a powerful global brand in a relatively short period of time, in large part because of their recruiting practice of seeking out partners (employees) who are truly passionate about their coffee and are eager to explore the global landscape of coffee, along with its history and culture.

By focusing on passion over experience, Starbucks ensures that as they educate their partners about the world of coffee, a never-ending process, partners will be just as passionate about sharing what they have learned with customers. Starbucks partners love to experience and talk about every nook and cranny of the global coffee culture. The dialogue they create with customers, in turn, causes customers to share their experiences, which provides an even richer quilt of stories for the partners to share with each other and other customers. Starbucks' 12,000-plus locations in 35 countries delivered over $7 billion of revenue in 2006.

Nordstrom: Sales People Who Understand Customer Focused Inefficiency
Nordstrom, a U.S. clothing retailer, is nearly synonymous with exceptional personal service. What is their recruiting secret? Nordstrom looks for people who are "willing to serve." Many employees feel that serving others somehow demeans them. Nordstrom's sales associates know that a willingness to serve others is the key to loyal customers that are consistently willing to pay more for the same branded items they could buy elsewhere for less because Nordstrom makes the shopping experience easier.

Because Nordstrom pays double the average industry commission, they naturally attract a large pool of proven sales superstars from their competitors. But Nordstrom looks deeper for those candidates who understand that what is counter-intuitive to most retailers is exactly the right way to serve customers. Nordstrom sales associates regularly sacrifice overall efficiency for the sake of a single customer. Nordstrom employees have been known to spend more delivering an item than the item is worth, take back merchandise Nordstrom doesn't sell, iron a shirt or tailor a suit for a customer who needs to wear it right away, and even gift wrap merchandise from another retailer!

These examples may sound absurd or even fictitious on the surface, but they are just a few of the truly extraordinary stories you will hear from Nordstrom customers. Nordstrom sales associates are experts at building their own personal clientele and are encouraged to do so. And they know that what may seem counter-intuitive on the surface is exactly the right way to keep customers loyal for life.

The Take-away:

As you read the examples I've provided, what should be most striking is how different is the *focus* and *method* for each of these companies. These brand leaders could not exchange recruiting strategies and philosophies among one another without disastrous damage to their brands. Each company has a clear understanding of the essence of their brand and how their people contribute to it. It is this clarity that makes their recruiting processes both *different* and *easier*. Having a clear profile of exactly who they are seeking makes the screening process easy. Each candidate clearly fits or not, and once hired, their personal match with the company's brand and culture ensures that their assimilation will be both rapid and smooth.

So put away the one-size-fits-all recruiting strategies you inherited from the personnel consultants and think deeply about what your people must do to extend your brand at the Human TouchPoint. Then think deeply about how you will screen for the unique talents that will make your people memorable representatives of your brand. Your recruiting methods should be as unique as your brand.

Action Items:

1. Get clear about what will differentiate your company in the marketplace and articulate it clearly in your Overpromise.

2. Define clearly the *specific* Human TouchPoint behaviors that will Overdeliver to your customers by fulfilling your Overpromise.

3. Define clearly the characteristics of the people you must hire who will behave that way naturally.

4. Design several methodologies that will enable you to screen for the traits and behaviors that are consistent with your brand.

Rick Barrera is president of Overpromise, Inc., a customer experience consulting firm that designs and executes differentiating marketing strategies for companies of all sizes. An influential business lecturer for many Fortune 500 companies, he is also co-author of Non-Manipulative Selling and Collaborative Selling. "Overpromise and Overdeliver" is published by Portfolio and China Machine Press. An excerpt is available at www.overpromise.com. Barrera lives in Rancho Santa Fe, Calif. and can be reached at (858) 759-2559.

How You Look Is What You're Saying
Three Steps to Achieving a Clear Visual Brand Message
By Daniel H. Stark

Over the years, the question that I get asked most often is "Why is design so important to me and my business? We do very well with what we have." Generally, this question comes from small business people or those looking to start their own businesses after working for large corporations their entire career. The question strikes me as odd because, generally, these are well-educated people with rich and diverse backgrounds. They are creative, at least in the profession they have chosen, and articulate. The companies for which they have worked already have these structures in place, so often they don't even think about them or their importance until after they have left. Why is consistent visual design so important? Why indeed!

In short, how you look (both as an individual and as a business) is what you're saying about your brand. A clear, relevant, unique, and consistent visual design will always win. Just look at any large corporation and imagine their logo or advertising. Generally, it speaks the same language in terms of color, form, words, and attitude. This is the goal for any business. So, the first step is to model yourself on their success and study the elements and underpinnings of those communications.

The next concept to understand and embrace is that a clear visual brand message is attained through a *process* and adherence to it. Your relationship to the process is what invariably dictates your success in the long run. Plus, because it is a process, it also means that you are never "done" with it. Rather, it is an organically growing facet of your business like any other process. It's no different than an accounting process, management process, or sales process. With these two things in mind, modeling your success and understanding that it's a process, you can move on to the vital criteria of a clear visual brand design.

Relevance

What message are you trying to convey? Who is your audience? How do they get their information? Why should they care? Are you telling them at the right time? If you can succinctly answer these questions, you will have the beginning of a plan.

Try to come up with a short list of words that describe your brand, company, or project. Be discerning and challenging with the list and make sure each one really describes you. These words will be your sounding board, which you'll revisit over and over. If you create something visually that doesn't measure up to any and all of them, then you may not be there yet.

Is your audience conservative or liberal? Wordy or visual? Old or young? Knowing who they are and how they digest their information is critical. It will inform you about how best to talk to them, making whatever you do "land" for them to hear, understand, and digest. Also, if you're delivering a visual message that matters and is compelling *to them* (either to take notice or take action), the communication will be effective. Do this by being clear about your *unique selling proposition*, or USP. This is what you offer that your competition does not. Finding a way to visually communicate that can be difficult sometimes, but it's made easier by knowing your audience, understanding their behaviors, and *how* and *when* they get their information. This will make the message—whatever it may happen to be—relevant and have a chance of sticking.

Uniqueness

Standing apart from the crowd is more important now in marketing and in life than it has ever been. Companies large and small take the process of defining their brands very seriously because communicating who you are and what you do better (or differently) than others could turn them into a customer.

Creating a unique visual identity—whether it be for a logo, ad, or other piece of marketing material, is vital to letting the world know what you are and what you stand for. Some brands rely heavily on photography or moving image while others define themselves with the words and copy in their ads. Still others create brand mascots or use illustration. Notice how companies or products advertise themselves and what mediums they use to determine the type (or types) of media that suit your USP, and begin shaping a unique message. First do it using just words, as in a mission statement or business plan. Describe it, then illustrate it with pictures, type, or drawings that correspond to the initial list of words you created. This "image board" will help define your brand as you develop and refine it.

Once you have created the message, think of the medium in which you deliver it. Can you be original and unique here, too? If your audience primarily reads newspapers, then you'll need to speak to them where they are. But can you do something interesting with the space, frequency, type, or color? If your audience is used to seeing your competition's logos as simple typeset names, like a law firm often does, would you be better served with an icon or logo that illustrates your unique point of view? Ponder these notions and find the combination that's right—and unique—for you.

Consistency

The hardest part is making sure that whatever you do—from your name, to the logo and business cards, to forms, presentations, advertising, uniforms, vehicles, physical offices, and so on—*all* needs to come from the same voice. Consistency is key to communicating a clear, visual brand message.

Take an iconic company and study their materials. Apple Computer, for example, has had a consistent message in everything they do since their *very first day*. The simplicity and ease of their ads translates seamlessly into what they do— it's who they are at their core. Because of this, the words that define their brand also exemplify their visual messages as strategically as possible. And their products. The words that you use to define yourself (in Step #1) come up again and again. That is why this is a process that will change over time. Even the words that define you might change, though they do so in the course of a process that continually grows and changes to suit you and your company's needs, so they remain relevant and thoughtful.

Another facet of consistency is putting the right people into place to steward this for the company. Many do this through their advertising agency or in-house design firm. There are no large companies that I know of who do not have a steward, agency, in-house department, or even, at the basic level, a graphic standards manual for their corporate identity program. Most major companies that work with multiple vendors, suppliers, and satellite offices have a marketing officer in charge of making sure everyone operates in the same way and with the same materials right down to the same typefaces, color palettes, and imagery. Throughout, they ensure a clear, consistent message and presentation of their brand.

Controlling and maintaining your identity, once you create it, is just as important as creating it the right way in the first place. If you can follow these initial steps, you will be well prepared to face your competition and your customers with a compelling message and identity that will ensure your success!

Action Items:

1. Create a list of 10 to 15 adjectives that describe your business in its look, feel, and approach. Try to limit your list to single words and not phrases or sentences.

2. Using the same criteria, create a list of 10 to 15 adjectives that describe your audience and how they get their information.

3. Gather examples of brand communications that inspire you or speak in the same way (visually or with words) that you wish to.

4. Look at your two lists and the examples of communications you have gathered and create a list of only five things you can do differently from your competition to have breakthrough communications. Remember to think of the media you use, like photography or type, as well as the medium you use to communicate it (radio, newspapers, direct mail, TV, etc.).

5. Carefully observe and question the consistency of what is created throughout all of your communications. Does it measure up to your first list of adjectives? If it does, then your message is likely to be consistent.

Daniel H. Stark is the principal and creative director of Stark Design in New York and is an internationally recognized art director and graphic designer whose work has appeared in numerous books and publications. He has served on the editorial staffs of Harper's Bazaar, GQ and US magazines, to name a few, and has consulted for several others worldwide.

He co-authored Stoked: The Evolution of Action Sports, a photography and art book of acclaim. Stark has worked with venerable brands and many of the iconic personalities in the fashion, entertainment, beauty, financial and luxury goods sectors. Stark currently resides in New York City and can be found on the web at www.starkdesignny.com.

Become a Top Advisor – a Household Name – and You Won't Need a Marketing Strategy

By Dennis Sommer

How would you like to run a successful business that didn't need any marketing? You have customers calling you 24 hours a day non-stop, more business than you can handle, and no need for a marketing budget. This is what can happen when you become a household name, or a "Top Adviser" in your industry. A Top Adviser is that person or business whom everyone thinks of when they have a serious problem that must be fixed. They are the expert, specialist, or guru that immediately comes to mind.

If you are in need of investment help, do the names Charles Schwab and Peter Block come to mind? Do you think of Tom Peters and Stephen Covey when you are having management issues? If you are having real-estate development issues, does the name Donald Trump come to mind? When you are faced with sales and leadership challenges, do you immediately start dialing Dennis Sommer at BTRC Business Advisers? If not, you should; that's me. You get my point. Do you think any of these Top Advisers really need to market their businesses? I don't think so. How different would your business be if your name was the first thing that comes to mind when your customer needs help? When you think about it, becoming a Top Adviser should be your highest business priority.

Let's take a look at how you can become the Top Adviser in your market and industry.

First, follow the successful marketing advice in this book. You will find very successful tips, techniques, and examples used by leaders in the field. Every Top Adviser had to start somewhere. Most likely they were in the same position you're in today. Start by implementing one marketing idea, then another. Monitor your success and adjust your strategy accordingly. As the advice from this book increases your market share and name recognition you must also focus on your second step toward Top Adviser status.

Your second step involves developing the characteristics of a Top Adviser. These characteristics are what make a person or business a Household Name instead of just someone that is in business. These characteristics make you stand out above everyone else. In your customer's mind, you will be the only one that can help them solve their problem. When these Top Adviser characteristics become second nature to you and your organization, you will be well on your way to success beyond your dreams.

Let's take a look at the key characteristics of Top Advisers broken out by Customer Service, Communication, Knowledge, and Building Strong Relationships.

Customer Service

I recently received a call from the CEO of a highly successful start-up firm. Jerry, the CEO, was very concerned about reports showing customer satisfaction was at an all-time low. During the initial launch of the firm, they expected to have a few bumps in the road. But two years after the initial launch, their customer satisfaction numbers were still low – and declining.

After reviewing their performance measurements, expectations, and the impact this challenge was taking on the firm, we decided to perform a complete Customer Service Assessment covering Sales, Finance, Services, and Management teams. Our objective was to pinpoint specific areas where customer service could be improved and make recommendations on how these improvements could be implemented. Jerry wanted his company to become a household name.

Here is what we found. The firm's ability to deliver a superior service and their knowledge of the industry was beyond reproach. These were the two factors that made them successful. The root cause of their customer satisfaction challenges was their customer service philosophy. Their focus on customer service started once a client complained; at which point they were committed to resolving the issue and did everything to keep the client as a customer.

The solution to this challenge was focusing on customer service even *before* a client became a client. By focusing on customer service from the first initial client meeting, the firm could eliminate customer complaints instead of reacting to them once they occur. Even though it is too soon to measure the impact of our training and mentoring solution, customer complaints from new clients have been declining drastically.

Top Advisers always provide superior customer service. The focus on great customer service turns satisfied customers into lifelong loyal customers.
- A positive attitude, focused attention, and commitment to resolving customer complaints will have a huge impact on customer satisfaction and the likelihood your customer will buy from you again and again.

- Guarantee your offering and stand by it. Offer an unconditional money back guarantee on all products and services.

- Help customers achieve their goals, not yours. Your goals will be exceeded when you help customers solve their problems.

- Have the best interest of the customer in mind. Try to bring a customer with a problem together with an offering that helps them solve it. If you don't have the exact solution needed, recommend other business solutions that could help them.

- Customers are not "always right." Disagree with a customer, in a polite professional manner, in order to help them make a better decision.

Communication

Take a moment and think about a Top Adviser (household name) in your industry. Do they rattle off statistics, techno jargon, and other mumbo jumbo that could only be understood by a NASA scientist? Do they go on forever lecturing you on incomprehensible topics, never giving you a chance to talk? Most likely your answer is, "No."

Top Advisers have the ability to sit down and listen to their clients. Then, they translate a very complex solution into terms that even a six-year-old can understand. They keep it simple.

Top Advisers focus on improving their written, verbal, and listening skills. When dealing with customers you must become the master communicator.

- Always tell your customer why they should buy/use your solution. Use plain English (no technical terminology) and describe the benefits. Example, "Produce a widget in half the time," or "Services are performed in half the time and at half the cost."

- Listen naïvely instead of defending and debating. Maintaining an open, unbiased mind and keeping the customer talking, provides valuable information that can be addressed in the future.

- Customers will better understand information if told as a story. Instead of showing numbers, statistics, and technical points, tell them a story about customer experiences with the offering, how they used it, and the value they received.

- You have a 50 percent greater chance of success by translating raw data into simple words, knowledge, and wisdom that customers can use to make smart decisions. Turn raw data into a story.

- Highlight and demonstrate how easy your solution is to use.

Knowledge

One of my favorite conversations to have with salesman, consultants, business owners, and so-called experts when I am on the road is this: "Tell me about the solutions you provide and how they compare to your competition." I find this to be the most enlightening question to determine how knowledgeable this professional is in their industry. My unofficial findings might surprise you. Only 50 percent of them carry on a fulfilling conversation about their own solutions. Even more depressing is that only 10 percent of these professionals can describe the pros and cons comparing their solution to their primary competitor. My favorite response is, "I just sell what I'm told to. I don't need to understand the product or my competitors' products."

Would you hire a professional or purchase a solution from someone who didn't take the time to learn about their industry or their products? Would you have confidence in their solution? I didn't think so. So what impression do you leave with your customers?

Top Advisers not only become the expert in their own solutions, they also become an expert on their competitors, their customers, and their industry.

- Spend 60 percent of your time with customers, 20 percent learning more about your offering and trade craft, and 20 percent on other business needs like management and administration.

- No one should know more about your offering and your competitors' offerings than you. Build confidence by knowing both the technical specifications and their applications.

- Learn more about your industry. The more you read and learn, the greater your likelihood to be among the first to identify meaningful solutions.

- Learn to talk more about your competition, what the customers like, and what they dislike.

Building Strong Relationships

A big portion of my work with clients focuses on improving sales by improving their relationship with the customer. In this fast-paced world, many professionals and organizations are so focused on short-term goals, that they have forgotten one of the most important success factors. People buy relationships, not products. It's hard to focus on the customer when you are dealing with monthly quota goals, internal politics, investors, organizational changes, and the overflow of email and voicemail requests that want responses immediately. Unfortunately, if you ignore your customer, they won't be a customer for long.

Robert, the president of a small technology company and long time-client of mine, came to me with a challenge. His goal was to improve customer retention by 30 percent while improving sales margins by 25 percent. The organization as a whole was so busy growing and focusing on short-term issues, they forgot how they became successful. They were so focused on internal issues, they forgot about the customer. We called this project "Getting Back to Basics."

To improve customer retention, we worked on developing relationships with their customers instead of just taking orders. The customer became top priority for every employee. Everything else was a lower priority. Secondly, we revamped the selling and billing processes to make it easier for the customer to do business with them. This improved customer satisfaction and reduced the sales cycle by 50 percent. These changes have dramatically improved their business and have turned average customers into loyal customers. Within 18 months, customer retention improved 37 percent while sales margins improved 26 percent. In the end, building strong customer relationships—getting back to the basics—has exceeded everyone's expectations.

Connecting with customers on a personal and professional level will build strong customer relationships, turning them into lifetime loyal customers.

• Reduce customer stress. The easier it is for the customer to do business with you, the greater their likelihood of repurchasing. For example, make the selling process as easy as possible. A long, complex selling process will turn off customers and drive them to your competitors.

• Top Advisers pay attention to detail. Customers make a direct connection between attention to detail and competence. Pay attention to spelling, what you say, out of place items, grooming, dress, etc.

• Do a 20-customer road show twice a year. Nothing beats going into the field and meeting customers face-to-face to better understand what they need and show them what you have to offer.

• Create a pattern of dependability by making small promises and over-delivering on results.

• Be an honest adviser. Present both the strengths and weaknesses of your offering. It is better for the customer to learn about your weaknesses now than to discovering them later.

• Keep your tone upbeat. Make a point to elevate everyone you come in contact with. When they hear your name, their mood will be lifted.

• Customers prefer to buy from people they like. Being likeable is as simple as helping customers feel happy, relaxed, and even feel good about themselves.

Are you ready to go beyond marketing and become a household name?
Are you prepared to become your industry's Top Adviser?
Think big, take action, and get started today!

Best of luck to you. Don't forget to send me a note on your success. You can contact me at www.btrconline.com.

Dennis Sommer is a widely respected and world renowned authority on sales and leadership performance improvement. He is a leading business adviser, author, and speaker providing clients with practical strategies to increase sales revenues and margins, improve customer loyalty, and transform managers and executives into leaders. Sommer has over 20 years of management consulting, sales, technology and business leadership experience. He has delivered over 250 successful client engagements for Fortune 1000 companies. He has held numerous leadership level positions with Accenture, Jo-Ann Stores, and CA Inc. Sommer is President of BTRC Business Advisers, an international firm located in Akron, Ohio. He also volunteers his time as a business counselor for SCORE (www.score.org, www.akronscore.org) a premier source of free and confidential small business advice for entrepreneurs. Sommer can be reached 330-676-1876 or www.btrconline.com.

When it's Time to Bring in the Professionals
Marketing a Knowledge-Based Business
By Bob Kustka

I'd seen the look before. At one of the many networking events that I attended when I launched my consulting practice, I had just been asked what I did for business. When I replied that I was an HR Consultant, eyes glazed over. "That's nice," was the reply, with either little interest in what I did, or worse yet no understanding of the value that I could provide. Having spent considerable time as an HR executive in a major corporation, I knew first hand how much good HR practices could add to the bottom line. Before I started my business, I had spent time developing my business plan. The marketing challenge I was faced with was to help a prospective client to understand the value of the knowledge that I would be able to provide.

There were a number of steps I took when I first began that were important to establishing my business. In creating my business plan, I developed a model that I used to explain what I did. I came up with a name, logo, and tagline to describe my company and create a brand. Immediately, I set up a website that had a corporate look to it, and more importantly explained who I was and what I did. I developed collateral materials such as brochures, letterhead and business cards that helped to establish the brand.

Many consultants first start out of a home office, use a P.O. Box address and don't have resources such as dedicated phone and fax lines, websites or company based email. I wanted to make sure that I wasn't seen as just another HR guy operating out of his house.

In order to have the "curb appeal" of a legitimate business, I selected an office in a small executive center a short distance from my home. I began to follow the three major rules for consultants: network, network, network. During the early days I attended a variety of different association events, from chambers of commerce to various professional associations. I met a lot of people, ate a lot of rubber chicken, and slowly developed clients. My business was building. But business plans are not static, or at least they shouldn't be if you want to be successful. With the help of a business mentor, I highly recommend that everyone have one, I had come to realize that I was not selling HR consultancy. I was not selling CHR Partners, the name of my firm. I was selling me. The value to my prospective client came from the body of knowledge that I had acquired in 25 years in my field. It was the fact that as a subject matter expert in this field, my expertise would help my client improve their profitability in their business.

The realization of this caused me to begin to rethink my marketing strategy. I needed to get myself out of the "HR bucket," where people categorized what I did without fully understanding how I added value. I had learned that once I had spent enough time with a potential client so that they could gain a fuller understanding of my expertise, I could get their business. Ironically, many people, once they reached this point, would say to me, "You are really more than just an HR consultant." I needed to breakout of this mold and build brand awareness around my subject matter expertise. Having reached this conclusion, it was not a challenge to articulate what my brand was. Remember, I had been at this for a while. The challenge was to develop a marketing strategy that would increase my exposure in the market as a far greater rate than my networking had allowed and to break out of the HR bucket.

As an HR professional, one of my core competencies is the ability to assess people's strengths and weaknesses. In an objective fashion, I assessed myself. In the first two years in business, I had done a reasonable job in marketing myself. But I was not a marketing or public relations professional. I could continue to promote myself on my own and grow at a slow steady rate. Or I could engage someone who would have the core expertise in this field and would accelerate the promotion. To reach this point I asked myself the following questions:
• What was I trying to achieve?
• At what rate and at what level was I interested in reaching?
• What was I willing to pay, both in time and money?
• What could I do myself and where did I need help?

It would have been easy to stay the course. The things that I was doing to date to build my clientele were all the right things to do. But in answering these questions, I realized that my goals were higher. In order to achieve them in the time frame that I was targeting, I needed to engage someone with the right competency.

Having reached this conclusion, I followed these steps:
- I outlined what I was currently doing and where I wanted to go.
- I researched and networked to identify several firms that could help me.
- I presented to each of them and asked them to respond with a proposal.
- I engaged my business mentor to help me assess the proposal.
- I decided on my budget.
- I assessed the program based on my goals, timetable, budget and the confidence in the resources of the firms.

Within months, we created a new brand and began the promotion at a far greater speed than I would have imagined. It has not been without pain, as it has been both hard work and there have been many lessons along the way. But the results are there.

The lessons I've learned come not only from what I have done or not done but also from my observations of other entrepreneurs in knowledge-based businesses. So let me share with you several of those lessons as well.

Honestly assess what your core competencies are and where you get the greatest value. If, for instance, your greatest competency is selling, but you are also developing the promotional materials and handling all the administration, are you putting your resources against the highest value activities? Getting someone to write your copy or do your paperwork not only shifts your valuable time to higher level activities, but allows you to focus on what you do best. Coincidentally, this usually is what you enjoy most.

Make sure that you do a good job of selecting the individual or organization that you will use. You need to make sure that what they will do for you will complement your competencies and add value to your business in a way you can measure. Careful assessment of the type of service that you need, selection of the most capable provider, and benchmarks and targets for measuring performance are key to making sure that you get your money's worth.

Be willing to pay for this and don't necessarily wait until you can afford it. No, I am not suggesting that you take on unreasonable debt. But too often I see entrepreneurs waiting too long to get services that will accelerate their growth, and when I ask them why, they reply that they can't afford it yet. The old adage that you have to spend money to make money holds some truth here. Look at your cash flow and determine what is a reasonable amount to stretch and what you can expect as a payback. Those questions will give you a better answer than, "Do I have the money in the bank?" Successful businesses usually say they wish they had invested in these things sooner. If you want to take your business to the next level, you've got to take some chances.

A former HR executive at The Gillette Company and founder of HRAuto. org, Bob Kustka works as an HR/Management consultant for companies like W.B. Mason, Draper Laboratories, and Fidelity Investments. Kustka uses his unique HR experiences to help his clients develop people strategies that fuse with their business plan to make them money. From hiring, to recruiting, to developing new managers, Kustka's ahead-of-the-curve insights provide the edge his clients need to keep their bottom-line razor sharp, and their companies continuously moving three steps ahead of the competition. Now, as the creator of The Fusion Factor, Kustka adapts the techniques he honed at Gillette to the unique needs of entrepreneurs and growing businesses, implementing HR strategies that help them protect and maximize ROI from their most important asset: people. Kustka is also the Co-founder of HRAuto.org, the only HR Development Forum of its kind for the Retail Automotive industry, and a writer. His management articles have appeared on Businessweek.com and in Dealer Magazine. For more information, please visit www.thefusionfactor.com.

Media Strategies
By Ron Finklestein

I recently heard on the radio that, in the course of our daily lives, Americans receive over 3,200 marketing messages a day. Wow! I don't know if it's true, but I can believe it. After hearing this bit of information I started noticing how we are bombarded with marketing messages almost everywhere we turn: radio, newspapers, magazines, television, billboards, bumper stickers, signs, T-shirts, web sites, emails. So the question then becomes: How do you get your message out and break through this clutter?

In this section you will learn how to get your message out and have it heard. What makes this so special is that anyone can do it, and it can be done for little or no cost. I love hearing about great ways to market my business, especially when they are free.

When you read this section you will understand how to market yourself, your company, and your products and services by simply writing articles and posting them on the Internet for the entire world to read. And once you know how to market your article by making it available for the entire world, how do you break through all the marketing clutter and capture the reader's attention? You write an article that provokes others to read it: you create controversy. People love to read about a good controversy.

Creating controversy is not as hard as it sounds. Just pick up and scan a newspaper to find out what is going on in the world (or your market) and use this knowledge to differentiate yourself from your competition: write an article on a hot topic and talk about it in such a way that others know you are an expert.

Your only real limitation in applying the tools in this section is your imagination. As you read these articles, take note on how you can use this information to create visibility for yourself and your company. What are the best websites for posting articles? What topics are best for you to write about? How can you break through the noise and be noticed?

Press Releases
Huge Return for Minimal Investment
By Kathryn Seifert, Ph.D.

Mail, documents, receipts—you name it—pile up on my desk on a regular basis. As an expert in family violence and youth trauma who balances her time between patients, conferences, research, book-writing, and media appearances, I rarely have time to keep my office organized. So my desk always looks busy—or cluttered, depending on your point of view. One Friday afternoon, I methodically attacked the foot-high piles, designating one stack for the trash, one to file, one to pass on to someone else, and one to act on. Grasping the next large envelope, I saw an invitation to attend a "People to People" trip for psychologists to visit South Africa.

What a dream trip! It offered visits to hospitals, townships, and Kruger National Park, as well as personal encounters with other psychology experts in my field across the Republic of South Africa. I had to go, and I knew that besides taking a great adventure and enriching my knowledge base, others would be interested in learning about my trip as well. To generate media coverage, I put some other pressing work on hold and took the time to write a press release: "Psychology Expert to Discuss Violence and Mental Heath Issues in South Africa." Busy life or not, it was imperative that I found a couple of hours to inform the media about this important event. And by writing this press release, I was able to take the trip of a lifetime, *and* achieve publicity.

Press releases are an economical tool that can be used to announce anything new and exciting about you, your business, or what you may be working on at the moment. The operative words here are "new" and "exciting" ("economical" is an important one too, but I'll get to that later). I read newspapers, listen to the radio, and watch the television to see if my commentary can help explain any news-related issues, from college lacrosse gang rape to mothers who brutally kill their babies. Press releases should inform the public (your reading audience) of your work and give you, whether you're an expert, a small business, or any other sort of professional, name recognition. This could include the release of a new book, speaking engagements, honors and awards, leadership roles in organizations, and promotions. In this manner, the press release further establishes you and/or your business in whatever field or industry you're in. But wait. Press releases aren't official unless they are written in appropriate press release form. Not only do they have to be timely and interesting enough to catch a journalist's attention, they must be written in an objective voice—no first person, please—in the same tone articles are written in the newspaper. That means the who, what, where, why, how, and when must come in the first graph, and it must be written clearly and concisely so that there is no question what this press release will be about. After that first lead paragraph, I will insert a quote, whether it's from me or another expert who is qualified to speak on the topic. Journalists like it when the release has everything mapped out for them, so providing quotes and background information heightens the likelihood they'll pick up your story.

There are several other nuts and bolts you won't want to leave out of your press release. At the top, in bold all caps, it should read: **FOR IMMEDIATE RELEASE**. Underneath should go your public relation specialist's or your contact information, including email, website, and phone number. After the body of my press release, which is usually just over one page long, I insert a short bio that outlines my expertise, accomplishments, a new psychology study or book I've published, as well as my website one more time. At the very, very end, three hash marks signal to whoever is reading my release that no more information will follow. Stop. You're not done yet. Don't forget to proof your own writing and have someone else proof it for you as well. If you have too many typos or are inconsistent in your press release style, journalists will not take you seriously.

I like to try new and fun ways of making my press releases stand out among hundreds of other releases out there. Press releases can be targeted towards local media (e.g. "hometown person does well"), which is always a good angle if your market is local. If you'd like to target national media, I'd recommend staying abreast of issues in the news that arise in your topic of expertise. In the news world, one breaking news story can filter down into myriad feature stories, character profiles, and human interest stories. You could be an interviewee or the subject of any of these if your timing is right. Also, think long and hard about your headline. It should not only be enticing, but be made up of key words that journalists look for when they are searching the Internet and press release networking systems. The headline should be informative and make the reader want to click and read on. It can even be controversial, but I prefer staying within the bounds of good taste.

Applying for awards is a great idea to create buzz and opportunities for press releases. There are business awards, such as the Stevie Awards, http://www.stevieawards.com, and Diversity Business, http://www.div2000.com, not to mention countless other awards in an array of industries. Do some research, see what's out there, and apply for awards. If you're a finalist—or you win—that's the perfect opportunity for a press release.

All of this information took me years to gather. Experimenting with the different types of do-it-yourself and paid services has made me a believer in high quality paid services. I may write a few of my press releases from time to time, but I rely on my public relations specialist to proof my work and do the bulk of my publicity efforts. I figure I know my own field, but I want professionals who know the marketing/promotion business and can compensate for my lack of knowledge in this area. The bottom line is: Press releases that are well crafted and professionally executed get your name out there to the buying public. Name recognition and someone saying your product or service is great is what you're looking for.

Action Items:
There are several price levels of press release wire services, some more economical than others. When you get started, look for a service that fits your budget. Some have worked wonders for me, while others, well, let's just say you get what you pay for. With some, you must get referrals from other people who have used their services and be invited in. If you feel you can write a compelling and coherent press release on your own, I've outlined a few of these options here.

1. At www.i-newswire.com, and www.free-press-release.com you can submit free press releases that you have written and there is the option of upgrading to a paid service.

2. On www.Prweb.com you write your own press release and post it, paying for each press release. There are levels of service including basic, SEO tools, and distribution to social media. They use Vocus software to help your press release get to the right media. Prices range from $40 to $200-plus per press release.

3. Create online business profiles and press releases at www.fastpitchnetworking.com/ index.cfm. They have three levels; you can create your profile for free or upgrade to more services.

4. Write the press release yourself and pay for a yearly subscription at www. NewsReleaseWire.com. A yearly subscription will allow you 52 press releases per year. You can add audio and images to your releases as well. Distribution is to local, state, and national journalists.

5. Have help in writing a professional press release. There are a plethora of qualified public relations specialists throughout the country. At www.IctusInitiative.com you can find professionals experienced in writing press releases that capture the media's attention on a regular basis. They use relationships with the media to get your services to the journalist who is looking for you.

Oh, and in case you're wondering, I sent the press release of my trip to South Africa out to local media. The final product had substance, was interesting, related to today's issues of violence and mental health, and provided background information. A local Salisbury, Md. journalist called me and was interested in writing a story about my trip. While we were on our tour in South Africa, my husband was accidentally locked in one of the rooms of the public psychiatric hospital with a professor. Dreading being left behind, and locked in this under-funded, understaffed psychiatric hospital in serious disrepair in the hinterland of Africa, they were frantic. They were finally able to get out by jimmying the lock open with a pen knife. It may not have been newsworthy-enough for a press release, but the debacle gave me great material for my talk the next day.

Kathryn Seifert, Ph.D. is a psychotherapist, author, speaker, and researcher who specializes in family violence and trauma and has over 30 years

of experience in mental health, addictions, and criminal justice work. She is Founder and CEO of Eastern Shore Psychological Services (www.ESPSMD.com), a private practice that focuses on serving children, adolescents, and at-risk youth and their families. Her new book, How Children Become Violent: Keeping Your Kids Out of Gangs, Terrorist Organizations, and Cults is available on Amazon.com and major national booksellers. For more information about Dr. Seifert please visit her website at www.drkathyseifert.com.

Hop on the Controversy Brandwagon

By Jeff Bukantz

Creating controversy is something that many of the most successful businesses, television stations, and individuals do to gain visibility (think about Ann Coulter, the Daily Show, and *Playboy*). And it's a strategy that small-business owners should embrace as well. As Bill O'Reilly once said of his show, "If you're not providing controversy and excitement, people won't listen, or watch." The same holds true for your product and your company.

But how can you market a small business (assuming its not selling mature magazines or generating money for stem cell research) by creating controversy? Well, here's a three-step plan from my own experience marketing my new book, *Closing the Distance: Chasing a Father's Olympic Fencing Legacy*—a feel-good account of my journey captaining the US fencing team to a gold medal (not the most controversial book ever written):

1. Figure out your message and what you genuinely want your product to stand for

2. Re-word, or present your message in such a way that it creates excitement and controversy

3. Leverage this controversy to sell more product

1. What do you want your business or product to stand for?

When I was writing my book, everyone would ask me what it was about. I would tell them, "It's my memoir. I want the reader to realize that it's not the destination that's important, but the journey. We're all winners if we give our all every chance we get." Well, as you probably just did, anyone I told this to rolled their eyes, gave me a fake smile, or just tuned out halfway through what I was saying. Clearly not the response I wanted if I was ever going to sell my book. However, I still believed in my message, and I wanted the reader to feel uplifted after reading my manuscript. I just didn't know how to get people excited enough to open the first page. As a small business, you need to figure out what you want to stand for. Make a name for yourself by having a message and believing in it—customers appreciate businesses that stand for something, even if it's something as basic as having great customer service.

2. Wording your message so that it generates interest.
After I realized what message I wanted to send with my book, I had to figure out how to market it effectively so people would want to read my story. One day, I stumbled across a quote from Hall of Fame Football coach, Vince Lombardi. He said, "I firmly believe that any man's finest hour ... is that moment when he has worked his heart out in a good cause and lies exhausted on the field of battle—victorious." Immediately, I knew I had my hook. Lombardi qualified everything he said about what makes a man's finest hour on whether or not he ultimately won, precisely the idea I was arguing against. So I started telling people that my message was, "Legendary coach Vince Lombardi is dead wrong!" And you know what? I was met with gasps, puzzled looks, and genuine interest. So the challenge for you is to figure out how to convey your message in a way that creates interest. Be creative. Look at advertising campaigns that you think are the most effective and see how they leverage controversy to generate interest. Or look at your competitors. What are they doing to make their products seem exciting?

3. How do you leverage controversy to sell products?
For me, that was easy. I generated controversial interest in my book, then backed up my claim with my credentials and my content. The controversy was the hook that generated widespread acknowledgment and my story and journey through the Olympics were the substance that ultimately made people buy the book.

Another example of leveraging controversy to sell products is an ad campaign for Apple Computers, Inc™. Apple has followed this three-step plan and generated incredible publicity for their 2006-2007 line of computers. The message Apple is trying to send was that they create excellent products. However, all computer makers send the message that their products are top-of-the-line, and Apple faced the added opposition that PC's dominated the industry. So to send out their message and generate buzz and controversy, Apple launched an ad campaign featuring one man who represents a young, hip Mac, and the other a slightly overweight, boring man—the old PC. In each commercial, the PC demonstrates his faults, while the Mac shows why he's the more elite machine. By challenging the mainstream idea that a PC is the better choice, Apple created controversy and in turn had a 61 percent increase in their computer sales in 2006[1].

So, do what clearly works. Hop aboard the controversy brandwagon and increase your visibility and your sales.

Jeff Bukantz was the captain of the 2004 U.S. Fencing Team and a former top-ranked medalist in the sport. At the Athens Olympics in 2004, Bukantz led his team to the first gold medal in fencing for the United States in one hundred years, and their first medal of any kind since 1984. Bukantz is a member of the International Fencing Federation (FIE) Rules Commission, the United States Fencing Association (USFA) High Performance Committee, and Chairman of the USFA Fencing Officials Commission. He has brought his success in the game to success on the speaker's podium, and is available to speak about overcoming natural limitations, brushing off impossible pressure, how to lead like a champion—and be a class act through it all. His book, Closing the Distance: Chasing a Father's Olympic Fencing Legacy, is available at Amazon.com and major booksellers nationwide. Bukantz was born in Queens, N.Y. and currently resides with his wife and two children in Livingston, N.J.

[1] Hesseldahl, Arik. How Do You Like Them Apples? The computer maker silenced skeptics with an avalanche of notebook sales. iPod sales held steady—and brought PC users into Mac stores. http://yahoo.businessweek.com/technology/content/jul2006/tc20060719_557792.htm. July 20, 2006.

China-Proof Your Business in 10 Minutes

By John Blakeney

Immediately following the tragic events of September 11th, the media across our nation began telling stories about the trauma experienced by the public. The American public's level of awareness could actually be characterized as a lack of awareness. The old "80/20" rule was in full effect. About 80 percent of the population could not believe such a thing could ever happen on American soil, while the other 20 percent felt that an attack on America had been inevitable. Why the disparity? Why did some know while the majority had no clue?

In business today, this same 80/20 disparity exists. Consider these 2005 statistics: 672,000 small businesses were started, and 545,000 of those same businesses—80 percent—failed. Why? What is the difference between businesses that make it and those that don't? What the facts point to is an extraordinary lack of knowledge about the changing state of the world around us. Here's one example of our changing world.

Have you ever noticed that 90 percent of the products you purchase are manufactured (household items, clothing, electronics, cars—you name it!)? Did you notice that you can get on the Internet and purchase almost anything you can think of, from anyplace in the world, at any time, and have it delivered anywhere you want? Have you noticed when you call companies for service you are helped by people in another country? Did you know services you depend on like credit card companies, insurance companies, accounting firms, law firms, and airlines use people in other countries to handle time-consuming activities such as research, analysis, and customer service? Did you know in 2007, pay for outsourced labor ranged from $ 1.35 to $5.85 per month (and they are generally very appreciative of the work). Did you know in 1776, General George Washington's Continental Army fought for American independence from England and were paid wages of $ 8.00 per month? 1776, $8.00 per month. 2007, $ 1.35 per month. Have Americans done the math? How much will you be making in three years? Who else will gladly do your job for less? Walmart is hiring.

Did you know big American companies like General Motors and Ford (there are others), who conduct business around the world lost *hundreds of billions* of dollars last year? They also permanently cut and are continuing to cut tens of thousands of jobs. Do you know why they lost all that money? Despite all their power, money, and political influence, they made a very simple mistake in planning by ignoring how their business, customers, and competitors were changing in America and around the world. Did you know the secret information the auto makers (and other businesses) needed to know to prevent their billions of dollars in losses, was available to them in an easy-to-find place? Like the billion dollar companies, 80 percent of small businesses ignore the same secret information that holds the key to opportunities and their future economic stability.

Can you see what these three have in common? Poor public awareness of September 11th, the 80 percent failure rate of small businesses, and billion-dollar losses by global companies: they were all lacking the secret knowledge. This secret knowledge is the reality that America is now significantly impacted by economic events in other countries and the smart businessperson can no longer ignore these events. The essential news you need to ensure your career and economic future is not in your local paper or on TV. It is found in international news sources. American economics have shifted dramatically in past 10 years and people in all businesses have flat-out ignored the changes and are now paying the price.

"In the Information Age, knowledge is king, innovation is queen, and speed of execution is the ace of spades!"

All it will take to become globally savvy is 10 minutes a day, five days a week. You must stick to this program for a month. Okay, time for you to learn the secret that has tripped up the best and brightest minds in business. Remember, "China-proofing" is insignificant, what we are really addressing in this article is how to "ignorance-proof" our thinking and our financial future. Every problem we see in business has a root cause of failing to accept and react to reality. Business is all about profits, and global opportunity awaits for those who pay attention. Do exactly as we say for 10 minutes a day, and the results will blow you away (Isn't that a Johnny Cash song?).

Take out your wallet. Pull out a credit card and call the *Wall Street Journal* at (800) 568-7625 and sign up for a trial subscription discount offer delivered to your door at 6am (reading it on-line is not as effective). Your eyes can interpret 10 times more information at a faster pace than you can read on a monitor. You will cover the business events in eight countries and an interview with Bill Gates in the time it takes your IT guy to count the pens in his pocket protector and clean the smudge from his glasses. Ready? Let's roll!

Get the paper in your hands. Skim. Don't try to soak up a lot of details now; it will all flow right into your brain later if you learn this technique first. It is going to take you 20 days to develop the rhythm. The main idea is to hit the high points and skim the paper in 10-12 minutes maximum. Your purpose during this period is to pay attention to significant economic current events and anything relevant to your industry or life.

Begin with the first section and read "What's News" in the center of the page for current events, then move on and skim the headlines on the entire front page. Next, turn to page two; this is where you will find pressing economic issues. Just skim the headlines; if you want to read one or two lines for the main idea, that's fine. Next, flip to the last page in section A, the Editorial/Opinion section. Again, skim the headlines and read the first and last paragraph of each editorial story. Put section A down and pick up the B (Market Place) section. Skim all the headlines on the B section. While you read, continue to ask yourself if the content is related to your industry. If not, move on; if yes, read the beginning, middle, and ending paragraphs. If an article is very important, clip it and save it where you can find it in a file market "Business News." Put down the B section and pick up section C ("Money & Investing"). Follow the same rules from reading A and B. Scan and skim the page for significant headlines. For anything that sounds like it is explaining key issues of money works: skim the articles, beginning, middle, end. Anything you really like, save it to read on the weekend, then toss out the rest in your recycling bin. If you miss reading a paper, you will feel compelled to save it for later. Don't do this! Throw them out today; by now it's old news.

We wish you well!

John Blakeney is a managing partner of Idea Firm, LLC, which provides business strategy training in management, marketing, leadership, and innovation and has worked with the gamut of industries and products from start-ups to AT&T. Blakeney lectures on the topic of innovation and change in business and is a career innovator-problem solver with a passion for creating and executing new ideas. His experience and insight are the result of 30 years working in diverse industries including manufacturing, engineering, automotive, construction, building, transportation, TV/radio production, advertising, Internet, telecommunications, and professional athletics. Blakeney received business degrees from the University of Cal.-Poly Pomona's School of Management and in International Business. He is married and has three children. For more, please visit www.ideafirm.com.

Making Waves
Leveraging the Power of Talk Radio
By George Kasparian

Talk radio is a fabulous one-to-many marketing strategy that allows you to showcase your expertise, promote your products and services, drive traffic to your website, and ask people to sign up for your complimentary email newsletter. And the best part: it doesn't cost a dime! Yes, there are a lot of people on the radio whom you may not want to be associated with. But there are some excellent talk show hosts that, if you can get yourself on their radar screen, can provide you with wonderful exposure in your geographic market at no cost.

There are really four ways to get yourself on talk radio so that you can strut your stuff and increase your visibility in the markets where you want to be recognized as a marketplace authority:
1. Comment on stories happening in breaking news
2. Get yourself featured as an expert for an entire segment
3. Become a regular guest commentator
4. Own your own radio show

Be an Expert on Breaking News Stories
I have subject-matter expertise in a couple of different areas. I taught political science at Tufts University before I went to law school, and I was a computer programmer before I became a tax lawyer. So I have been able to market myself as an expert commentator on breaking news stories in the areas of law, economics, politics, technology, and estate planning.

Talk show hosts (and their producers) are always looking for well-spoken people who can come on the air on very short notice and offer insightful analysis of what is happening in the news of the day. Radio talk show hosts need someone to talk to. They also need people who can state positions—the more controversial the better—that will make the phones ring. If you can get yourself in the Rolodex of a radio show producer as a great guest, you will be invited back again and again.

What's in it for you? Everyone in your geographic area will hear you on the air being referred to as an expert. This is the kind of marketing you could not possibly pay for. And all you had to do was talk on the phone for 7 to 10 minutes about things that you love to discuss anyway. How good is that? When you are on the air offering expert commentary on a news story you probably will not have the opportunity to do a lot of self-promoting. But I've always been fine with that, because the status that I gained in the community as a result of these appearances more than outweighed the lack of advertising.

Do a Feature for an Entire Segment

Radio shows are divided up into segments of a fixed length. These vary from show to show, but are the periods of actual content sandwiched between the commercials usually anywhere from 11 to 17 minutes. Talk show hosts tend to structure their show content around these segments and often they will feature a topic or guest for an entire segment. Your goal is to get yourself invited to do an entire segment.

The easiest way to do this is to have a book published. If you are an author and your book is a good fit with the show content, you have an excellent chance of getting an entire segment. You want to pitch yourself (or have your PR firm do it) by sending your media kit and a review copy of the book to the producer. I recommend sending a list of sample interview questions or talking points as well. (The hosts almost never read the book—they wing it.) The host will plug the book for you and almost without exception will allow you to send people to your website, invite them to sign up for your e-newsletter, and say other self-promotional things that are not too overtly sales oriented.

It's a little more difficult if you don't have a book. An article published in a national magazine may get you a segment. Absent this, it's tough sledding unless you've been making frequent guest appearances and the host has decided to do a feature segment on a topic within your area of expertise. The bottom line is you really do need to be the expert and have the *bona fides* to support your credentials. If you have gotten past that hurdle, a feature segment is a wonderful promotional opportunity.

Become a Regular on the Show

I was able to leverage my occasional guest appearances on talk radio into a weekly gig. The show I appeared on wanted to format one of its segments as a political roundtable. The fact that I was well-versed and kept very current (meaning I read extensively) on all of my areas of expertise made me an attractive candidate for a roundtable discussion. I could comment on a Supreme Court ruling one week, the latest problems in the computer industry the next, monetary policy the next, and the machinations in Congress the next. My versatility and depth of knowledge earned me a regular gig.

Now, I did not make any money being on this show for two years, nor did it cost me any money. But, the name of my firm was mentioned often, my bio was on the website for the show with a link to my website, and I was able to say, everywhere I went, that I was the political commentator for *Financially Speaking*. The hosts were also very generous in discussing the nature of my practice and some of the things that were happening in my business as events transpired. The bottom line: I got a heck of a lot of personal publicity.

Own the Show Yourself

The final way to get yourself on the radio is to become the host of your own show. I was astonished to learn that the barriers to entry into the talk radio business are very low. You basically needed a compelling personality, a sponsor, and a checkbook. Personality is critical, because remember: on the radio you are promoting your expertise and being an entertainer at the same time. You need to be comfortable developing a rapport with your guests while managing the clock (the schedule of content and commercial breaks) and avoiding "dead air." Given all the choices in the media marketplace—other stations, iPods, and mp3s, just to name a few—how long will you hold your audience if you take 15-second pauses between questions?

Talk radio requires you to have a quick mouth and a quick mind. You have to be able to think on your feet, speak in snappy sound bites, and transition well from idea to idea because your audience has a limited attention span. You will want to link your expertise to a show concept that has broad consumer appeal such as health, business, real estate, or finance.

Once you decide that you have a solid concept, you must develop a format for the show and then go into a studio to cut a demo tape. The demo tape is used to shop your show concept to program directors (smaller independent stations are usually best) to see if they are interested in picking up your show. Obviously, it makes sense to approach stations with a format that fits your show concept. It probably would not be productive to approach a sports talk station about a real estate show. However, if you have a business and finance station in your community, they are likely to be very interested.

At this point, if the station is interested, you will probably need to take out your checkbook. Radio stations sell blocks of time (for example, Monday to Friday from 10 to 11 a.m.) to shows. The price for buying time on the radio is determined by the power of the station and the time of day. Morning and afternoon commuting time usually costs the most since they have the largest potential audience. Successful shows have sponsors who pay for these costs. However, when you're first starting out, you may have to pick up the tab yourself until you build audience share and attract one or more sponsors. One of the dirty little secrets of the industry is that most hosts pay to be on air early in their careers. But you have to invest money to make money, right? At a minimum you will be able to showcase your expertise, and who knows, maybe you could be the next Sean Hannity or Dr. Laura!

Whether you become a regular guest on someone else's radio show, or you are able to create your own show, I recommend undertaking marketing and PR initiatives to make the listening audience aware of your debut on the radio waves. This can include a combination of press releases, space ads, feature articles, advertising spots on other radio and TV shows and stations, and performing guest appearances. Talk radio itself may not ever be profitable for you; but the help it offers in establishing your reputation will be priceless, and it will pave the way for a very lucrative future.

George Kasparian is a graduate of Tufts University and Boston College Law School and is a member of the Massachusetts Bar. Leveraging his background in computer science, he has worked for several high-tech startups developing software and web-based applications for the legal,

tax, and financial services sectors. He served as co-host and political commentator for the radio show *Financially Speaking* and is a frequent contributor to law and tax publications. He now co-owns The Ictus Initiative (www.IctusInitiative.com), a multi-faceted marketing, web development, and PR firm located in Boston, MA.

Space Advertising
Zoltan Makes It Work with "7 Touches"
By Paige Stover Hague

Small business owners often call me and say they want to run an ad in the community newspaper, advertising their new landscaping business, or day care center, law practice, or life coaching business. My response? "You might as well take that money and throw it down the toilet!"

The operative words here are "an ad." A single space ad, in a single community newspaper, without any other supporting marketing will not deliver anything for you. I give you that as a written guarantee. Space advertising can be a very effective way to market a certain business with a specific geographic target market. But you need to be doing it as part of a coordinated marketing effort with reinforcement mechanisms built in. Here's what I am talking about…

The marketing gurus tell us that it takes 7 touches—or impressions—before a prospect will take action on a marketing message. That means that you have to get in front of your prospect's face and in their mind an average of 7 times before they will pick up the phone, or buy something off your website or return a direct response coupon. These 7 touches can include seeing your sign as they drive by your office, meeting your secretary in the grocery store, hearing your three-minute presentation at the Rotary, or checking out your website one night when they can't sleep. All of these count. Seeing a space ad in the community newspaper also counts. But all by itself, that ad is not going to get you anything—guaranteed.

My question when people tell me they want to run a space ad is: What is the marketing initiative that the ad is supporting? This question always stops people in their tracks. How many times have you picked up the phone and called a service provider the first time you saw their ad? You have no clue who this guy is who wants to remodel your kitchen. Who would leave their preschooler with someone they never met? Why would I tell my deepest darkest passions and frustrations to the licensed social worker whose office is in the same building as my dentist? You just don't make buying decisions that way. Here's how you make a buying decision: You attend a baby shower for someone in your office who has just remodeled her kitchen and it has exactly the look and functionality you would like in your kitchen. She writes the contractor's name on a piece of paper which you throw in your purse. 1) You go home and tell your husband how great her kitchen looks and confirm that your home equity line is in process. You look in your purse and can't find the paper with the contractor's name on it. Two weeks go by and you get a letter from the bank saying that your loan is approved; attached is a list of home improvement contractors that have met the rigorous quality standards of the bank and you recognize the name—Zoltan's Kitchen & Bath Remodeling, your friend's contractor. 2) You make a mental note. Another couple weeks go by and on the day of your 4th of July cookout your garbage disposal stops working. You are at your wit's end, still can't find the note in your purse and your husband has taken the loan approval letter to his office. You send an email to your friend asking her the name of the contractor again, which she sends with a link to Zoltan's website. 3) You check out his site and he has all kinds of fabulous pictures of kitchens he has done, lots of testimonials from satisfied customers, plus a picture of himself and his wife and kids. The following Monday you leave for a two-week vacation. When you get back the garbage disposal still isn't working, but somehow it doesn't matter so much. Now it's time to get your kids ready to go back to school. On the first day of the new school year, you take your third-grader in to his new classroom and who is sitting at the computer station but little Zoltan. 4) The following Tuesday the newsletter from the Chamber arrives and there's an announcement that Zoltan is chairing the Holiday Food & Wine event. 5) You grab your navy blue purse because you are going to your mother-in-law's for dinner (she always comments if your shoes don't match your purse) and lo and behold there is the note your friend gave you at the baby shower—you were looking in your black purse. 6) The next morning you run over the community newspaper as you back out of the driveway, but something compels you to jump out and pick it up. When you get to your office, while you are sipping your coffee before anyone else gets there, you open the paper. In the upper right-hand corner of page 2 is Zoltan's space ad—with his phone number in big letters so that you don't need your glasses to read them. 7) BINGO—you pick up your cell phone and dial. Zoltan clearly has a marketing plan in place and space advertising is a key component of it. In fact, Zoltan has signed a 52-week contract with the community newspaper so that his ad is always in the upper right-hand corner of page 2. Every week it's in exactly the same place, to the point that you would have a funny feeling that something wasn't right if his ad wasn't there. You may not even look at it every week, but subconsciously, you know it's there. If you need Zoltan's phone number you know where to look.

He also has a professionally designed website and his space ad instructs the reader to go to his website to download a free e-book called "Zoltan's Quick and Easy Guide to Designing Your New Kitchen." You enter your email address and Zoltan's web guy has everything set up so that the e-book gets sent to the prospect automatically and Zoltan is sent a message with the prospect's e-mail address. Zoltan waits a few days and sends a follow-up email asking if the prospect would like him to come by for a complimentary design consultation. Zoltan is also very active in the Chamber and its logo appears in his space ad. Even though he can't make every meeting he is sure to have a strong presence because he knows that in his community this is the business networking group that is the gatekeeper of influence. He runs exactly the same space ad in the Chamber directory that he runs in the community newspaper. He is chairing the Holiday Food & Wine event because there is a really good connection between food and wine and kitchen remodeling, but also his suppliers are bringing in some fancy wine storage units, some food warmers for the hot hors d'oeuvres, and a beautiful chocolate fondue machine that is a real showstopper. This will create quite a buzz, he speculates—everyone will be talking about him and what a great party he threw. The publisher of the community newspaper sits on the Board of the Chamber.

Zoltan put a lot of energy into getting himself on the list of recommended contractors that the bank sends out with the loan approval documentation. He has received very positive feedback from potential customers because they feel more comfortable doing business with someone who has been vetted by the bank. People are very concerned about being ripped off by home improvement contractors, and getting the "seal of approval" from the bank completely removed this fear element from his sales process. He also includes a statement in his space ad that he is on the list of the First National Bank's approved contractors.

The final piece of Zoltan's plan that he is doing really well is delivering a superior product for his customers so he gets the referral. The hostess of the baby shower was not only eager to share Zoltan's contact information, but she had it right at her fingertips. Zoltan always leaves a tastefully designed kitchen magnet on the refrigerator of every kitchen he works on. And when Zoltan finds out that a new prospect was the direct result of a previous customer's referral, he sends that customer a beautiful set of steak knives with a discreet "Z" embedded in the design of the handle. Whenever you see that "Z" you just can't help but think of Zoltan.

Zoltan has a very successful business, but he isn't working a million hours and isn't destroying his profitability by overspending on marketing. He formulated a very specific plan, with reinforcement vehicles built into it, and he has stuck with his plan, having tweaked it in the early days until he got the result he wanted. Space advertising is the core of his strategy, but it is solidly supported by networking, endorsements, affiliations, Internet marketing, promotional products, and public relations. The other less tangible but equally important component of Zoltan's strategy is something not often discussed as a marketing tool (until the last few presidential campaigns), and that is likeability. Zoltan is just a really good guy. You can't help but like him. He's personable and caring and he always makes you feel like he is genuinely interested in your project. You also feel that he is honest and ethical. You are not afraid to leave him your house all day while you're at work.

Zoltan has found a magical combination. If you asked him about his strategy, his "aw shucks" response would not persuade you that he is a marketing genius. But for a small business person, he has come up with a system that delivers for him with all the aspects of a professionally designed marketing plan, and it is 7 layers deeper than a space ad alone.

Paige Stover Hague is the owner of several Boston-based communications companies that provides strategic planning, public relations, marketing and business development services to professional services firms, small businesses, speakers and authors.

She is brought in by CEO's and owner managers throughout the United States to consult and conduct programs and retreats that launch or further company-wide initiatives that effect the way employees and stakeholders think about every aspect of their business. The reach of her presentations touches financial operations, human capital allocations, product development and employee engagement. She also presents continuing education programs for lawyers, accountants and financial advisors on art succession planning. She is co-author of *Life is Short, Art is Long—Maximizing Estate Planning Strategies for Collectors of Art, Antiques and Collectibles* **(Wealth Management Press 2007).**

Paige is a graduate of Duke University and Nova Southeastern University Law School and a member of the Florida and Massachusetts bars. For more information, please visit www.IctusInitiave.com.

Writing Articles
Increasing Your Visibility in Target Markets
By Kathryn Seifert, Ph.D.

This morning when I picked up the newspaper, my eyes groggy and coffee still brewing, I was unpleasantly greeted with the headline: "Prominent psychiatrist killed by patient." I was saddened and dumbfounded at the murder of Dr. Wayne S. Fenton, who was the associate director of the National Institute of Mental Health and an extremely important doctor who treated people with schizophrenia. I was upset about the loss of an important colleague, both personally and professionally. This, my instincts told me, could change the field of mental health as professionals know it.

As a psychotherapist with 30 years of practice under my belt, I see newsworthy events like Dr. Fenton's murder as opportunities for me to get my message of "stop the violence" out to the public. My experience in mental health, addictions, and criminal justice has led me to develop several violence assessment tools for men, women, and youth. I recently wrote a book, *How Children Become Violent: Keeping Your Kids out of Gangs, Terrorist Organizations, and Cults*, which is an invaluable anti-violence resource for therapists, parents, and victims alike—and how ironic, that the patient who's suspected of murdering Dr. Fenton is only 19 years old.

But if these people don't know my book and assessments are out there, they can't utilize them. Therefore, my quest right now has metamorphosed from one of clinical research to one of PR.

I make a practice of staying attuned to current events in my field. Whether it's Dr. Fenton's untimely death, the capital punishment trial of confessed terrorist and diagnosed schizophrenic Zacarias Moussaoui, or other horrible stories such as school shootings that are all-too-common today, if there is something in the news that helps me spread my message, I pounce on it. I do this not as a means of taking advantage of current news for my own purposes, but in the hopes of being able to direct people to what I consider to be a highly useful tool when more attention is focused on the issue. One way to do this is by writing articles about current events.

This is exactly what I did after I read this morning's nasty headline. My experience working with dangerous criminals and the mentally ill told me Dr. Fenton's murder would have at least two consequences. There is the immediate—his colleagues in mental health and those living with schizophrenia (there are 2.5 million in America alone) will lose the man's future contributions to psychology. And, secondly, there is the broad effect his murder will have on my profession. It rekindles the fear that so many in our line of work have about our day-to-day safety.

So I wrote my interpretation of these consequences in an article. My articles tend to run about 600 to 900 words—long enough for me to relay my information and engage readers, short enough to not bog them down. The PR firm I hired, The Ictus Initiative, pitches many of my articles to websites, magazines, and other media. Sometimes, like what recently happened with an article I wrote on women and violence, editors will use my article as background material and assign a staff writer to do a story on the same topic—and use me as the primary expert source. I submitted my article on Dr. Fenton to Expertclick. com on my own.

Articles are avenues for experts in two ways. They help the expert gain more media prominence and credibility. They are also a great way for experts to attract traffic to their websites, sell their products, and publicize their books. Again, while it is distasteful to think I may be capitalizing on the deaths and suffering of others, I tend to consider my maneuvers in a different light. What I am selling can save lives.

If you are interested in writing your own articles, here are some Action Steps:
1. Write on a subject you know well. Research which topics are popular and experiment with new topics that will interest those in your market.

2. Use key words. Internet search engines help people find your articles by using key words to organize and locate them. Decide on what key words should appear and reappear in your article. What words would you put in a search engine that would result in your article? Be generous in your use of key words—that is how the little spiders from the search engines will find you.

3. Proofread. Please use your spell checker! And the dictionary! Make sure everything is spelled correctly and that your sentence structure flows nicely. If there's anything I have learned in this business, it's that you must read and reread and reread your work and then rewrite, rewrite, rewrite until you never want to see it again. This is what makes a polished article. You can also hire an editor to look at your article when you think you are done. A good editor is invaluable and will make your work shine.

4. Watch and read the news. Keep your eyes and ears perked for news items that are related to your area of expertise. Relate what you know to these news items. For instance, I often write about children and violence. When there is a school shooting in the news, I write a short article about preventing youth violence. These are for the media, so they do not need to be long; like I said, 600 to 900 words are sufficient.

5. Use article distribution websites. Here are some websites I use:
- I Snare: http://www.isnare.com/login.php
- Ezine Articles: http://ezinearticles.com/submit/
- Article Marketer: http://www.articlemarketer.com/index.php
- PR Web: https://console.prweb.com/prweb/login.php
- Yearbook of Experts Online: http://expertclick.com/
- http://www.bookmarket.com/files.html

6. Get a website. The Ictus Initiative designed my website. It is professional looking and exactly how I envisioned it. However, when you're starting out and if you're limited with funds, you may want to utilize a service that helps you build your own website (such as Bravenet or Yahoo). While this will be relatively inexpensive, it is very time-consuming, and in the end you will still have an amateurish website. However, if this is what fits into your budget, it is a good way to get started. You need a web presence.

7. Social Bookmarks. Social bookmark sites tag, group, organize, and analyze sites. The idea is to make sites of a particular topic easier to find. Sites include del.icio.us, Flikr, Furl, Spurl.net, and eKstreme.com. Social bookmarks have become very popular and are a good way to get you articles known in appropriate networks of users looking for material on your topic.

8. Author and Reader Sites. I found a wonderful site, http://authorsden.com, an online community of writers and readers with a friendly atmosphere. You can join for free or you can pay a very small fee for more features. You can post links to your work for sale, as well as articles and poetry. As you make a circle of friends, it helps promote to your work. The site also offers paid promotions for your work.

Kathryn Seifert, Ph.D. is a psychotherapist, author, speaker, and researcher who specializes in family violence and trauma and has over 30 years of experience in mental health, addictions, and criminal justice work. She is Founder and CEO of Eastern Shore Psychological Services (www.ESPSMD.com), a private practice that focuses on serving children, adolescents, and at-risk youth and their families. Her new book, How Children Become Violent: Keeping Your Kids Out of Gangs, Terrorist Organizations, and Cults is available on Amazon.com and major national booksellers. For more information about Dr. Seifert please visit her website at www.drkathyseifert.com.

Networking Strategies
By Ron Finklestein

All of us understand unconsciously, if not consciously, that our success depends on how well we communicate, sell, motivate, inspire, manage, and treat others. What many people do not understand is the work it takes to create this type of clarity so that it can be communicated effectively.

In this section you will learn how to build a business by doing what you love to do. People will never buy a product or service from you; they will, however, buy an outcome. They will buy into the passion, conviction, and belief you have about your product and service. You need to understand your Unique Value Proposition (UVP). Once you understand it, you can communicate it to others as well. Your UVP is the one thing that differentiates you from your competitors. It is the value you provide.

How do you develop this UVP? You can use the Small Business Marketing Mastery Advisory Board (SBMMAB) to help you figure this out. Multiple minds and multiple experiences are far more effective and efficient than any single mind or experience in helping you understand the value of your product or service. So by tapping into the experiences and opinions of others, you receive valuable, objective feedback that can help you clarify your message and how it will be received.

After you clarify your UVP and have tested it in your SBMMAB, you are ready to rock and roll. The best way to encourage new business is to enlist others to help you. One of the best approaches is developing a referral process. A referral process is designed to usher you directly into the decision maker's office. The reason referrals work, if executed correctly, is that the person making the referral is passing along his relationship with his client (friend, family, etc.) to you. If this does not shorten the sales process, nothing will. The key is getting referrals from others who understand how to do this effectively. In this section you will learn the importance of creating a UVP and how to use an advisory board to help you create one, then use this information to close more business.

Networking for Referrals
Getting in the Door the Right Way
By Laura T. Leggett and James W. Hornyak

Cold calling. Just the word promotes dreadful thoughts of gatekeepers, "rejectionists," and a long haul toward getting to the right person, much less at the right time. Ever notice that most top-producing sales/business people rarely cold call?

They don't have to, because they focus every day on developing relationships that generate *business by referral.* And business by referral—when properly conducted—is equivalent to being ushered into the CEO's office with an escort! When that happens, your sales cycle could be dramatically condensed—from six months to perhaps six days.

No need to meander through the corporate ladder to get to the right person at the right time. No need to be rejected by gatekeepers. We've all heard that people do business with people they know, like, and trust. So the question becomes: How can a sales/business person be known, liked, and trusted by a prospect he's never met? It's easy when the sales person has a network of people *the prospect* already knows, likes, and trusts. In this context, we're talking about "who *they* know" being just as important as "who you know." As Verizon® so prominently advertises, "it's the network."

When you have the right network in place and you work it correctly for everyone's benefit, you'll be guided through the right door, at the right time, to the right person.

Here are two quick, cardinal rules about networking:
1. **You must have the mindset of helping others.** Networking must work both ways. Zig Ziglar said it best: "To get what you want, help others get what they want." If you don't have this mindset, no matter what type of networking you do, you'll experience mediocre results, if any.

2. **You are not selling when you're networking.** This is the most common mistake people make. Instead of selling, you are sorting to find contacts who are mutually beneficial.

Now that you know the "cardinal rules," here's how to best develop a quality network, then "work your network" to dramatically condense sales cycles without having to deploy the debilitating demands of prospecting:

Quickly Find People Who Target Similar Markets

First, stop wasting time on people whose Rolodexes don't complement yours! It's unfair to them as much as it is to you. You want to meet people who target similar markets in a non-competitive manner or work with the same personnel within organizations as you (i.e., the CIO or the CEO). Imagine the time wasted, for example, at a Chamber of Commerce mixer event when you allow yourself to get stuck talking to the Manager of Collections for ten minutes when you sell enterprise computer systems.

Your objective at business networking or social functions should be to meet people and quickly determine if it makes sense to schedule a later discussion. This can be done diplomatically and politely. After all, if there's no fit, they shouldn't be spending time with you either! This process is called, in the words of millionaire Mel Kaufmann, finding beneficial "links" in contacts (www.thelinksystem.com). Mr. Kaufmann recommends getting a conversation started with a general question like, "How did you hear about this event?" Then ask the following "link" questions that will allow you to see if the contact's Rolodex complements yours:

- What does your firm do?
- What do you do for your firm?
- What is your target market?
- How long have you been with your firm?

Then have a short dialogue, three to five minutes. If you think the person is a mutually beneficially contact, ask if you can have his or her card and say, "Maybe we should get together to see how we can help each other develop some business. When would be the best time to call?" Then be sure to make the call!

If you determine there is not a good fit, then politely excuse yourself by saying, "It was a pleasure meeting you. I'm sure you have other people you would like to meet, as do I. I look forward to seeing you again." And then move on!

Notice you are not selling but sorting. These conversations should take only several minutes. The key at business networking events is to meet as many people as possible. As you build your network, you build your opportunity pipeline. Join your local Chamber of Commerce or as many business organizations as time permits. Get involved on the committees within these organizations so people get to know you. While you might not think at first that these are business building activities, realize that they are. Your involvement will save a huge amount of time in prospecting and will inevitably put you in the right place, at the right time, ready to close business.

Attend or Organize a Structured Referral Group

The most focused way to network for referrals is to attend or organize a group that meets regularly for the sole purpose of exchanging personal referrals. This is not a "mixer" where you throw around business cards. It's not a coffee club. It's a structured meeting of professionals specifically designed to generate highly-qualified referrals.

The group you attend or organize should be appropriate for your type of business. Many "lead exchange" groups are consumer-oriented (B2C). If your business caters to other companies (B2B), a group with mixed membership or solely B2C will be a waste of time because Rolodexes are generally not complementary.

Here are some guidelines for an effective referral group:
1. *The group should preferably be made up of business owners who target the same type of market, either B2C or B2B (not both).*

2. Give attendees at least five minutes each to present their business, outlining:
   a. A brief description of business and why it's unique
   b. Mention of key clients currently served

3. *Clearly articulate and describe the types of business opportunities desired,*

including:

a. Specific prospects wanted for introduction or referral (by company name or description).

b. "Hot Buttons"—things group members should look for in a prospect that would make for a good referral.

4. *Give referrals to other people!* Make it a goal to give referrals, at least ten per month. This gets you talking to people and it's a universal rule that when you give you receive.

5. *Use a three-way call to introduce, edify, and transfer trust for a truly qualified referral.* Don't just tell someone to use your name (nor accept someone telling you to use their name). A three-way introduction call generates immediate credibility, and eliminates phone tag. The key factor in a three-way call is properly edifying the referral in front of the prospect.

As the structured referral group matures with regular attendees, you'll be amazed to see the synergy between members and the relationships that develop. Soon you'll have a "team" of people out there looking for opportunities to help grow your business. And more importantly, they'll dramatically cut your sales cycle by getting you in the right door at the right time with the right person. Say good-bye to cold calling!

Laura T. Leggett and James W. Hornyak are co-founders of *B-to-B Connect* (www.BtoBconnect.com), a business-to-business personal referral membership organization with chapters throughout the U.S. and Canada. Leggett and Hornyak are both seasoned sales professionals in the telecommunications industry.

Creating Customers for Life
Defining your Unique Value Proposition
By Jack R. Howe

The most difficult challenge for small business owners is to be limited to a single Unique Value Proposition (UVP). I am as guilty as any. In my third attempt to be more entrepreneur-like, I struggled for three years trying to be one thing and then the other, telling myself that I was adjusting to the market. Horse pucky! I was afraid to limit myself for fear of failure. And, sure enough, just like all the great authors tell us, what I focused on, I obtained—failure. Certainly not fall-down-and-die or bankrupt failure, but failure to accomplish my stated goals and objectives. My friends tried to help me find the right words to describe my business position. They would read my material and say, "Okay, but what do you offer? What do you want me to buy?" Deep inside the answer was, buy *me*. Believe in me! But that doesn't work unless you're an actor, artist, or entertainer—*or does it*?

The struggle to define your unique value to the market you want to serve is one of the most difficult, yet important aspects of starting your own business. Therefore coming up with a solution should precede all other activities in your development of an enterprise. Without a unique value to offer to the market, your service or product is just another commodity with limitless competition. But even the king of commodity, Wal-Mart™, has a UVP—"Your Low Price Leader." If Wal-Mart needs a UVP, how can you ignore the need in your small business?

A Unique Value Proposition is the foundation to creating a business relationship, one that weathers the storms and outlasts the competition. It helps you establish customers for life. It helps you cement your business as a presence in the community. For example, I don't have a long-term business relationship with the guy that currently mows my lawn, at least not one based on any UVP. He messes up and he is gone – period. Someone comes along and offers to do a comparable job for less and today's guy is history.

Conversely, Bob Sandlin, the fellow who mowed my lawn from the day I moved into my house until he retired to his farm in east Texas, I did have a business relationship with. Our relationship was based on a UVP—this was as much his yard as it was mine. Bob Sandlin took pride and care in his work, paid meticulous attention to detail, was committed to having things done right, and was always willing to go the extra mile for parties and open houses, making him as much a friend as a vendor. If he missed a day we worried about his health. We argued and insisted on giving him occasional increases in pay.

Bob started our business relationship with simple questions. He was driving by our new house and we were in the yard that was still dirt and dreams. He complimented us on the house we had designed and built. He then asked if we had decided on seed, mulch, or turf? We said we were leaning toward seed. He asked if we were thinking Bermuda, rye, fescue, or zoya? We were thinking Bermuda—he said good choice; in this climate, it would grow with the least amount of water and look really nice. He continued his subtle marketing and sales approach (heaven forbid he should hear me say this because that was not his approach—it was just his way). He asked if I owned a lawn mower. New homeowner that I was, the answer was no. "Well," says he, "no need to buy one. I will cut your yard for you when you get it ready and keep it looking great." He then went on to list all the neighbors whose lawns he tended to, homes we had admired, if we wanted references (we didn't). "So how much would that cost us?" I asked. He told me, and our business relationship never faltered for 20 years, until we shook hands and wished him well as we presented him and his wife with their new housewarming gift for the ranch.

Bob had made a customer for life—me. No cheaper deal. No bigger firm. No one could ever replace Bob. Bob was a friend who owned my yard more than I did. He was vested in its success and I knew it. And Bob had all the customers he ever wanted. He never advertised, although occasionally he might stop and say "Hi" to someone new in the neighborhood and ask if they were going to seed or mulch.

If the guy that cuts the yard can create a valued relationship that lasts for most of 20 years, can you do any less with your business?

Now, if I asked Bob if he had a UVP, he would look at me and think me sun-stroked. But he had one that he lived, and it was all the marketing he ever needed to obtain as much business as he wanted for his whole life. Can you say the same?

Bob Sandlin didn't mow grass. Bob Sandlin took pride in his work and wanted you to be proud of it as well. Bob was more concerned with how we felt than what he got paid. Consequently, he never wanted for customers. He lived his UVP.

At long last I came to understand what my third try at independent business was to be. The moment the idea crystallized in my head, everything changed. People began to want to help me, offers of opportunities came up in conversations without me so much as asking. People I had not spoken to in years called and reinforced that I was on the right path. The value was so clear, so unique, so compelling that it pulled opportunity to it like a magnet.

So is there a process for defining your UVP? Is there some method or rule you can follow?

Ask yourself—what do you love to do? What will get you up every morning excited to do? Why is this important to you? (I offer a single caution: if your answer is to change people's lives—make sure you have the right to do so.) Focus on your passion, and your unique value proposition will become clear. And when it does, you too can have customers for life!

Action Items
To create customers for life you need to adopt the following four principals, as demonstrated by Bob Sandlin, in all your business dealings:
1. Communication—Listen first; demonstrate respect; ask the customer how he wants to be treated; and keep your communication open, honest, sincere, and fair.

2. Responsibility—you should take full responsibility for your actions, your intentions, and your communications. Customers like to know they can rely on you.

3. Integrity—Look for ways to make a difference; extend trust; do right by those who do right; and keep your customers interest paramount in your dealings.

4. Results — Practice accountability; pay attention to the details; create transparency; and deliver on your commitments.

These principals will serve you well, both in business and in life. Remember: We judge ourselves by our intentions; others judge us by our actions.

Jack R. Howe has over 30 years' experience in business management, sales, and sales management in complex operational environments. His background includes experience in industry, a major accounting/consulting firm, and in private practice. Clients have included multi-billion dollar firms and aggressively growing start-ups. In private practice, he has developed innovative business tools and solutions to remodel business enterprises for greater profitability. Howe is a public speaker, mentor, coach, and the author of *Please Don't Tell My Mother I'm a Salesman, 30 Minutes to Prepare for the C-Suite Meeting*, and is about to reiease *The Tao of Customers for Life*. Visit www.30minsto.com or www.ceotoolbelt.com for more information, or email Howe at jack@ceotoolbelt.com.

Small Business Mastery Marketing Advisory Boards

By Ron Finklestein

Over 100 years ago Jules Vern wrote three books: *Around the World in Eighty Days*, *Twenty Thousand Leagues Under the Sea*, and *Journey to the Moon*. When those books were written Vern was called crazy, ignorant, and a dreamer—yet the concepts in each book became a reality and are taken for granted today.

Why do you care? Because you are a business owner with your own dreams, goals, and desires that you want to accomplish. You, like Jules Vern, have others who second-guess your vision, your direction, and sometimes think you're crazy too!

In order to succeed as a business owner, there are five marketing problems you want to address in your business:
1. Identifying your ideal customer
2. Getting in front of the right people
3. Keeping your marketing pipeline full of prospects
4. Maintaining contact with prospects, suspects, and clients
5. Having a marketing plan that works

How do I know? I am a business owner and I wanted to fix or avoid those things too.

Like Jules Vern, you may feel as though no one understands you or the challenges you face, the pressure you are under, or the opportunities that are available. It can get lonely. You don't know who to trust to help you solve your problems. But you know others did it and you know that you can do it too. You also know that in order to succeed, you need to create a measurable, repeatable, and predictable marketing process that anyone in your business can use.

You're not alone. There are people who you can trust. To find them, consider creating a Small Business Mastery Marketing Advisory Board (SBMMAB).

A SBMMAB is a group of friends, associates, and selected customers who are dedicated to providing feedback, advice, suggestions, accountability, and marketing best practices that allow the members to grow, flourish, and get results. After all, multiple brains and experiences are far smarter and efficient that any single brain or experience.

You know the old saying: *It's lonely at the top?* When you're a small business owner, you have no one to turn to but yourself. You are expected to make decisions that affect your employees and their families, vendors, customer, clients, and your family. It's nearly impossible to keep thinking straight when you have people coming at you from all directions: bills, payroll, client obligations, vendor problems, and production issues. That's where the SBMMAB can benefit you. Marketing can be complex and difficult. There are so many choices, options, and opportunities. How do you know what works? When you create or find a SBMMAB to participate in, you can put more money in your pocket! The SBMMAB will help you develop new business and increase your success. This Advisory Board can provide constructive feedback and great ideas that you can use to grow your business. This group can help you define and refine your marketing approach and message.

My experience has shown that the best decisions are made in a safe environment, with a group of people you trust, who can be objective and are willing to share what they know. Some of the things the SBMMAB will allow you to experience and implement include:

- Brainstorming and perfecting ideas to grow your business.

- Exploring marketing problems and opportunities in a safe, secure, and friendly environment.

- Masterminding solutions to your marketing problems.

- Creating a marketing team of objective, interested, concerned, and fearless advisors.

- Sharing your marketing knowledge to help others grow and prosper.

- Holding you accountable for taking the actions necessary to achieve your goals.

The process is very simple, but it is not for everyone. If you are not willing to play it out, please stop reading—this concept is not right for you. This group should be designed to help you create (or keep) the right attitude, provide the best marketing advice available, and hold you accountable for the results you want to achieve, but only if you're serious about growing your business.

Basic tips to start a SBMMAB:

1. **Define the purpose of the group**. Make sure it is marketing-based and that everyone is in agreement.

2. **Finding the right members**. You want to look for people who are willing to share what they know and are not afraid to provide constructive feedback.

3. **Meet at least once a month**. All members must treat this meeting time as sacred.

4. **Keep it short and to the point:** Each meeting should be no more that three to four hours in length. By keeping everyone focused and on-topic you will get more done and will make members believe in the integrity of the group.

5. **Respect the voice and needs of everyone.** Give each member of the group 30 minutes to put their marketing issues in front of the group to request feedback.

6. **Define action items that you will accomplish before the next meeting**. This is vital in order to hold yourself and each other member accountable. It will also ensure that the ideas of the group come to fruition and build each member's business.

The outcome you can expect are best defined by Alan Plastow, Founder of the Business Technology Consumer Network:

I know how difficult it can be to find honest, accurate, affordable answers to mission-critical questions. I know how isolated you can become from business expertise, simply due to fears of exposing too much, or too little. As a member of AKRIS Small Business Mastery Advisory Board, I've discovered an incredibly valuable resource—a group of knowledgeable business professionals with whom I can share advice, diverse perspectives, and expertise—even friendship. This group is demonstrably the most beneficial resource for unlimited personal and professional growth that I have found in over two decades of intense searching.

So what's the next step? There are two things you can do: find a group or start a group. Whatever you do, do it now. If you are like me, if you don't do it now, it won't get done because something else will get your attention and take you away from accomplishing your goals and dreams. Be like Jules Vern and dare to dream what your future can be like.

Action Items:
Here are a few quick ideas for finding or starting a group:
1. Find other business owner who are experiencing your same problem.

2. Create a structure for the meeting so everyone knows what to expect.

3. Give everyone an opportunity every month to share their challenges with the group.

4. Make sure there is no competition between members in the groups

5. Implement a rule in the group—no selling!

6. The best marketing ideas come from different industries that are applied to your industry, so be sure to invite a variety of different individuals from various industries.

7. Limit the group to 10 to 12 members. This will allow for enough people to meet each month and forgive the absentees that inevitably happen.

8. Create an agenda that is always followed.

Remember, multiple minds and multiple experiences are far more effective and efficient that one mind and one experience.

Ronald Finklestein, President of AKRIS, LLC, is a small business success expert, business coach, consultant, speaker, author, and trainer, and has published two books, *Celebrating Success! Fourteen Ways to a Successful Company and The Platinum Rule to Small Business Mastery.* **He contributed to** *101 Great Ways to Improve Your Life.* **Finklestein founded the Business Leadership Association, LLC and co-founded Celebrating Success! NEO Business Conference. Finklestein is available for coaching and consulting and for speaking engagements, workshops, and seminars. You can contact him at info@yourbusinesscoach.net or reach him at (330) 990-0788. Sign up for his newsletter at http://www.yourbusinesscoach.net.**

Technology-Based Marketing Strategies
By Ron Finklestein

When used correctly, technology can be a fun and exciting way to grow your business. Did I forget easy? Yes, technology can be easy. You can use teleseminars (if you know how to use the phone), email marketing (if you write emails), website promotion, and electronic newsletters to get the word out about your business and to communicate with suspects, prospects, and customer.

As with anything else, you may not have any experience with using this form of marketing. That's okay. Use this section and invest a bit of time learning about this new and exciting approach to marketing your business. Our authors describe how to use this approach and the benefits it can have for your business.

You should use these techniques to communicate with your customers regularly. You can announce special promotions, new products, new hires, and promotions, and discuss other aspects of your business that your customers want to hear about. You can use these techniques to reach out into new markets or inexpensively test different marketing approaches.

If you don't already have the infrastructure to support this technology, your friendly Information Technology Specialist can help. In many cases, having a technology infrastructure to support this approach is not necessary. There are legions of companies that exist to take the technology out of building technology marketing strategies.

I use what is called a Content Management System (CMS) to update my website and submit it to Google® for indexing. Using this CMS system, all I have to do to update my website is login, make the change, and save my work. This is very cost-effective and convenient. Through my website I can also create an email newsletter that allows for very easy email marketing. The tough part is not the technology, but the creation of strong, effective, useful context.

The problem is that we sometimes hide behind technology. People find it hard to contact us. We become an email address or a web site to our customers and not a real person. With technology we can remove the people element without thinking about it.

In this section you will learn some great strategies to allow you to use technology to make contact and build effective, profitable relationships. When we use technology with good relationship strategies we have an incredible combination for building our business. Like everything else, you need to make a business decision on whether to use these tools in your marketing. Feel free to write in the margins if something looks interesting. Use your advisory board (from the Networking Section) to help with this if necessary. But learn about these powerful tools before you dismiss them. Savvy Internet marketers are making a lot of money, and so can you.

Using Multimedia to Market High-Ticket Products And Services

By Robert Scheinfeld

In my 18 years as a direct marketer, I've designed and executed marketing models that included face-to-face components, telemarketing, direct mail, print advertising, and the Internet. I've always been obsessed with finding ways to increase efficiency, effectiveness, sales, and profits.

In the early days of my career, most of my marketing was text-based – print ads and sales letters – and I was able to produce extraordinary results that way. Then I added audio into the mix and got even better results. Then I added video into the mix and got even better results.

When you combine text, audio, and video, you create "multimedia" and when I discovered the magic and power of multimedia in marketing, everything changed for me in amazing ways. The only problem was that producing and distributing multimedia marketing was complicated and expensive.

Then the Internet came along and evolved to the point in recent years where things have become possible that multimedia direct marketers like me only dreamed about previously. I went on to develop a multimedia marketing model that I've used, with astonishing results—for myself and clients.

The model can be used to sell any product or service. I've used it to sell millions of dollars in multimedia home study courses, seminars, coaching, consulting, and software. To give you an idea of the power of the model, when I applied it to Blue Ocean Software, we grew from $1.2 million to $44 million in four years – with 50% margins – and then sold the company for $177 million cash.
The model will help you to:
• Sell more to your existing clients
• Create more new clients
• Increase the size of your average sale
• Decrease your expenses
• Send your profits – and the impact you have on your sphere of influence – soaring

There are three primary components to the model:
1. Isolating "The Best Of The Best"
2. Using Multimedia to communicate "The Best Of The Best"
3. Using the Internet in a specific way to distribute the Multimedia
I'm going to sketch out the components here, and then refer you to additional resources to get more detail and see examples of the model in action.

Isolating "The Best Of The Best"
In general, the best way to sell any product or service is in person, face-to-face, and most businesses have a proven process for doing that. Whether it's you or another member of your team, there's generally one person who's the best at selling your product or service, and that person does specific things whenever he/she sells.

For example, some salespeople are at their best speaking and referring to PowerPoint slides. Others are at their best using a pitch book with photos, graphs, illustrations, and testimonial letters. Others are at their best scribbling on a yellow pad, using a white board, or actually demonstrating the product or service. Still others combine several of the resources just listed, and/or use additional ones.

The first step in the model is finding one or more or your best "salespeople" and isolating what they do when they're at their best.

If you don't currently have a proven "live" sales process, or your current process is text and/or audio based, then the alternative is to simply let your creative juices flow, look at each step in your current sales process and ask yourself, "What would be the best way to communicate this point if I had no limitations?" Then you design the skeleton of a new sales process from the answers to those questions.

Using Multimedia to Communicate "The Best Of The Best"
Once you've isolated or designed a "Best of the Best" sales process, the next step is to use multimedia tools to mimic what you'd do at your best, live. There is a new breed of multimedia tool available so you can easily and cost-effectively present your process without anyone having to "be there" in person.

When the best way to communicate a point is through text, you use text. When the best way is by showing the face or head and shoulders of your best salesperson communicating "live," you do that. When the best way is to have your best salesperson demonstrating your product or service, or narrating while a graph, illustration, white board, or yellow pad is being shown, you do that.

Virtually anything someone could do live can be done remotely with these tools, and when done optimally, it yields astonishing results. All you need is a PC, camcorder, and software. You can stay simple or get very sophisticated. You can do the work yourself or hire it out to experts. I've gotten very sophisticated but still do all of it myself from a home office above my garage.

Using the Internet to Present The Multimedia

Once you've converted your Best of the Best sales process to multimedia, you can then offer the multimedia presentation via a CD or DVD or on the Internet. Because of the cost-effectiveness and international reach of the Internet, that's my preferred choice. When done on the Internet, I use a specific model I call my "T.O.T. System." The T.O.T. System rests on four foundational pillars:

1. A mind-set for designing websites

2. A methodology for applying sales strategies that complement that mind-set

3. A methodology for optimizing the results you get from applying the strategies

4. Using multimedia to turbo-charge the results you produce

The Mind-Set

I use the acronym "TOT" to describe the mind-set behind my model. The three letters stand for:

T = The
O = One
T = Thing

Internet users are notoriously "click happy." They're like bored kids with remote controls in their hands and 250 channels of satellite TV, looking for something to captivate them. Just like with a live or telemarketing sales call, if you get a visitor to your website and don't instantly grab their attention, hold it, and keep it focused where you want it to be, they're clicking off to another option.

Therefore, once a visitor gets to one of your TOT sites, you have only one thing you want them to do—only one decision to make. The whole site is very simple and designed to support the visitor in doing the one thing you want them to do.

Once they do the one thing you want them to do on your main page, you guide them to another page where they're once again motivated to do one thing only. You then keep them moving down a slope of "one thing only" decisions until the final decision is to buy your product or service, or contact you if the goal is lead generation.

It's absolute "death" on the Internet to have one website that has multiple, independent, non-strategic choices for people to choose from: "Click here for this, click there for that, click here to listen to my audio, click here to see a demo ...."—on and on. All your multimedia resources must be coordinated using an intelligent plan.

Would you walk into a prospect's office and bombard him/her with choices on what you could discuss with them? No! You'd get their attention, control their focus, and guide them where you want them to go using an intelligent and proven system. Don't lose that strategy on your website.

Methodology and Strategies

When I build TOT sites, it's almost always based on offering a free course or a guided tour, although other options are possible. I call it a free course if I'm actually teaching them something valuable as part of the sales process and I call it a guided tour if I'm just showing them how something works, why it works so well, and/or how it can help them. For purposes of discussion here, I'm going to use the example of the guided tour option.

Since a TOT site is based on motivating people to do one thing only, the one thing you want them to do when they visit the site is enroll in the tour. That's it. No other choices. Nothing else is visible on the site unless it supports the process of getting them to enroll in the tour. To gain access to the tour, they must give you their name and email address and they then get immediate access to the course.

The tour is as long as is needed to replicate your best salesperson at their best. Suppose your tour has six segments to it, which is the average length of one of my latest TOT sites. Once they enroll, the next "one thing" you want them to do is experience the first segment. The next one thing would be to experience the second segment and so on.

All the Tour segments, except the final one, are designed to educate, inspire, and filter your visitors. In fact, with a TOT site, the prospect may not even know you have anything for sale in the initial segments!

Each Tour segment is linked to the next through a "cliff hanger" like you see on TV shows and in novels. Why? To ensure that they keep sliding down the slippery slope of your one decision at a time until the final decision is to buy. In the final segment, you shift to a sales pitch (using an elegant and effective transition), and invite them to buy your product or service. If you did your job well in the early segments, the prospect is already positively pre-disposed towards you and you don't have to "close" hard or play any games to close the sale or generate a highly-qualified lead.

Optimizing Your Results

The TOT model is very effective and consistently out-performs other models for selling on the Internet because:

1. It's different. Most people don't use it, or if they do offer a free course, it's done by email, which isn't as effective.

2. The look and feel of a tour or course versus a "sales letter" is different.

3. The educational and inspirational aspects, when done well, build greater rapport and trust and facilitate the sale with less or no "live" human involvement.

4. You capture the name, email address, and phone (if you choose) of the visitor so you can follow-up with them.

Beyond that, however, there's another major advantage to the model. When you use this model, you divide your sales process into pieces:
- The main page of the website
- The educational segments
- The final segment that does the selling

By breaking the whole into smaller pieces, you can then study what are called "web logs" for your website and see what's happening with each piece. Behind the scenes on all websites, large blocks of information are captured and stored, including exactly what your visitor does when they visit—someone came to this page, stayed two minutes, then went to that page, stayed four minutes, etc.

By using free or low-cost software to analyze the web logs, you can find out exactly where you have "problems" in your sales process. For example, if you see that 100 people visited your site and only 20 enrolled in your tour, you know you need to revise the main page. You can the make a change, study the logs again, and keep repeating the process until you optimize the enrollment percentage. This is very easy to do and you don't need any technical skill or knowledge.

If, as another example, 100 people visit your site, 70 enroll in your tour, and only 40 go from the first segment to the second, you know you have a problem in the first segment and you need to revise it—or punch up the cliffhanger that links to the segment that follows.

Plus, since the web logs show how much time someone spends on a page, if you see a pattern that people consistently exit a segment at the three-minute point, you know exactly where "the problem" is and you can then test different changes to the segment in that specific part until another review of the logs shows you've fixed the problem.

Having this kind of "X-Ray Vision" is a salesperson's and marketers dream and it's not possible with other types of web sites, nor in offline ads or sales letters.

So take action today, and market your company and its products with all the resources available to you.

In order to take immediate action on what you just learned, follow these five simple steps:

1. Visit this website and download the additional resources available there to support you in executing what you just discovered and to see examples of multimedia and T.O.T. sites in action: http://www.bobscheinfeld.com/100secrets.html.

2. Study the PowerPoint presentation available there, which will give you additional detail beyond what this short chapter provided.

3. Open and study the two resource documents, select the tools you think would help you, order them, and get them installed.

4. Work on isolating or designing your "Best of the Best" sales process and then use the tools to help you convert it into a multimedia presentation.

5. Start distributing the multimedia presentation on and off the Internet.

For more than 20 years, Robert Scheinfeld has been helping people create extraordinary results, in less time, with less effort, and much more fun. His passion is helping others carve out and live what he calls their "Ultimate Lifestyle." Scheinfeld is an 11-year veteran of applying cutting-edge sales and marketing strategies and has had in-the-trenches experience of creating hugely profitable multi-million dollar businesses (on and off the Internet). He has helped tens of thousands of people in more than 170 countries transform their definitions of success, and the pathways they follow to create success in their lives. For more information, please visit www.BobScheinfeld.com.

Teleseminars
Great Marketing for Products and Services
By Marsha Egan

In this age of globalization, decentralization, and increasingly expensive travel, teleclasses and teleseminars are becoming a very popular means of connecting, communicating, and educating. They are also a new-found solution to people looking for a new and different marketing medium.

First, just a little bit of background... By simply dialing in to a predetermined telephone bridge line, a participant is able to join people interested in his or her topic from virtually all over the world, while eliminating considerable travel time and expense. Teleseminars can range from a very few people to very, very many. They can be free or for a fee. Some teleseminars are interactive; some are not. The formats can vary from a lecture, to two-person interviews, to roundtable discussions, to interviews with celebrity guests. The only limit to how these can be used is your own creativity. Teleseminars are simply an inexpensive and efficient method of delivery that can touch your clients and prospects all over the world for just pennies.

So how can you use teleseminars to market your business?

Here is an example: You hold a free one-hour teleseminar on a subject of interest to your target market. The subject relates in some way to your business. You give them great information that they can use. You even provide them a handout that they download by going to your website. After you've spent a content-rich hour, you've developed a relationship with each person on the line. As they become comfortable with you, it builds the trust that is needed to develop loyal customers. Because you provide them information that they truly need, they appreciate you and your business more. They are exposed to helpful solutions that your product or service can provide, and therefore you have a higher percentage opportunity of making a follow-up sale. They have just entered your product funnel.

It is important to note that running teleseminars is not rocket science. For anyone who has conducted a seminar or facilitated a meeting, the actual practice of putting on a teleseminar is similar. For anyone who has marketed an event, the marketing is similar. The difference is the medium. It is a relatively new, time-saving, value-rich, and inexpensive marketing tool.

Teleseminars that market your business can take many forms:
- Providing useful information that drives your market to your products or services
- Informing clients about new procedures or practices
- Conducting "Ask the CEO" sessions
- Updating prospects and suspects on industry trends
- Interviewing experts who can help your market stay current
- Training clients' employees in a skill they need
- Holding Q&A sessions

Finding participants for your teleseminars depends on your defined target market, and the purpose and subject of your teleseminar. Depending on the specificity or niche of the teleseminar, you may have a small or very large prospect base. You can find potential attendees in your database, through personal contacts, by advertising, emailing, mailing, calling etc. The key point is that you should match the people you are inviting to the teleseminar with a subject that will be very interesting or helpful to them.

It is critical that the teleseminars that you sponsor are run well. Failure to provide great value for the time that people invest will almost guarantee that they will not return. So, here are a few points to help you run a teleseminar that successfully markets your business:

In advance:
- Publish your start and end times, noting the time zone
- Send reminders with the bridge line information three days and again one day in advance

On the call:
- Call from a land line, and have a backup telephone nearby
- Have a strong and capable moderator/facilitator
- Start on time, and end on time
- Prepare yourself thoroughly, and follow an agenda

- Prepare any interviewees in advance
- Make the call extremely content-rich
- Manage the quality of the call; i.e. address background noises by asking participants to mute
- Keep the teleseminar moving energetically and engage the participants
  After the teleseminar:
- Follow up, thanking your participants for their involvement
- Provide information on your products or services, and how to contact you
- Stay in touch with your attendees periodically using all of your other marketing know-how

Any time you have an opportunity to spend an hour or two with people in your target market, you should be able to build relationships that will help your business. As with giving public speeches, taking people to lunch, or playing a game of golf, teleseminars can do this.

Today's technologies, and people's increasing familiarity with using conference calling to communicate, make teleseminars a natural progression in the marketing arena. As we said previously, it's not rocket science, it's just a new medium of doing previously successful things. They are easy, inexpensive, convenient, effective, and here to stay.

So, what's keeping you? When will you offer your next teleseminar?

Marsha D. Egan, CPCU, PCC, CEO, is a celebrated keynoter, facilitator, author and ICF-certified coach. Egan "speaks from experience" as president of the energetic success coaching firm, The Egan Group, Inc. An ATHENA Foundation Award recipient, one of PA's 50 Best Women in Business, and 25-year veteran of corporate and volunteer America, Egan intuitively reinvents leadership by igniting leaders with positive change and innovation. Services include keynotes, half- or full-day programs, and one-on-one coaching designed to inspire individuals and organizations to maximize their potential. Her firm publishes and produces numerous "how-to" eBooks, CD's, and a bi-weekly eZine, The SIGNAL for more than 20,000 success-seekers worldwide. Egan can be reached at marsha@marshaegan.com.

Lead Generation With Webinars

By Don Philabaum

How much are you spending on leads? I used to spend as much as $1,000 for a lead until I found a way to generate a lead for virtually nothing. In addition, I found a way to increase the number of leads from a marketing activity from an average of 10 per mailing to as much as 250 from just one mailing!
Are you interested in learning my secret? Then read on!

In 1994 AOL, GeoCities, and Tripod were emerging online communities that were growing by leaps and bounds. They, along with pioneer online communities like The Well, brought people together in a virtual community. Anxious to build a business around the Internet, I read at least 30 books and spent hours online learning to research from a user and provider prospective. By 1995 I had found my niche. I envisioned all groups and organizations would benefit from using Internet technology that would help them communicate at less cost and network their members. My business plan was built around providing private, password-protected, online communities to groups and organizations worldwide—for a fee!

When I looked around the marketplace, there were two obvious places for me to offer a fee-based online community service. One was to national associations like the National Association of Dental Hygienists and the other was the 3,000 plus alumni associations. I gravitated to providing the online community product to alumni associations for three reasons. First, alumni associations already provided their alumni with a printed directory listing the names of all other alumni. Second, focus groups I held indicated they were receptive to moving it to the web. Finally, I was familiar with the education market. While in college myself, I founded a company that pioneered the photographing of students when they received their diploma on graduation day. By the time I founded IAC, my firm was photographing 200,000 students at 550 colleges, universities, and high schools.

I reasoned it would be easier for me to break into this market because I could use my current client list and continue to expand it. Because my product was entirely new to the market, I found myself spending a great deal of time educating the prospect base on the value of the product.

When I built my list up to 1,000 prospects, I felt it was time to do a mass mailing. After spending a great deal of time creating an attractive flyer, writing an incredible letter with the appropriate call for action, we sat back waiting breathlessly for the deluge of bounce-back cards. We received two bounce-backs. Two bounce-backs! When I totaled the graphic design, printing, postage, and labor cost, each bounce-back cost me $1,000! And neither lead was ready to buy. Having no alternative, we kept building our list and making calls. When the list hit 2,500, we did a second mailing. We received 12 bounce-backs!

After analyzing my costs again, my lead cost had dropped to $208. We were moving in the right direction! By the second year of business we significantly ramped up our marketing strategy. We decided to send a flyer every month to the target group of 2,500 prospects. Leads were coming in and the lead cost was hovering about $180. Even though we were spending $40,000 a year sending mass mailings, we were receiving a positive ROI for each mailing. Keep in mind, during the 1990's small businesses were also paying 20 to 35 cents per minute for 800 calls. It wasn't cheap to prospect.

By 2000, email had become a standard business tool among our prospects and we began to reduce our mailing budget and using monthly emails to generate leads. By 2002 we completely eliminated mass mailings. However, after a period of time we began to see a serious drop in the leads coming from our broadcast emails. People were becoming immune to our pitch and offer. We realized that we needed to do something different to rise above the significant clutter of other emails our prospects were receiving.

That's when we decided to try online conferencing, or webinars, as we call them.

Our first webinar offered an opportunity for anyone to see how our product would benefit them. In reality it was simply a demonstration of our product.

We attracted 20 people to our offer, of whom 10 showed up. Our sales team was happy because the process made them 10 times more effective. Normally they would find a prospect and do one-on-one demos with them. That led them to setting up regularly scheduled demos where they did group presentations. Some sales people loved it because this technique gave them more prospecting time, others didn't like it because they liked the one-on-one relationship they were able to develop with prospects. Eventually a blend of ideas grew that made everyone more productive, and sales soared.

Then by happenstance, we attended a couple of free online conferences on marketing. After we had attended these, it dawned on us that, in addition to demo webinars, we should offer educational webinars. After all, we had written white papers and reports, provided a monthly eNewsletter, and even published a book entitled, Create a NET-Centered College Campus. We reasoned, why not use that knowledge to educate the market and sell more products?

It worked! After a series of webinars that attracted 50 or more attendees, we hit a particularly hot button in the industry when we held a series of webinars built around my report "Facing UP to the Facebook/Myspace Generation." This series attracted over 750 attendees at three webinars!

Today, we use mail to send out automated letter campaigns set up by our sales team to continually connect with their prospects. Direct mail campaigns are only used on rare occasion to reach new market areas.

As you contemplate adopting webinars to develop "no cost" leads, there are ten lessons we learned along the way that will benefit you:

1. Keep your email short
In evaluating the responses to our broadcast emails that offered free webinars, we found that shorter emails worked best. Through trial and error we learned that three short paragraphs were most effective, two of which could be no more than four sentences. The offer had to be short, compelling, and/or a call to action that revolved around "reply to this email and say 'I'm in.'"

2. Share knowledge
Your webinars should focus on sharing knowledge. Your target audience will more likely respond to an offer if they know they are going to learn something.

Your webinar goal should be to offer statistics, best practices, and examples. Only at the end of your webinar should you talk about how your product can improve the numbers or issues shared in the presentation.

3. Offer a report or "whitepaper"

A short report from four to ten pages became a valuable draw to increase attendance. We found authoring these also increased our credibility. For the most part, I wrote the reports, but there are many reports you can buy and give to attendees. You will also have to decide when you want to give them your report/white paper. There is some logic to sending it prior to the event, but we've always thought it important to require attendance in order to get the report/white paper.

4. Bring in industry experts

While you are hosting the webinar, it's important to include an industry expert. This could be a customer or noted consultant. Most customers enjoy being recognized for their achievements, and consultants love additional exposure. The formula that worked best for us was a simple interview technique. We prepared a series of questions for the expert in advance to give them a chance to formulate their responses. It's casual and requires the least amount of preparation for all parties.

5. Decide if you want to let attendees ask questions

You have to decide if you want to let attendees ask questions. Do you let them ask questions during the presentation, or after the presentation is done? Generally with groups of four or more, I'd suggest you hold questions until the end. You will have to be prepared to politely handle people who monopolize the question-and-answer sessions.

6. Record the sessions

After conducting at least 20 webinars, we finally realized that we should be recording them. The sessions are a great way for your sales team to continue to stay in touch with prospects. Recording them also allows others who were not able to attend the opportunity to listen at their convenience.

7. Provide handouts

People like handouts. We found the best way to increase participation at the event is to mail them a PDF of the PowerPoint the morning before the webinar.

8. Know your conference software

Every conference call software is different. You and your team should spend time going through the conference software demos so you thoroughly know how to use the software.

9. Incorporate survey questions

Most online conferencing software will enable you to ask the audience to respond to questions. This is a fantastic way to gauge who is a prospect. We've learned to incorporate three to four questions per webinar. Your conferencing software will enable you to isolate each participant's responses. Knowing their responses provides a powerful tool to your sales team.

10. Analyze your results

Always go back and analyze the results of each campaign. Review the number of emails, how many responded, how many showed up, and how many turned into leads and then customers. Don't be afraid to ask for feedback on the quality and value of your webinar. It's important to learn from each one, what you can do better the next time.

Webinars will provide powerful prospecting tools for you and your organization. Not only will it position you as the experts, but you and your staff will enjoy being in a consulting/educational role to prospects. Use your expertise and experience to educate your prospects and along the way you will see orders increase.

Here are three simple steps to begin generating easier leads through webinars:

1. Grab all the business cards you have accumulated from visits, conferences, and networking events and create an email list.

2. Identify something that everyone wants related to your product and create a short PowerPoint and white paper. If you don't consider yourself a writer,

outsource the report to someone. Elance.com has thousands of people with the expertise to write your report for a reasonable fee

3. Send an invitation to your email list.
It really is that easy. If you don't think you have the personality and skills to conduct a webinar, don't let that stop you. Let people with skills in this area help you. But most important, if you remember to keep your webinars entertaining and informative, you'll offer a product that will build your success.

Don Philabaum is President and CEO of IAC, a world-wide provider of private social networking solutions for groups and organizations. Don has written two books, *Create a NET-Centered College Campus* and *Alumni Web Strategies*. He authors a blog called www.wiredcommunities.com and has written numerous articles and reports about social networking communities. His new division, Internet Strategies Group www.internetstrategiesgroup.com, helps organizations create Internet strategies to increase sales, reduce cost, and increase customer retention. Don can be reached at don@iaccorp.com

Does Anyone Know Your Fabulous Website Exists?

By Julie D'Aloiso

You have created a wonderful website. Maybe you had it redesigned; maybe it is brand new. Now what do you do? What you can't do is build it and expect them to just come. You must stay active on your end to ensure that your website works as much for you as you worked on it.

In order to ensure your website is seen, you must make sure you are marketing it both on- and offline. You must also make it easy to find on the Internet.

Marketing Your Website Offline

It is essential to market your website offline. There are so many opportunities to do this, and they may be easier than you think!

Update your business cards to include your web address as well as your email address. When you hand your card to a potential client, they will know where to go online to learn more about it.

Do you have a company car? Make sure it has a sign or sticker directing people to your amazing website! You never know who is stuck in traffic next to you – maybe your next client!

When you do print advertising, always include your web address with your contact information. When you put out a good ad, and customers want to know more, they can go directly to your website without searching for it. Convenience for the customer could result in profits for your company!

Don't forget the importance of public relations in alerting the world to your fabulous new website. Put out a press release to notify the media that your business can now be found on the Internet.

If one aspect of your marketing strategy is writing articles, make sure to include a reference to your site either in your bio or, better yet, send them to your site to download a free supplemental resource.

Marketing Your Website Online

You already know the importance of the Internet in marketing your business – that's why you created your website! Now, you have to use the Internet to market your website. Fortunately, there are many opportunities to do this.

Chances are, there are a number of websites related to your topics. They don't have to all be competitors! In fact, you can work with related websites to promote your own website. See if you can work out a deal with them. Maybe you can put their link on your website and they will do the same for you. You can also sign up to put banner advertisements on them. You may want to return the favor by putting their banner on your website. (Not only is this a polite thing to do, but when people click on their link through your site, you profit!) Start a blog! Blogs are an increasingly popular and entertaining way to inform and advertise. Why not start one? And when you do, be sure to promote your website on it! Keep up with the blog and you will have repeat customers visiting your site to see what you are blogging about.

Do you belong to any groups, organizations, or associations? If so, get your website linked to their online directory. That way, other members of the group can see your company's name, click your link, and be taken directly to your website.

When people do visit your website, encourage them to sign up for your newsletter or mailing list. That way you can ensure that they don't forget about your site, by sending them the occasional reminder of the great services you provide, along with other information. Just be sure not to flood their inboxes. Not only is that rude, they'll get tired of hearing from you and unsubscribe from your mailing list. They may even stop visiting your website. This isn't meant to discourage you from sending out a newsletter – just don't send it out every day!

Making Your Website Easier to Find on the Internet

Websites are often found through search engines. Search engines look for websites that are informative, frequently updated, and popular. Most of the search engines have different criteria and they do not let us know their specific requirements. However, there are some guidelines to keep in mind when you construct your website that can result in your site being featured in a search.

The content of your website is crucial in leading people to your website. Make sure your content includes keywords. Keywords are words that people type into search engines to find websites on these topics. Find out what keywords you should be using by doing keyword analysis. This area requires professional assistance, so be sure to hire someone with expertise in this area to help you.

If a keyword is important to you, create a page just for information regarding that subject. For example, if one of your main products is oranges, create a page with lots of information about oranges and call it "oranges.htm." The title of the page should include oranges, and other pages will link to the oranges page.

On your website's homepage, have a great keyword-packed paragraph. You should have pages related to your main keywords, so link to them from this paragraph. (This is where you should link your oranges page!)

If you include meta tags in your website, make sure that you have used those words in your content on the page. This is called 'keyword relevance' and it is a good thing!

It is a good idea to create pages that will inform people about your product or service. For example, create a page that is titled "How to Buy Oranges." Be sure to include a site map on your website. It will include links to all of your pages and make it easier for people to find the specific information they are looking for.

Also make sure to include bottom text links to all of your main pages in a navigation bar on very page of your website. This will allow viewers of your website to easily find what they need, and to move around all the information of your website with ease.

If you have a local business or headquarters, include your address and phone number in text format on every page. Be sure not to do so in image format, as search engines cannot read images. In fact, if viewers have a hand-help device, they can click on your phone number and call you if it's displayed in text format.

Lastly, update your website often. Visitors want to see your latest and greatest information.

It is always helpful to hire a professional to make your website look its best.

There are many good web designers, web masters, and search engine optimization consultants out there. Don't go it alone, and don't risk not publicizing your website. If you do, you could have a fabulous website, but not one will know that it exists!

Julie D'Aloiso's Webjazz Web Design, Inc. is a full-service web design and marketing company that focuses on positive Internet marketing outcomes for their clients. Services include web design, application development, managing website content via Content Management System, writing copy for client websites, Internet marketing, writing press releases, email marketing, and search engine optimization. Contact D'Aloiso for more information at (330) 467-0515 (office), (330) 998-0600 (cell) or by email a designer@dwebjazz.com. To find her online, go to www.dwebjazz.com.

Electronic Newsletters
Building a Personal Marketing Database
By Dr. Tony Alessandra

Having a free newsletter or eZine is an essential marketing tool for any business, individual, or organization. Upon first consideration, it may seem like a third-rate marketing ploy, or not worth the hassle to maintain. However, when you create a newsletter, you not only provide your subscribers with valuable information, you also create a mechanism to reach out and touch your subscribers every month or week, or any time period of your choosing.

Everyone who receives your eZine is a potential customer. Whether you are selling your services or products, each newsletter is an opportunity to generate revenue. It is also a chance to increase recognition and grow your business.

And the reason it's free? You want as many names in your database as you can get. In order for someone to give you their valuable, personal information, you need to provide them with something equally valuable in return. Also, if you ask people to pay for your newsletter, some may if they perceive significant value above and beyond the fee, but most will just move on to someone who will give them the equivalent information for free.

Your eZine can be created in either plain text or HTML (HyperText Markup Language) formats, or both. HTML is the same code that is used to create web pages, so it allows you to incorporate design elements such as colors, graphics, photos, and links in your eZine. At one point, plain text vs. HTML format for newsletters was a highly debated topic and the vote was pretty evenly split. With the advancement of technology, such as increased storage capacity in inboxes, this is no longer such a pressing issue; however, there are a couple of things to know.

First and foremost, you want your readers to be able to read your newsletter. There are a couple of great websites that will help you manage and send out your newsletter with this priority in mind; I use Aweber (http://www.aweber.com). This site sends out both types and then the receiver's email software chooses which format will be the most readable. However, if you cannot send out both, there are certain advantages and disadvantages to either type.

Text: Text documents are the easiest to read because all email servers can receive them. They also are less likely to be caught in spam filters, so you can be sure that your subscribers are receiving your newsletter (see tip 9 for more information on spamming). However, you have to worry about "wrapping" the text so that it looks the same in everyone's inbox. And, you can only work with text color to make your content and product presentations flashy and visually exciting and interesting.

HTML: As noted above, an eZine in HTML format will display like a web page. However, not all email programs will be able to read it properly. While the technology has improved, many people still own older machines that cannot decipher HTML embedded in an email. Also, the spam rating for this type of newsletter is significantly higher than it is for a text document, so there's a chance it may end up in your readers' spam folders. The possibilities for design, color-scheme, and product placement are endless, and usually make it worth your time to explore this option.

Best of both worlds: Another option for format is to send out a plain text message that simply introduces that issue of your eZine, then provides a live link to the full version online, which can include as many graphics and media as you want. This ensures that your email will get through, but also allows you to take full advantage of online resources. Keep in mind, however, that not all readers will be willing to click out of the message to another web page. Consider what's best for your readers.

Content

It is essential that you take your newsletter or eZine seriously and create high-value content. If you deliver sub-par information, you will quickly lose subscribers. At the same time, however, don't overwhelm your readers with too much information, even good information. Short is better than long. Many people are inundated with emails every day; they are not going to take the time to read your weekly novel. If you can condense your message into three really pithy paragraphs and deliver great value to your reader, you are golden.

Ideal target: Try limiting each issue of your eZine to 350 words of text. This will fit on most viewers' screens, without having to scroll down. Subscribers really appreciate having all the content at their immediate view.

Once you've struck this balance and engaged your readers, you can then use your content to promote your products, speaking engagements, or your media placements. If you can incorporate a plug for your latest eBook, mp3, or any other item into your newsletter, you will sell infinitely more merchandise. You will do best if you can make a connection between the message you are sending and the product you are presenting. If your message is all about reading body language and you can say, "For more about the subtle messages you send with your body language, check out my new eBook on …" By giving readers a bit of useful information, you are creating an interest in the specific topic, and you can build on that by immediately offering to expand their knowledge of the topic with a related product.

The best balance: While each issue of your eZine is a great marketing tool, there's good reason to give your readers a break from promotions once in awhile. They'll surely appreciate the occasional reminder that you are providing a worthwhile service outside of your product plugs, and that might make them even more willing to purchase a product the next time. A good balance is a 3:1 ratio of issues without and with product plugs.

Sell Your Products

Having products to sell and incorporating them into your eZine are obviously a great way to generate income and make your newsletter profitable. I currently make on average about $8,000 a month from products people buy off of my newsletter. That's a lot of money! I've been able to accomplish this by taking the time to create 70 pieces of merchandise. These range from eBooks and mp3s to assessments and soft-cover books. I am also in the process of creating Podcasts and video downloads to complete my range of media offerings.

Explore all of your options. Your products do not have to be tangible; they can be electronic. Things like eBooks and mp3s are great items because there are no manufacturing, distributing, or shipping costs. Once you pay to create the file, that's it. It's pure profit!

Also, your products should be as specific as possible. If your newsletter is on a broad topic, such as cooking, create products that address specific issues. You may have "how to grill the perfect steak," or "when a vegetarian menu is your best option," or "the top 25 chocolate recipes." By breaking down your expertise into specific titles that solve a certain problem or meet a specific need, you will be able to easily generate products and start earning money off of your "free" newsletter.

In order to sell products in your eZine, you will need some type of online shopping cart to process the transactions. Most of these systems have the capability to automatically handle the purchase and distribution of eProducts such as mp3s and eBooks (I use AutomatedShoppingCarts.com). Another useful feature called "Ad-Tracking" allows you to track which purchases were made from each eZine so you can monitor your most and least effective product sales copy. Ad-Tracking also allows you to do "split testing," which enables you to track the results of several versions of sales copy for the same product. This process will let you see which sales copy is the most effective at generating sales. By dividing your web traffic for a product between several destination pages, each with different sales copy, you will be able to easily determine which page is performing best. There are also software programs available to help you test and optimize your online ads.

Promotional Content
There are three approaches to newsletter content: the type that exists to sell products, the type that exists to promote the author, and the type that purely gives information.

Obviously, if you have a lot of products and are using your newsletter to generate income, the first option is the best. However, make sure that the content of your newsletter doesn't suffer. You are still providing your readers a service and feeding them valuable content. If your content suffers because you are trying too hard to sell your products, you will lose subscribers and ultimately lose money.

If you are a speaker, author, consultant, personal coach, or expert who wants to gain recognition, you should promote yourself in your newsletter. You should talk about what you've been doing, your recent articles and media mentions, your speaking engagements, problems you have helped your clients solve, opportunities you have helped your clients seize, and how potential clients can contact you. After all, there is no better product than yourself, so you need to market your services as effectively as possible.

If you don't like the idea of using your newsletter as a promotional device, the solely informational option is probably what you'll choose. Companies can use newsletters to educate customers on effective product usage or share ideas from other customers. While your newsletter is still valuable as a database generator, I would advise against abstaining from all promotional copy. If you are going to take the time to create a newsletter, you want it to work for you as much as it can. There is always a way to find a balance between maintaining the integrity of your newsletter and either promoting yourself or your new project/product.

Auto Responder vs. Here & Now Tips

There are two different types of newsletter formats, the auto responder and the Here & Now time sensitive tip.

Auto-responders (or evergreen eZines) are a series of tips or eZines that are created in advance and sent out at set intervals (weekly, monthly, etc). First, you must write several tips or newsletters that you put into a reserve database of eZines. When someone subscribes to your newsletter or tip series, they receive issue #1. Consequently, if person A signed up for your weekly tip a year ago and person B signed up yesterday, person A would be on tip #50, while person B would only be on tip #1. This is a great system if you do not want to create a new newsletter every month or week. Once you write enough tips, you can sit back and wait as your subscriber network reads through them all. However, you need to monitor your newsletters and subscribers carefully. Once your readers start to catch up on the eZines you've already written, you need to create more. The downside of this system is that you cannot make your tips relevant to items in the breaking news or seasonal happenings. The topics need to be able to stand on their own.

The Here & Now time sensitive tip is an eZine you write each week or month. If you enjoy relating your advice to current events, holidays, or seasons, or just like writing a newsletter every so often, this is the best option for you. It is also a great way to promote your speaking engagements, current articles, or recent sightings to keep your readers up-to-date on your activities. If you are just starting out and don't have a lot of products to promote, this might be your best option because it allows you to create visibility for your marketing efforts before you have product.

The Layout

Laying out your newsletter is extremely important. You have many more options with HTML, which makes your eZine display like a web page, than you do with plain text. However, if you are confined to text, play with color, spacing, and font to be as creative as possible.

In HTML, it is important to create continuity between your website and the newsletter. If you have a logo, a slogan, or any type of branding on your website, make sure that it is also on your newsletter. I am a proponent of creating a column that takes up one third of the page either on the left or right side. While your content goes in the middle two-thirds of the page, this side column is purely promotional. You can use this space to write catchy copy about yourself and your products or services. Or, you can create buttons that make it easy for people to buy merchandise directly from your eZine. But most importantly, the best way to promote your products and your services is to make your newsletter as visually interesting as possible. Use of color, pictures, and design will entice people to buy and help them remember you.

HTML layout also enables you to create hyperlinks within your message to pages on your website, particularly your shopping cart. (You can also do this in plain text, but it is clunky and intimidating.)

All the Stuff That Goes on the Bottom

There are a couple of items that need to be included in every newsletter, regardless of its intended use. Most important is an easy way for your readers to subscribe and unsubscribe. Most newsletter service providers insert this link automatically and make it user-friendly.

You also need:

- A link to update contact information. If your subscriber is changing email addresses, make it easy for them to keep subscribing to your eZine.
- A phrase about the author, i.e. "Check out Dr. Alessandra's website at … " to keep referring your readers back to your site and products.
- A copyright notice — for your own protection.
- A link that they can click on if they want to share the newsletter with their friends.
- If you are a speaker or author, contact information where interested parties can book you for a speaking engagement.
- A privacy policy.
- A legal disclaimer.

Don't Spam!

Every newsletter or eZine you send out gets rated by the recipient's spam filter, and could, if you're not careful, end up in their spam folder! You want to keep this rating as low as possible. To do this, be conscious of your word choice, color scheme, and background template. Certain words, like "free" or "guarantee," and certain non-web colors or excessive use of graphics trigger spam alerts. Also, limit your database to people who have signed up to receive your newsletter and to those who you've done business with. By sending mail to parties who have "opted in," you will be less likely to be flagged as a spammer.

But why care about spamming?

Well, there are a couple of reasons. First, if your message has a high spam rating, it will never make it to your subscribers' inboxes. Many eZine systems allow you to monitor what percentage of your emails is actually getting through. It is a good idea to keep on top of these stats. A newsletter is worthless if your readers aren't reading it. Secondly, there are anti-spam laws in place, both on the federal and state levels. While they aren't generally enforced unless the violation is egregious, just being aware of these laws is essential.

The federal anti-spam law, called the CAN-SPAM Act, was passed by Congress in 2003. It contains several important provisions that you should know about:

- Your email's "From," "To," and routing information – including the originating domain name and email address – must be accurate and identify the person who initiated the email.

- The subject line cannot mislead the recipient about the contents or subject matter of the message.

- You must not send to anyone unless they "opted-in" to your list by signing up or you have an existing business relationship with them.

- You must provide recipients with a mechanism to "opt-out" of receiving future emails.

- Each violation is subject to fines of up to $11,000.

But most importantly, if you consistently spam your subscribers, the ISP (e.g., AOL, Comcast, etc.) can block your domain name. These big ISPs provide their users with spam-flagging tools. If enough people flag your newsletter as spam, these providers will block EVERYTHING you send. That means that no one from AOL will be able to receive newsletters, emails, or anything else from you. And, unlike the spam legislation, these ISP providers monitor spam very closely because they want to keep their subscribers happy. And if they do decide to block you, there is no warning; they can just flip the switch. Once blocked, it is also extremely difficult to get unblocked, and you must provide the ISP with evidence that you are not in fact a spammer.

Monetizing Your List

Deciding to offer access to your subscriber base to someone else, or sell your list of subscribers, is a slippery slope that will take you down a path of consumerism that may or may not hurt your business. Selling your list to another vendor may result in customer dissatisfaction, spam issues, and most importantly, loss of subscribers. I wouldn't do it.

However, you can partner with another vendor or exchange your list with someone in a data-share arrangement. If someone has a product that you think would benefit your customers, you can make an arrangement with the seller to give him or her access to your list of subscribers. You can put an advertisement in your newsletter and tie your content to this other product or service. However, make sure that the product you are promoting is not, in any way, in competition with your products or services. Also, you should create an agreement with the other vendors with whom you are exchanging marketing lists so that they promote your products and services in their newsletters. This type of agreement, or exchange of lists, is a great way to expand your marketing reach and also maintain the integrity of your newsletter and the loyalty of your readers.

Keep in mind that a list exchange, or joint venture as it's sometimes called, is not the same as selling your list. You don't give up control of the information in your database; you simply agree to mail them your list without giving them access to your actual database. They only get access to your list through you. Another important issue to keep in mind is to make sure that the person who you are exchanging lists with has a list that's comparable to yours in some way. Size can matter; if you have a list of 5,000 subscribers, it's not usually a good idea to exchange your list with someone who only has 1,000. Sometimes, however, the content of the list is more important than its size. If the list contains information on the best 1,000 people out there to whom you wouldn't otherwise have access, then that would be a good deal. Try to keep the exchange even and in mutual benefit to both parties. This way, your readers get the benefit of exposure to new information, and you get the benefit of expanding your reach through all of your hard work on your newsletters!

Dr. Tony Alessandra helps companies achieve market dominance through specific strategies designed to outmarket, outsell, and outservice the competition. Alessandra has a street-wise, college-smart perspective on business. He earned his Ph.D. in Marketing from Georgia State University in 1976. Alessandra is president of AssessmentBusinessCenter.com, a company that offers online 360° assessments; Chairman of BrainX.com, a company that created the first Online Learning Mastery System™; and is the founding partner of Platinum Rule Group (www. PlatinumRuleGroup. com), a company that provides corporate training and consulting based on The Platinum Rule®. Alessandra is a widely-published author with 15 books translated into 17 foreign languages. Alessandra's television

program, "People I.Q." is currently aired on the DISH Satellite Network and on TSTN—The Success Training Network. Recognized by *Meetings & Conventions Magazine* as "one of America's most electrifying speakers," Alessandra was inducted into the Speakers Hall of Fame in 1985. For more information, please visit www.Alessandra.com.

Use Email Effectively and Increase Your Productivity

By Marsha Egan

Great marketing can take many forms.

The technology gift of email is an opportunity great marketers should not miss. Email is very inexpensive. It is efficient. And when managed correctly, it can be a very effective marketing tool.

In days gone by, marketing via mailings, billboards, radio, or TV were expensive. Email is not. (Comparatively.) The use of email, in combination with a database management program, can be a boon to any business's marketing efforts. With database management software, such as Act or GoldMine, you can enable personalized emailings, keep diaries, and maintain of records of contacts with your clients and prospects. Here are a few examples of how you can use these technologies to your marketing advantage:

Categorize contacts: I recommend to my clients that they categorize the contacts in their database into different levels, such as A, B, C, and D. Your A contacts are your top priority contacts—these are contacts who you may want to stay in touch with on a monthly basis. Your B contacts could be those that you care to write on a quarterly basis, and so on. With a database manager, is very easy to sort and identify the contacts who you have not touched, or to set diaries to assure that you don't miss an opportunity.

Personalized mail merges: Using your database manager in combination with your email system, you can insert personalized fields into a mail merge so that the email has a personal touch, using the person's first name, town, or place of business. Many of the database managers automatically record the subject of the email into the contact's record, without you having to enter it separately.

Sharing your contact information: By having all of your contact information in your email signature on every email correspondence, you enable your customers and prospects to easily transfer your information into their databases. I recommend to my clients that whenever they meet a new prospect, and receive a business card, they send an email – not a letter – to the contact within 24 hours. This not only assures that that person's information is now in your database, but you have just given them a very easy way to do the same with your contact information.

While email and database technology can be a real advantage, beware of the traps and the negative side of using email. First and foremost, never spam your prospects or clients. It just isn't right. If you do it, it will hurt your marketing efforts—not help them. And second, proactively manage your email, rather than having it manage you.

One of the biggest challenges in dealing with email is the mishandling and mismanagement of it.

While the email technology itself could be the best thing since sliced bread, the people side of misusing email has become a real challenge. People have developed nasty email handling habits that have severely sabotaged their productivity, and have truly gotten in the way of their ability to achieve their business goals. And that includes you and your marketing efforts.

Examples of those nasty habits include, but are certainly not limited to:
- Allowing yourself to be interrupted by each individual email as it is received. "Ding! You have mail."

- Holding a large number of emails in your Inbox, forcing you to review and sort through these items many more times than necessary.

- Surfing your email for "quick hits"—items that can be handled quickly—regardless of their importance.

- Spending an inordinate amount of time trying to find emails.

- Sending emails to yourself as reminders to get things done, rather than using the technology available in your email system.

If any of these sound familiar, you more than likely have an opportunity to make space for more important efforts—including marketing your business.

The reality is that many of these actions have turned into habits we have brought on ourselves. And we have a choice of ingraining productive habits instead of energy-sapping habits.

So, the better we can manage ourselves and the way we manage our email, the more our marketing efforts can benefit or even flourish.

Here are some of the tips that are contained in my popular e-book, *Help! I've Fallen into my Inbox and Can't Climb Out! Five Email Self-management Solutions that will Add Hours to Your Days*:

1. **Turn off Automatic Send and Receive.** This is a feature that is available on most email systems, and it allows you to control when you receive your email, rather than notifying you every time an email is received in your system. We recommend that you set your Automatic Send and Received to a minimum of 90 minutes.

2. **Keep your inbox clean.** By viewing the inbox only as a receptacle to receive work, and taking all items received, and filing them in places that you can access to determine your daily, weekly, and/or monthly plan, you will take control of your work—rather than it controlling you.

3. **Set times to work your email.** When you schedule time to handle your email in your daily schedule, it becomes part are of your work, rather than an interruption.

4. **Work your email into your daily planning process**. Instead of viewing email as a task, view email as a deliverer of other tasks to be done. Meld the tasks you receive by email into the tasks you receive from other sources, whether it is your boss, the telephone, US Postal Service mail, etc.

5. **Believe that you control your email**. Too many people take a reactive approach to email, and have become romanced by reacting to and handling emails that may or may not be important or significant. They get their jollies

by checking them off the list, rather than by dealing with what is important. When you take control of your email, you have taken back your life.

By making space for and working on what is truly important, you will be able to take your business to the next level. Obviously, you believe that marketing is a key aspect to your business, or you would not be reading this book. Therefore, making the time to market your business is key to your success.

Use the technology. Invest in database management software. Creatively use that software to market to your clients and prospects. And build effective, proactive habits that will help you manage all that email you will get from interested clients and prospects!

Marsha Egan, CPCU, PCC, is CEO of Egan Email Solutions, a division of The Egan Group, Inc. As a celebrated speaker, facilitator, author, and certified professional coach, she has tirelessly labored to add value in her quest to help others save thousands of hours and reclaim their lives due to the waste that she has seen email mismanagement cause.

She is an award-winning authority on email productivity, authoring the eBooks *Help! I've Fallen into My Inbox and Can't Climb Out! Five Email Self management Strategies that Will Add Hours to Your Week and Reclaim Your Workplace Email Productivity: Add BIG BUCKS to Your Bottom Line*. For more time-saving hints and a bi-weekly newsletter of email productivity tips, Visit http://EganEmailSolutions.com. She can be reached at Marsha@MarshaEgan.com

High Tech Has Got to Include High Touch

By Timothy A Dimoff

We all are part of the "High Tech" society—whether we want to be or not. Supposedly, high technology was going to free us up, allow shorter work days, quicker and more efficient service, and, most of all, a much more satisfied customer.

However, it didn't quite turn out according to the plan. We didn't see the end result of the totally satisfied customer in many situations. Why? This turns out to be a simple answer: we have become much too dependent on the high tech aspect and have absolutely forgotten about "High Touch." No matter who you are, where you live, or what you do, we *all* desire to have that special ingredient in our personal and business experience that I define as High Touch. I don't just mean a little customer service; I mean that "special" customer service with all the extras!

A great example is Starbucks. Their national average monthly visit by each of their customers is 17 times per month. Is that due to the fact that their coffee is the least expensive? Absolutely not, since their coffee is on the higher price end. Simply put, Starbucks delivers High Touch service to each and every customer that walks in the door. Their goal is to make each customer feel special and unique. To support this culture in each of their stores, they have mandatory training on how to provide the High Touch to each and every customer!

A few years ago I was deciding which printing service to utilize for my business. My company printing needs are substantial, since we are engaged in a variety of training programs for corporations, so this was an important choice.

I narrowed the potential list down to three different printing service companies. I asked them all one last question: What is going to separate your service from the other printing services that benefit my company?

The first two printing services responded separately in typical fashion. "Mr. Dimoff, we will give you the best prices in relation to the best quality print and your product will be ready on time." This is great service! But, I wouldn't have even considered any of these companies if I wasn't confident that each of them would provide quality service, quality product, and state of the art equipment – all of the High Tech aspects. I was looking for and desired more!

The third printing vender said, "Mr. Dimoff, we already talked price and quality, but my service will go the extra mile. You and your employees are too busy to pick up your print orders; you have a business to run. Time is crucial in today's working environment. All of your orders, no matter how large or small, will be delivered to your business by a member of my staff every time you place an order, for no additional charge." Now *that* is what I call High Touch!

The companies that think that just high tech service is good enough are thinking too narrowly and will not be in business in the future. I believe there is a cultural change taking place in the United States. People, clients, and customers want to be *pampered with high touch,* not just *serviced with high tech*! Look around and you will see the evolution already taking place. The business that can provide the High Touch best is the business that will grow the most in the future.

The most important question to ask is when that customer leaves your shop, your building, your meeting, your business, and/or hangs up that phone after talking with you, did they feel they received that little extra? If you're not sure, it probably didn't happen.

If the answer to my question is you *don't know or no*, then be prepared to loose that customer to another business that answered it with a *yes*!

Over the past decade, we have seen countless false and failed starts in online retailing. Experts were saying that the market and technology wasn't ready. Electronic relationships still are attempting to grow and the feeling is that it is just a matter of time before this segment explodes. But, many retailers are still struggling to maintain a presence on the web, and substantial retail business on the Internet may not be far away. Retailers are learning some new techniques that are increasing customer comfort and sales.

So, what is the secret? Surprise! It's the human touch. Sales growth on retail websites is now being attributed in large part to the increase in interactive aspects of these websites, including personal touch orientation toward customers, questions answered instantly using online chats, and prompt product information from well-trained customer service associates who know their stores, merchandise, pricing, delivery, and techniques to assure customers are always happy and satisfied. The High Tech Internet is finding out it can only grow when it also embraces and becomes a High Touch Internet!

How do you start or improve your High Touch service? It is very simple – ask the best consultants in your industry, your employees, and customers! Your employees will be able to identify those aspects of your company's service most appreciated by your customers. Focus, expand, and improve on these areas. Next, ask your clients for specific suggestions on service that they would appreciate receiving that would make their job easier and/or more pleasant. The additional value of this system is that your current customer base will inform more potential customers of your extra effort and concern for them personally!

High Touch will not only help your company survive, but it will be the difference in stimulating your company to grow! The results will be more than all the advertising money can buy.

Timothy A. Dimoff, President and Founder of SACS Consulting, is a nationally recognized author, speaker, trainer, and registered expert. Dimoff is an author of six national books and numerous nationally copyrighted training programs. He has been featured on CNN, Dateline, NBC, the *Wall Street Journal*, the *New York Times*, the *Los Angeles Times*, the *Chicago Tribune*, the *Washington Post* and several other national media formats. Additionally, he is a member of the National Speaker Association (NSA) and is often sought after for key note and professional presentations. You can contact Dimoff at SACS at 1-888-722-7937, by email, TADimoff@ sacsconsulting.com, at SACS Consulting, www.sacsconsulting.com, or on his speaker website at www.TimothyDimoff.com.

R-Commerce
Using Technology to Build Relationships
By Terry L. Brock

The term "E-Commerce" came out a several years ago, around the era of the Dot-Com Boom; it was a time of heady cheering. Many were talking about a "New Economy" that had replaced the old. Everything was different and the old models didn't work.

Well, that silly idea encountered a thing called reality. Booms and false ideas of a "new era" have come and gone throughout history. This is not new.

It seems that many people throughout history have thought that their era was a "new" way of doing everything. Yes, technology has changed how we do what we do. We don't have to depend on horses and animals to power our economy. The steam engine revolutionized much of our world today. However, even that great invention is out of the picture today.

Oil was not a part of the economy in 1776 when the Americans decided to break off from the greatest military power in the world and form their own nation. Yet, today oil is a primary tool in fueling the economy of many nations. Relationships were critical to the foundation of the American Republic. People would gather in taverns, churches, and other public meeting places to socialize and exchange thoughts.

In the Industrial era, new concepts emerged that produced wondrous technologies. Transportation in the form of railroads, clipper ships and even flying dirigibles emerged that changed the way people moved about. With the advent of air transportation in the early 20th Century, a new and unparalleled way of living emerged that enabled people to get goods from various places around the world. Yet, even in this time, relationships were vital for functioning and forming ideas.

So, yes, there are changes in life and people adapt into different eras. However, throughout all these changes, what stays constant is the need for the connection with people.

That is why I say that it is not about the E-Commerce—it is about the R-Commerce. It is not about the Electronics of Commerce; it is all about the Relationships that we build with others that fuels commerce.

These relationships that we build transcend technology. Whatever the technology is today, it will change. We have to focus not on the current cool technology (have to use the word "cool" somehow when you talk about technology!), but on the people. It is the people who always have and always will matter most.

Relationships affect our business in many ways. It is about how you can connect with the right people and strengthen those relationships.

You would be wise to invest more in developing relationships than in technology. History has shown us this truism time and time again. This runs against the grain of many of my friends in techie-ville. They often put more emphasis on getting the latest, coolest gadgets and gizmos. It is much wiser—and a better investment of funds—to focus on helping people and forging relationships than just investing in new tools. Yes, we need the tools and they are helpful. However, the new tools must always help to strengthen relationships.

Yes, those gadgets and gizmos are nice. Hey, I use them and find that many of these tools really help to build relationships and make the strong. However, when focusing on the people, you grow.

Table 1 illustrates some of the differences between 20th century business practices and where we are today:

Principles for Success

20th Century	Today
Need Lots of Capital	Need Lots of Ideas
Seniority Matters and Rules	Results Matter and Rule
Big is Better	Fast and Nimble is Better
Traditional Industry Ruled	Best and Fastest Thinkers Rule
Owning Means of Production	Having Access to Means of Production
Principles Matter Most	Principles Matter Most
Relationships Are Critical	Relationships Are Critical

Let's look at these important differences. In the 20th century, to be successful in business, you needed a lot of money behind you. You had to build a plant and buy equipment. You had to create the big smokestack industries that churned out steel, cars, telephones, etc.

Today you need a different way of thinking. We've seen companies like Microsoft emerge as major players. Bill Gates didn't become the richest man in the world by producing cars. In 1960 if someone were to offer advice on how to become rich, the advice might have been something along the lines of getting into cars, oil, or even, as we saw in The Graduate in 1968—plastics!

Today Bill Gates, Steve Ballmer, and their team of leaders have assembled the brightest and smartest people from around the world. The real strength of Microsoft, Google, Yahoo or other high technology companies is not in the CDs or DVDs in their warehouses. It is the ideas of their people. What they know and how they apply that knowledge is what separates them for the masses.

You can succeed today if you come up with great ideas that are valuable to other people. You can't do it on just "a smile and a shoe shine" alone as Willie Loman in Death of a Salesman would tell us.

In the 20th century, seniority mattered a lot. I remember growing up in the Midwest where a lot of people worked in the auto industry. I worked my way through undergraduate school working at Goodyear Tire and Rubber Company in Jackson, Michigan. In order to work in that factory, you were required to join the union. You didn't have a choice it the matter. It was mandatory.

The way to get ahead there was to stick around for a long, long time. They had this thing called seniority, which meant those who had been there the longest got first choice in jobs, hours, and any of the extra goodies that came along. Those of use who had just joined were at the bottom of the food chain and had to settle for whatever we could get.

Today things are different. Results are what matter and rule. It means that if you produce and come out with great ideas that are valuable in the marketplace, you can do well. This is true if you have been around longer than anyone at work or if you just started.

This has both good and bad news. It means that you must produce. You can't just sit on your laurels thinking of what it was like "in the good ole' days." You must come up with fresh, new ideas that are valuable to others today. If you can do that, you'll succeed. If you can't break out of the old ways of doing things, you are going to fail and fail miserably.

In the 20th century, big was better. The larger the company, the more likely it was to stick around and succeed. You also wanted to have the biggest plant and equipment and get bigger all the time. Today bulk can be junk. If all you have is a big, old company, you might not do very well. You must come up with new fresh ideas that are valuable to the marketplace (Do you see a trend here? Ideas that are compelling.)

Oh, and the most important, you have to be fast and nimble. Big and bulky can't compete with fast and nimble. Being fast means you are alert to changing market conditions. As buyers change and want different items, you must be able to change with that. You have to reach and constantly grow.

Being limber and quick in your thinking means that you keep an open mind. Always be open to new ideas and new ways of dong old things. Regularly feed your mind with new information. Learn, read, listen to quality educational audio, regularly attend seminars, and always learn new, valuable information. Most important, hang around smart, intellectually curious people who are progressing and making new advances.

In the 20th century, traditional industry ruled. In Michigan, we'd look to the big car companies in Detroit. They were the tradition in the State of Michigan and around the country. Today, the best and fastest thinkers rule. People like Bill Gates come up with innovative ideas that can help others get ahead. People like Sergey Brin and Larry Paige, who founded Google, surround themselves with other smart people who constantly learn and look at new possibilities. Other companies will grow and prosper as they also bring in new ways to think faster and serve more customers.

In the 20th century, you were successful if you owned the means of production. In Michigan the auto companies owned their plants, and it was important to have lots of these. Banks liked that. The plant and equipment were assets and collateral they could attach to loans.

Today, you want to have access to the means of production. That means you might not necessarily own a piece of equipment. You might rent it. You might lease it. You might even engage in a barter or trade with someone to use what they have for a period of time.

Sometimes it does make financial sense to own property or equipment. Each case is different. However, think about getting access to valuable income-generating equipment, not just owning it. If you wait to own, you might miss the market opportunity to use a technology that is good today but obsolete tomorrow. Think quickly and act quick!

Back in the 20th century, principles mattered most. Ideas and concepts like discipline, integrity, character, honesty, doing what you say you're going to do, and being dependable were valuable traits. These are principles that matter around the world.

Today, those same principles matter most in building a truly successful business and life. Without character, honesty, and dependability, you will be found out and people will avoid you.

Some things in life don't change.

In fact, I would submit that in an age of fast technology with many people who are less than dependable, your ability to consistently have integrity, honesty, and dependability give you a strong competitive advantage. As more and more people get to know you as a person who is dependable, whose word is his bond, who has integrity, and who does the right things, in the right way, at the right time, they will want to do business with you. They will trust you.

Never forget that trust is the key to building relationships. Trust is the bedrock and the support system for any relationship. The more trust you have in someone, the more likely you are to have a successful relationship. When trust erodes, the relationship suffers. Sometimes it can be restored, but any erosion of trust in a relationship can have serious long-term ramifications.

Finally, in the 20th century, relationships were critical. The people you knew helped you get ahead. If you were able to win the approval of key people because of your skills and the experience they had with you, your success was much more likely.

Today those principles are still vital. Relationships are more important than ever. We can hide behind 24/7 television, always-changing web pages, and a barrage of commercial information. But what we desire—what we need to exist—is a network of connections with people whom we trust. Relationships in business make all the difference. With them, you succeed. Without them, you will have a very difficult time and probably will not succeed in business as you would have with them.

Brian Tracy said in his audio cassette series, Getting Rich in America, " Your success in life will largely be determined by the number of people that know you in a favorable way." Make it your goal to generate many positive relationships with key people. Your success in business will be stronger.

Make it your goal in business to focus on relationships in business. R-Commerce, Relationship Commerce, is and always will be more important than the Electronics of E-Commerce. Yes, we'll continue to use electronics, but remember the technology is there to support the human relationships.

Terry L. Brock, President and CEO Achievement Systems, Inc., is a professional speaker and a columnist for *Business Journals* around the United States. He writes about technology, marketing, and the Internet in his weekly column, *Succeeding Today*. Brock speaks about productivity and increasing profitability for businesses in industries such as banking, distribution, sales, marketing, real estate, and finance. He boasts fun, informative sessions, and change-your-life-for-the-better advice. His sessions are entertaining and packed with useful, "put-it-to-work-right-now" information. His MBA in Marketing and background in radio and

newspapers helps him bring excitement and zest to the speaking platform. Reach Brock at terry@terrybrock.com, or visit www.terrybrock.com for more information.

Fill Sales Positions You Don't Have to Pay
Hire the Internet to Sell
By Don Philabaum

How would you like to have a salesperson work for you around the clock who requires no pay, no benefits, is never sick, never requires a day off, provides you reports daily and does exactly what you tell him/her to do?

If you are interested, read on!

Over the last three years, we've seen a number of new products, services and concepts on the Internet. Our banks have made it all but unnecessary for us to visit their branches with the introduction of online services that include the capability to transfer money from accounts, check our balance and even pay bills online. And yet, just four years ago consumers were concerned about using their credit card and personal information online. Fast forward to today—we see billions of dollars donated to victims of national and international crisis online and online shopping is at a record high. We can research practically anything we want from our computer wherever we happen to be in the world. While some industries are benefiting from the web, others are beginning to become disintermediated. Small travel agents have all but been put out of business by the convenience airlines have provided their customers of not only enabling them to make their own reservations online but printing out their boarding tickets. Brokers have had to significantly cut their transaction rates as investors were courted by trading rates a fraction of what they used to spend. The retail music industry has seen a number of large scale providers like Tower Records fold under the disintermediating forces the Internet imposed on them. The Encyclopedia Britannica sales person has all but disappeared from our neighborhoods as consumers understood the power and potential of the Internet.

In less than three years, MySpace grew to 130 million users and in only 18 months YouTube grew to 70 million users. The point I'm driving at is human behavior is catching up with the power and capability of the Internet. America and the world are turning on to the Internet via their computers and cell phones. People worldwide are embracing and using the Internet because tens of thousands of organizations are making it easier for them to do their job by offering them more options at a lower cost.

The Internet is turning out to be a powerful sales tool because of its reach and low cost. Not only can you send out thousands of emails at virtually no cost, but via your online ecommerce/ordering tools, it can take the order, fill in forms, calculate costs and forward the order to shipping. It could become one of your best salespersons!

Let's put into perspective the potential reach and opportunity the Internet will provide you:
• Worldwide there are over a billion people accessing the Internet.

• Internet buying growth increased overall by 11 percent in 2006 vs. 3.5 percent in 2005. Meanwhile, retail growth increased by 3 percent in 2006, online retail grew 24 percent.

• Today there are more cell phones that access the Internet than computers that are capable of accessing the Internet.

That presents an enormous opportunity for your company. However, if you are not actively working on your Internet strategy, you will see your Internet opportunity slip by. Worse, a competitor might figure this out before you. Even worse is someone who you had no idea was a competitor. The cell phone industry is trying to get into the music business. Currently eight percent of all music sold is cell phone ring tones. Skype.com grew to 100 million users and has the potential to become a major player in the phone industry. *If you are not seriously evaluating how your firm can benefit from the Internet, you need to stop everything you are doing right now.*

Never in the history of my business career, or for that matter any that preceded us, has one tool given us so many opportunities to reinvent our businesses. When I entered the workforce, I carried around a 60 pound IBM electric typewriter as I traveled throughout Ohio and the surrounding states. At night when I got to my hotel room, I'd plug it in and type letters to follow up on my visits that day. Much later, I had enough business to buy an IBM card reader typewriter. Every time I walked by the selective typewriter and saw the little ball head automatically typing a sales letter. I'd smile knowing I was using "one to one" marketing techniques and providing my prospects very professional looking letters. I loved it. My smile grew wider when I'd realize that I was not paying it a salary and benefits.

The PC began to make our sales and marketing efforts more effective and by 1985 we developed an in house contact management tool that enabled us to keep better notes on prospects and write letters faster. Now look at the Internet and how much it's impacted your company in the last three years. Most people wonder how they ever lived without the Internet.

To successfully run a business today, each department in your firm has to create an Internet strategy that rolls up into the business plan and overall strategy. There are few companies that can't benefit from better communication, faster product development, better customer service and higher profits by using the Internet.
The Internet will enable you and your organization to:
• Go national and global
• Decrease the cost to acquire leads
• Enter niche markets
• Get more in touch with your customers

Go National & Global
The Internet will help all organizations expand beyond their current customer base. In the past a firm's customer base was limited by the number of sales people they had, the coverage of their Yellow Pages or the borders of their country. The Internet takes all of that away. With Search Engine Marketing anyone anywhere in the world has an opportunity to stumble onto your web page and your offer.

Decrease the Cost to Acquire Leads
Remember the Yellow Pages? As the behavior of consumers and business to business consumers change, they will be using the Internet to find the products, service and information they need. With nearly 60 percent of America using some form of broadband access to the Internet, their computers are in a ready

state, always on, available to do a search. All search companies are working towards localizing, as they see the writing on the wall.

As the Yellow Pages loses its significance, Search Engine Marketing (SEM) will become more important to all organizations interested in reaching their client base. When you think about it, search engine marketing is similar to putting an ad in the Yellow Pages except you have a free option or pay-per-lead option. It takes a bit more work than placing an ad, but you must remember you are opening your product to the world, not your local phone book or professional directory.

You'll want to be concerned about SEM in two ways: 1) Designing your website so search engines put you on the first results page; and 2) Purchasing keywords that will put your company product or service first.

There are specific techniques you can employ to increase the likelihood that your website will be found by search engines. You should have someone in your organization spend some time online to learn about this or, do like I did and hire an intern from a local college. You will find a student will pick up on the idea faster and for less cost!

If you are a consultant you will want to purchase key words that describe your business. Let's assume you help companies develop new applications for polymer rubber. You need to anticipate what names your prospective customers will search under at search sites like Google, Yahoo, and others. Armed with the names you want to be found by, you have the option of indicating what you will pay when someone clicks on a link to visit your website as a result of being found in the search. If your sales organization is selling a special grade of wood that has been harvested from the 55 degree waters of reservoirs, you will do the same. Every group and organization who is selling something today will benefit by putting some time and effort into SEM.

Enter Niche Markets

The Internet gives you an opportunity to explore smaller niche markets that may not have been profitable to develop through your standard sales force. Many firms over the past decade have been modifying their sales efforts by building in house account representatives who call on small to medium clients. This cut the sales cost for companies who were sending high priced sales people on the road. It enabled the sales people to focus on the premium accounts which produced more revenue and profit.

In a recent book, The Long Tail: Why the Future of Business is Selling More of Less, Chris Simpson shares proven facts that organizations can make more money when they provide an unlimited product offering. The Internet will enable you to sell more because you almost eliminate the sales cost.

Get More in Touch with Your Customer

Social networking at sites like MySpace, Facebook, and YouTube has caught the eyes and ears of marketing professionals. In a culture where most of us are exposed to 3,000 ads in a single day, testimonials and recommendations from our friends, colleagues and family are becoming increasingly important. As consumers are introduced to online tools like Amazon.com, which allows them to post comments, they will come to expect it from organizations like yours.

The Internet will also enable you to survey customers more frequently, enable customers to provide feedback effortlessly, and engage your customers in the development of new products. Companies like P&G are creating clubs where, in their case, 250,000 teens are receiving special updates, samples and services in exchange for their feedback and willingness to share the "buzz" with their friends.

Your Internet Future Starts with a Plan

Most business Internet sites are brochure ware. They are designed to be an extension of the brochures the sales force is handing out. In many cases, companies are not investing enough time, talent, and resources to get the return on investment they could be making on their website. As a result they are leaving thousands, if not hundreds of thousands of dollars on the virtual table.

What's really appalling is some organizations spend more time discussing what to do for their company picnic or Christmas party than they do in developing their Internet strategy. I suggest that your organization form an Internet strategy committee with individuals representing the key departments within your organization including, finance, sales, marketing, customer service, manufacturing, and fulfillment.

To prevent your organization from being disintermediated by the Internet, you should immediately consider creating an Internet strategy. Like a marketing plan, your Internet strategy should outline the following:
• Products and Services offered
• Goals
• eMarketing
• Internet tools and services
• Analysis/Benchmarks
• Responsibilities

While most of these are familiar to you, eMarketing and Internet tools and services may not be. Let's take a look at what you should be considering in each of these areas:

eMarketing

All of us are familiar with traditional marketing techniques through direct mail, conventions, phone calls, distributors, retail, etc. There are a number of new tools and services available to you while marketing on the web:
• Broadcast emails
• HTML emails
• Multi-media emails
• Landing pages
• eNewsletters
• Blogs

Broadcast emails have given my firm the opportunity to send 8,000 emails with a simple keystroke at no cost and wait for the response. In addition to simple text broadcast emails we now have the ability to send magazine quality pages designed to appeal to prospects. Multi-media cards are like brochures that include video, audio, photos, and can capture as much as a minute of your prospects time. As you know there is no printing, postage or mailing cost.

Many companies are now moving toward a landing page for each product and service they offer and tie in with their search engine words they purchase to them. For example, if you offer sprinkler heads among the 100 products you offer, instead of driving people to your home page, consider developing a "landing page" for the product. Kind of like a flyer, the page should have a compelling offer, designed to get the person to buy. Technology is available where the person could begin chatting with your in house sales team, or let the prospect call over the Web.

eNewsletters and Blogs are excellent ways to keep your product and service in front of current buyers and to attract new ones. Blogs, particularly, are becoming powerful public relations and marketing tools. I've recently hired part-time college students majoring in eMarketing to find blogs that are relevant to our product and services and to begin to send them press releases and news feeds about our firm.

Internet Tools & Services

In consulting with businesses, I've found that most do not have the resources or skill sets within their organization to develop the necessary tools to offer products and services online. If an organization has an IT department, they are normally swamped with projects and work orders keeping everyone operating. I'm a good example of that. I've got an IT staff of 15 who are fully competent to do what I need, but no time to accomplish it. So I've used www.elance.com to find writers, programmers, designers, and other skills I need. Not only is it affordable, it's amazingly effortless to post a job and have dozens of interested professionals offer their service. The most difficult part will be deciding who to work with. About half of the twenty jobs I've outsourced have been done by individuals or organizations in a diverse set of countries from Russia, Argentina, India, Pakistan, and throughout the United States.

How much do you currently pay for a sales position? $30,000? $50,000, or more? How much do you spend on postage, printing, and the cost to put brochures and flyers together? How much do you spend going to conventions, for travel and related costs? Now think about how much you are spending on your Internet strategy.

At the beginning of this article I wanted to bring to your attention that much like Bob Dylan's song: *The Times They are a-Changin.* Businesses that once survived for decades, that employed tens of thousands, are being disintermediated by the Internet. Throughout history businesses have had to change with the times. American Express started out delivering mail and money by pony. They migrated into a business after the train ran over their business strategy!

I want you to take advantage of the benefits the Internet provides by setting aside time in your organization to develop an Internet strategy that will expand your market, reduce your costs, increase your revenue and give you a sales person who is willing to work 24/7/365 without pay, benefits, who is never sick, never requires a day off, provides you with reports daily, and does exactly what you tell him to do.

Things to do:
- Get together with your key department leaders and talk about the opportunities and risks the Internet presents to your existing business strategy

- Require each department to develop their own Internet strategy and integrate this into a company wide Internet strategy

- Use the Internet to test market new and emerging markets for your products and services

Don is President and CEO of IAC, a world-wide provider of private social networking solutions for groups and organizations. Don has written two books, *Create a NET-Centered College Campus* and *Alumni Web Strategies*. He authors a blog called www.wiredcommunities.com and has written numerous articles and reports about social networking communities. His new division, Internet Strategies Group www.internetstrategiesgroup. com, helps organizations create Internet strategies to increase sales, reduce cost, and increase customer retention. Don can be reached at don@ iaccorp.com.

Event Strategies
By Ron Finklestein

This section discusses some of the more traditional ways to market and grow your business. There are several different approaches you can use—some of the more popular ones are listed below.

Public speaking: Don't panic. You will not die if you speak in front of a group. This is just a new and exciting skill to add to your marketing repertoire. If you are not experienced in public speaking, join a local Toastmasters group. Toastmasters is a safe and inexpensive way to develop your public speaking skills.

One of the biggest advantages of public speaking is that you can get your message out quickly to a large audience. I particularly like this approach because it keeps me in close touch with people who can use my services, and through discussions with the attendees I get first-hand exposure about what's important to my potential clients.

With any public event, visuals play an important role. Whether you are doing public speaking, presentations, seminars, or other events that require visuals, it is important to understand that visuals are to be used to convey a message. They should never be used as a crutch for the speaker. What do I mean by this? I have been to presentations where the speaker read word-for-word what was on the visual. Don't do this. I can read; what I am looking for is the speaker to expand on the points that are on the visual. Visuals should be clean, reflect your brand, and used to clarify your message. Done right they can be powerful.

Event sponsorship is one of my favorite marketing activities. I sponsor an event each year that attracts around 300 business people who are my prime audience. I get the list and I market to my audience using other techniques discussed in this book. As long as your event attracts the correct audience, helps you build your brand, and is professionally done, it is a great way to develop hundreds of leads in a very short time.

Seminars are another great way to attract people who are interested in what you do. Many people will not involve themselves in a seminar because they are afraid people will not attend. If you utilize techniques from the Thinking to Win section as well as this one, you can put that fear to rest. A word of caution: People come to seminars expecting to learn something of value. They know that you will be selling something, but make sure you give them something of value in return; word travels fast if people go to a seminar and got what they expected. Give them a reason to come to your next seminar, and hopefully they'll bring their colleagues as well.

Everyone loves a party. When you're holding an event as a promotional tool, the most important thing to do is make it fun. You can have semiannual clearance sales, customer appreciation events such as a clam bake, special promotions for existing customers, or any event that makes sense in your business setting.

As you read this section, decide what type of event is most suitable to the marketing and promotion of your business. Try to think differently and ask yourself how you can take an event and apply it in your business. Take something that is successful in another industry, refine it, and use it in your industry. This kind of thinking is what will make you different. It gives people a reason to come visit you.

Speaking Before Groups
Making the Most of Your Moment at the Mic
By Dennis Sommer

You have just completed your sales and marketing strategy. You have taken your business experience and proven marketing ideas from this book to create a strategy that will propel you to the top of your industry. Now what?

Keeping your strategy locked in your computer or file cabinet will not help your business. Your next step is to deliver your message.

There is one small problem. Research surveys have shown that most professionals fear public speaking more than death. I don't believe most professionals would actually rather die instead of speaking to a group, but this does show why so many professionals have trouble speaking in front of an audience. Based on my personal experience working with thousands of sales, service and consulting professionals, I believe only 15 percent of them actually enjoy speaking to groups. The other 85 percent are not comfortable communicating in person, and when they must, they prefer reading off canned questions, speeches, or presentations that leave the audience turned off by the experience.

You need to persuade and inspire others for your message to be successful. You will need to meet directly with employees, stakeholders, investors, media and customers in person, delivering an awe-inspiring message that will motivate everyone to embrace your strategy and purchase your product or service.

Let's take a look at two proven speaking techniques that will propel you and your business to the top of your industry: 1) Talk with your body; and 2) Persuade listeners with your voice.

Talk With Your Body
Confidence, power, and excitement are communicated through your body language. Body language enhances your believability and emphasizes your main points and recommendations.

Imagine attending a promotional kickoff meeting where the speaker's goal is to inspire and excite the audience about a new product line for the coming year. The speaker stands stiffly before the group, not moving or looking at the audience. His words say he is excited, but his body language says the opposite. What is the result? You are not motivated to go out and sell that new product. Your body language will have the same effect on your audience. Get them excited about your topic. Get them inspired about your ideas and recommendations. Let's take a look at the five body language expressions.

1. Moving Around: Movement during your presentation attracts your audience's attention and gets them involved as their eyes and heads follow you from one position to another. It also adds variety for the audience.

Your first opportunity to display body language is when you leave your seat and walk to the front of the room. You should appear eager and confident. Walk with your head up and shoulders back at a purposeful, quick pace. When you are done speaking, walk back the same way.

During your presentation, talk from one spot then move two or three steps as you move on to another topic. This movement provides a great transition between topics or main points. To emphasize critical points, step toward your audience. To dramatize a point, act out your description just before your verbal description. For example, if you were describing a very cold situation, you might act out shivering right before the description.

Below is a list of distracting movements that you should avoid:
• Pacing
• Fidgeting
• Swaying from side to side
• Bouncing up and down

2. Standing in Place: We just discussed moving around during your presentation, but there are times when you should be standing in place. During your opening and closing, the stance you take is important because it indicates your comfort level, confidence, and poise. To be most effective, stand with your feet slightly apart and your weight evenly distributed.

Avoid habits and stances that indicate shyness, weakness, nervousness, or being uncomfortable, such as:
- Eyes fixed on the floor or ceiling
- Slouching shoulders
- Shifting weight from one foot to the other

3. Eye Contact: Eye contact plays a significant role in how your audience perceives you. While speaking, you should pay special attention to how your eyes interact with the audience.

Have you ever been in an audience when another professional was talking and would not look at you directly? The professional looked at the floor, ceiling, or back wall—and never directly at you. Did you get the impression she was less than honest and lacked confidence? Did she inspire or persuade you to back her ideas? I doubt she did.

When you make eye contact with the audience, they believe you are honest, credible, and sincere. Audiences will then be more willing to accept and back your ideas. Another benefit from good eye contact is the bonding it creates. As your eyes meet, you get their undivided attention and they will have a hard time ignoring you.

During your presentation, look directly at your audience. Look directly into the eyes of one person until you finish a thought and then move on to another. Make eye contact with the audience randomly throughout the entire room. If the room is small, you will most likely be able to make direct eye contact with everyone in the room. If the room is large and packed, you will not be able to make eye contract with everyone. In this case, make direct eye contact with someone in each section of the room—the front, middle, back, right side, and left side.

Avoid these bad habits:
- Gazing around the room; no direct eye contact
- Moving your head back and forth like an oscillating fan, distracting the audience
- Staring at one person for a long time, making him uncomfortable

• Glancing quickly from one person to the other, making you look untrustworthy

4. Facial Expressions: Your face conveys how your audience should react or feel about the information being presented. Your facial expressions must be consistent and demonstrate those feelings. If you are talking about achieving record profits, yet you are frowning with your head hung low, your audience will be confused, not excited and happy with the results.

Show happiness and excitement by smiling broadly. Show sadness by frowning slightly and bowing your head. Widening your eyes and raising your eyebrows will display surprise. When you display these feelings, your audience will then emulate them.

5. Hand and Arm Gestures: Gestures are the most expressive body language and help drive home key topic points. The most effective gestures are those made above the elbow and away from your body. They should be definite and vigorous to show your enthusiasm and conviction. Repeating the same movement is very distracting; therefore, vary your gestures. For larger rooms, gestures should be larger to ensure everyone in the back can see them.

Try some of these gestures the next time you are speaking to an audience:
• Repeated up-and-down motion of your head to indicate approval
• Clenched fist to indicate power or anger
• Hitting your clenched fist into an open palm to indicate an important point being made
• Open palms to indicate generosity and caring
• Folded arms across your chest to indicate strength and determination
• Clasping hands in from of your chest to indicate unity
• Hands moving in unison to indicate similarities
• Hands moving in opposite directions to indicate differences

Gestures can mean many things and will vary culture to culture, so be sensitive to your location and audience.

Persuade Listeners with Your Voice
What kind of voice do you have? Is it easy to listen to, exciting, deep, and rich?

Your voice is how you convey information to your audience and gain their acceptance. If your voice is annoying, they stop paying attention and your ideas will not be heard.

Top advisers have four voice characteristics that gain the audience's full attention:
- Easily heard: They clearly articulate words and use proper volume.
- Pleasant: They convey friendliness.
- Natural: They project sincerity, reflecting their personality.
- Expressive: They demonstrate various meanings, never emotionless or monotone.

Balancing the levels of extremes between your voice quality, speed, pitch, volume, and silence is also critical for successful delivery.

1. **Quality**: Your voice should be easy to listen to. It should be enjoyable, friendly, natural, and confident. If your voice is harsh, shrill, nasal or breathy, you need to eliminate the tension in your voice.

2. **Speed**: Speak fast and your audience won't be able to keep up. Speak slowly and they will lose interest. Keeping your speech at approximately 125 to 160 words per minute will be fast enough to keep their attention and slow enough for them to digest your ideas. This is not to say you should speak at a constant rate the entire time. Slow down to emphasize a main point. Speed up through other, less important material.

3. **Pitch**: On a music scale, how high and low your voice sounds is the pitch. Vary your pitch throughout your presentation. Never keep the same monotone voice. This will quickly put your audiences to sleep. On the other end, a constant high-pitched voice will make them cover their ears or leave the room.

Adapt your pitch to the topic. For excitement and enthusiasm, use a higher-pitched voice. For thoughtfulness and sadness, use a lower-pitched voice.

4. **Volume**: Controlling the softness and loudness of your voice will keep your audience's interest in your topic. Vary your volume level to emphasize key

points. Increase the volume for anger or making a final point. Decrease the volume when being secretive or sad. Also remember that your volume depends on the size of the room. Adjust accordingly.

5.Silence: Well-placed silence or pauses in your presentation will have a tremendous impact on your words and the points you are making. This is a very powerful speaking tool that is not used enough.

Silence can be used to:
• Emphasize. Silence before and after a critical statement tells the audience this is an important point.
• Punctuate. Silence tells the audience you have completed a sentence or thought.
• Gain Attention. When audiences get distracted or it looks like they are losing interest insert a pause. This silence will attract their attention back to you.

You have now perfected the use of your voice and body during a presentation!

Dennis Sommer is a widely respected and world-renowned authority on sales and leadership performance improvement. He is a leading business adviser, author, and speaker providing clients with practical strategies to increase sales revenues and margins, improve customer loyalty, and transform managers and executives into leaders. Sommer has over 20 years of management consulting, sales, technology and business leadership experience. He has delivered over 250 successful client engagements for Fortune 1000 companies. He has held numerous leadership level positions with Accenture, Jo-Ann Stores, and CA Inc. Sommer is President of BTRC Business Advisers, an international firm located in Akron, Ohio. He also volunteers his time as a business counselor for SCORE (www. score.org, www.akronscore.org) a premier source of free and confidential small business advice for entrepreneurs. Sommer can be reached 330-676-1876 or www.btrconline.com.

Making Your Message Memorable Using High-Impact Visuals and Obtaining
Audience Buy-In
By Dennis Sommer

In "Speaking Before Groups – Making the Most of Your Moment at the Mic," we reviewed two powerful techniques for delivering your message. In this chapter we will be looking at an additional two techniques that will propel you and your business to the top of your industry: 1) Making a visual impact; and 2) Persuading your audience with involvement.

Making a Visual Impact
Audiences remember best what they see and hear simultaneously. Use visual aids to compliment and enhance your presentation, not to replace your presentation or be used as a crutch for lack of preparation. Charts, graphs, and diagrams, and other visually stimulating objects will increase your audience's retention of your ideas and recommendations.

Visual Aid Benefits
1. **Reinforcing Topic Points**: Visual aids show your audience that what was said, or is about to be said, is very important and something to remember.

2. **Increasing Understanding**: Most of what audiences learn is through their eyes, not their ears. Visual aids help audiences understand things like dimensions, relationships, statistics, and other numerical information.

3. **Improving Retention**: Audiences will remember only 10 percent of what you say. However, when visual aids are included, audiences will remember 66 percent of what they both hear and see.

4. **Improving Attention**. Audience's minds tend to wander during presentations because they think much faster than you talk. Visual aids keep their minds focused on you.

5. **Communicating Faster**. Ideas presented in a visual format are communicated faster and better when using visual aids rather than spoken words.

Popular Visualization Tools

Common visualization tools in use today include: product, computer-generated, flip charts, and white boards. The best choice for your audience will depend on several factors:

- Audience profile
- Topic points you want to emphasize
- Type of information you wish to display
- Equipment available

Let's take a look at these visual aids in more detail. These guidelines will help you select the correct visual aid for your purposes.

1. **Product**: A product can be an actual product you are recommending. It can also be an object that helps you make a point or helps the audience better understand and remember your ideas. You will need to consider the size of the object and the space available in your room. You may need a table to place the product on and a cloth to cover the product until it is needed.

2. **Computer-Generated**: Computer-based visualization is becoming standard for most presentations. Using a notebook computer, software, and LCD projector you can produce and display dramatic visuals with a click of the mouse. You can display simple as well as very complex information. Your visual options include presentation slides, pictures, software applications, and video. You can also walk around the room talking while changing your visuals using a remote control. This allows you more freedom to use gestures and movement while you talk. Here are a few things to consider when using computer-generated visuals:

- Do you have the equipment or should it be rented?
- Do you have the skills to develop the visuals or should you staff this out?
- Plan enough time to create the visuals in advance.
- Make sure all components work together. Rehearse before your planned presentation date.
- Have a backup plan in case you have technical difficulties before or during your presentation (yes, this does happen, and often!).

3.Flip Charts: Flip charts are great for small room briefings, training, or brainstorming sessions. They are used for displaying key topic points or recording audience responses. You can prepare pages in advance and will have the flexibility to add items during your talk. Writing down information during your talk will help reinforce points and improve audience retention. You can also tear off pages and hang them on the walls for easy viewing. An added benefit of flip charts is the actual recording of key topic points, questions, issues, etc., that can be reviewed at a later time.

4.White Boards: White boards are very common in meeting rooms. They work well when you need to display your key topic points or make small lists. However, there are a few drawbacks. If the white board is not cleaned well, it is difficult to read. Markers dry out quickly, so you need to test the markers to make sure they are readable. Finally, there is no way to save the information on the white board. If you need to document this information, you need to transcribe it onto your notebook computer or a piece of paper.

Visualization Design Tips

Effective visual aids are pleasing to view, easy to understand, and easy to read. Consider these top adviser tips when developing your visual aids:

1.Visible: The visual aid must be easily seen by everyone in the room. Use the largest letter size possible. Use blank space to make the words stand out. Make sure text, diagram, or picture coloring is not similar to the background color – you want your items to be prominent. For example, yellow letters on a black background really add punch to the visual.

2.One-Topic Point: Limit each visual to one main topic point or idea. The audience will be distracted when viewing more than one.

3.6x6 Method: Have no more than 6 words and 6 lines per visual. This will allow you to keep the letters large, making them easy and quick to read. Your audience will then be able to focus on you, the speaker.

4. Add Variety: Variety in your visuals will maintain the audience's interest. If you are using a computer slide show, don't show text on all the slides or just diagrams. Mix it up a bit. For example, follow a text slide with a diagram or chart.

5.Eye Candy: Use consistent style formats for fonts, colors, and artwork. Consistency in the visual will be more pleasing to the audience's eyes.

6.Simple: Your audience should be able to identify the point quickly. Avoid using fancy graphics or multiple diagrams bunched together.

Visualization Display Tips

There are many things that can go wrong when displaying your visuals. Each one of these will lessen the impact of your message and lower your credibility. Let's take a look at a few top adviser tips that will help you deliver a memorable visual:

1.Display before Talking: Display your visual aid before you start talking about it. The moment your visual aid is displayed, the audience will begin absorbing the content. Display your visual aid, pause while the audience absorbs the content, and then begin talking.

2.Keep Audience Eye Contact: Maintain eye contact with your audience (don't turn your back on them) while displaying your visual aid. Don't face the visual aid and read from it. This only shows your audience that you are not prepared and you will lose credibility.

3.Timely Removal: Display your visual aid for as long as it takes to discuss the topic point it supports. When complete, remove it from view. When using flip charts, have a black page between visuals. When done with one page, flip to the next (blank) page. If you are using a notebook computer and PowerPoint slides, have a blank slide between visuals or hit the "B" key to turn the screen black. To redisplay the slide hit the "B" key again.

4. Don't Block the View: Every person in the room must be able to view your visual aid. Stand to the side of your visual aid. If you need to point something out, use a pointer or your hand. If you are displaying a product that you can pick up, hold it to the left or right of your body at shoulder height.

5. Don't Talk and Write: When using a white board or flip chart, don't talk while you are writing. When you are done writing, turn back to the audience and begin speaking.

6. Be Ready: Prior to your presentation, put all the visual aids in their appropriate spot. Check their positioning to make sure everyone will have a clear view. Triple-check all electronic equipment to make sure they are functioning properly. Don't forget to bring backup batteries.

7. Practice: Confidence and composure will be your key to effective speaking. The more you practice, the more familiar you will be with your voice and material, and the more comfortable you will be in front of the audience.

If you have access to a tape or digital recorder, use it to record your practice sessions. Review the results and make changes that will improve your effectiveness. Your voice should be natural and consistent with the meaning of the material. Listen for your voice volume, speed, pitch, quality, and appropriate pauses. Make notes on where and how these can be improved.

Practice in front of a mirror to improve your body language. Does your body language show confidence, power, and excitement? Does it enhance your believability and emphasize your main points and recommendations? Watch your head, arm, and hand movements. Make sure you move around.

Persuading Your Audience with Involvement

More than 70 percent of the presentations I have witnessed are missing a key component for achieving audience buy-in. This component is audience involvement. Getting your audience involved is one of the most powerful ways to persuade your audience and ultimately get them to say "Yes" to your request, or "I Agree" with your point of view.

Why are presenters not involving the audience? Here are a few reasons. Have you used the same excuses at one time or another?
- I am not comfortable interacting with the audience.
- I did not have enough time to prepare.

- I don't know the best way to involve the audience.
- I am nervous enough already; why add unpredictable components?

If you want to dramatically increase your success by persuading your audience, try inserting a few of these "Involvement" strategies into your next presentation:

1. **Ask a Thought-Provoking Question**: Ask the audience an open-ended question that makes them use their imagination or reflects on a current situation. There is no right or wrong answer for this type of question. For example, "What could you accomplish if you had an additional two hours of uninterrupted time a day?"

2. **Raise Your Hand If...** This involvement technique will get your audience involved and also provides visual support for the audience response. You could say, "Raise your hand if you have ever missed a quarterly goal." Then, "As you can see from the response, 9 out of 10 of you have had this unfortunate experience."

3. **Ask a Multiple-Choice Question**: Ask a question about your topic and provide the audience with a list of possible answers. This technique makes it easier to answer and still makes the audience put some thought into their response. For example, "What percentage of technology projects are considered successful? A) 23 percent, B) 37 percent, C) 62 percent, or D) 99 percent?" Your audience will retain this information longer by putting some thought into their answer and will be more comfortable answering since they have a one in four chance of being correct.

4. **Fill in the Answer**: Studies show that you are more likely to remember important facts if you write them down. A great way to make sure your audience is writing down the key facts you want them to remember is to provide presentation handouts with fill-in-the-blank answers. For example, you might have a slide that reads "Implementing this unique sales approach can improve sales revenue by _____%, equivalent to $_____ increase in sales this year." This is a great technique that energizes your audience while helping them retain the critical facts you are presenting.

5. **Ask a Simple Question**: Nobody wants to look foolish in front of a crowd of people. By asking easy questions that are focused on the audience's experiences, you will see an increase in participation. When everyone gets involved in the discussion, they will be more enthusiastic and will also have the opportunity to learn from their peers. You might ask a question like, "What is your number-one priority this year?" or, "What leadership skill do you think is most important?"

6. **Hand out a Questionnaire**: Writing answers down is much more powerful than simply thinking about them. Provide your audience with a short questionnaire listing three to five open-ended questions that are relevant to your discussion and provide your audience with valuable personal insight they can take back and work with the following day. For example, if you were delivering a presentation on starting a small business, you might ask questions like: "1) What is your product? 2) Who is your competition? 3) Who will be your target audiences?"

7. **End with an Action Plan**: Every presentation should end with a way for the audience to use the information you have presented. One of the best tools to use is the "Action Plan." At the end or your presentation, ask the audience to take out a pen and paper. At the top of a fresh page, write the words "Action Plan". Under this list the numbers 1, 2, and 3. This is where they can fill in the actions they will take right after your presentation. For example, if you were giving a workshop on Technology Cost Reductions, ask the audience to write down the top three actions they will take tomorrow to reduce technology costs.

You don't need to include all seven involvement techniques in your presentations. Doing this might overwhelm the audience. For shorter presentations you might include two or three of these techniques. Give it a try. You will see a dramatic increase in positive responses to your topic.

Next Steps

Now you are ready to take your winning sales and marketing strategy out and inspire your employees, stakeholders, investors, media, and customers in person, and deliver an awe-inspiring message that will motivate everyone to embrace your strategy and purchase your product or service.

When preparing your presentation, consider the four proven speaking techniques that will propel you and your business to the top of your industry:
1. Talking with your body
2. Persuading listeners with your voice
3. Making a visual impact
4. Persuading your audience with involvement.

Now all you have to do is utilize these techniques to sell yourself and market your business!

Dennis Sommer is a widely respected and world-renowned authority on sales and leadership performance improvement. He is a leading business adviser, author, and speaker providing clients with practical strategies to increase sales revenues and margins, improve customer loyalty, and transform managers and executives into leaders. Sommer has over 20 years of management consulting, sales, technology and business leadership experience. He has delivered over 250 successful client engagements for Fortune 1000 companies. He has held numerous leadership level positions with Accenture, Jo-Ann Stores, and CA Inc. Sommer is President of BTRC Business Advisers, an international firm located in Akron, Ohio. He also volunteers his time as a business counselor for SCORE (www. score.org, www.akronscore.org) a premier source of free and confidential small business advice for entrepreneurs. Sommer can be reached 330-676-1876 or www.btrconline.com.

Sponsor a Charitable Event
Prospecting Made Easy
By Michael A. Mendelsohn and Suzy Peterfriend-Ross

Donating money to organizations and sponsoring events is a great way to generate publicity. Why else would big corporations spend millions of dollars to put their names on music halls and sponsor major charitable events? But if you are just starting your own law firm, consulting organization, or any other business, you probably don't have the type of budget larger corporations such as Mellon Bank® and Gillette® have for philanthropy and/or advertising. However, there are ways to financially support your favorite charity or organization and drive traffic to your small business that cost less money than a local paper would charge you to run an ad.

Corporations sponsor seminars and art symposiums. These events, running anywhere from an afternoon to a three-day lecture series, are a great way to benefit a charitable organization and acquire new clients. They are also some of my favorites to attend. With my company, Briddge Art Strategies Ltd., I have been involved in many of these lecture series, giving advice on art succession planning, collecting, and planning for antiques like one would any other asset. I enjoy presenting at these events because they benefit everyone. For me, they are a great way to increase recognition for what I do. For the museum or charitable organization, they are an easy way to raise money. And for the sponsor, they are a perfect way to get a group of ideal potential clients in one room where they can network.

If you are a small business, sponsoring an event like this is one of the cost-efficient, most effective forms of advertising and improving your client base. For example, if you have started your own investment firm, you need to build a client portfolio. You could place ads in all of the trade magazines, run commercials, show up at events and hand out your card, and call up potential investors and take them out to lunch, but these expenses add up quickly and might not significantly improve traffic to your front door. To save yourself money, the best way to advertise to your target market is to get everyone you want to meet in one room listening first-hand to what you have to say. And the best way to do this is to sponsor an event that high-net worth individuals want to attend. As a sponsor, you will be able to introduce the speakers, distribute all of your marketing brochures, socialize, and network with all of the attendees throughout the event. In addition, the only cost to you will be the coffee and hors d'oeuvres at the reception!

Here are some simple steps to organize an effective event:

1. **Figure out what type of client you want to attract and what common interests they might share.** My experience has shown me that the types of people who attend my speaking engagements are the individuals with enough assets to worry about how they are going to plan for their expensive art and antiques. If these are the types of people that you are also trying to attract, consider sponsoring an artistic information session.

2. **Contact local charitable organizations that would be interested in hosting such an event.** Again, in my experience, this has been museums and artistic societies. They will most likely be more than happy to host such an event, since they will benefit from the charitable donations.

3. **Solicit speakers and information providers.** Given the nature of these events and the enormous possibility for exposure, many speakers and experts will be happy to speak pro bono, considering this is a chance as much for them as it is for you to network and distribute their material.

4. **Spread the word.** The organization will usually provide most of the marketing material for the event. However, as the sponsor, make sure that they include your name on everything that goes out and approve all of the ads to make sure that you are adequately represented. Next, provide them with your database of contacts. Make sure that everyone you know, everyone they know, and anyone who you've ever coveted as a client is invited and aware that you are going to be there. Don't be shy about contacting local papers, television stations, radio stations, etc. The more buzz you can generate, the better.

5. **Make sure that your marketing materials are up-to-date and cater to your audience.** If you are sponsoring an art event, you are going to be targeting people who pay attention to design, color, and detail. Don't show

up with text-heavy, visually boring brochures. Also, ensure that you've printed enough pamphlets, brochures, and business cards and give one, or multiple copies, to everyone – it is always better to have too many than too few. Encourage the attendees to distribute your cards to their friends or anyone else who may be interested in your services.

6. **Once the event commences, don't just sit back and relax**. This is when your work really beings. You must network, network, network. What better opportunity are you going to find that has all of your ideal clients in one room just waiting to hear what you have to say and what services you can offer them? Make sure that the introduction you give to the speaker has some self-promotional content (i.e. when you introduce the speaker say how much they've helped you turn your business into one of the leading profit earners for the year). Then, during the reception, talk to everyone. Even if your potential clients already do business with one of your competitors, don't despair. Give them your card, encourage them to call with any questions, and tell them to spread the word. Who knows, they may be unhappy and looking for a new company, or they may be so impressed with the information they gained during the event that they will want to make the switch to you. Regardless, talking to everyone can only help your business. So don't be shy—get out there and mingle.

Michael A. Mendelsohn is Founder and President of Briddge Art Strategies Ltd., the premier art succession planning firm in the country. He is a world-class art collector, philanthropist, lecturer, and writer on inheritance planning and preservation of art assets. With a background in accounting, taxation, and philanthropic studies, Michael is a frequent continuing education presenter on lifetime and postmortem planning strategies for art assets and has been an invited speaker at the Smithsonian American Art Museum, Philadelphia Museum of Fine Art, Bank of America, U.S. Trust, Museum Trustee Association, Estate Planning Council of Philadelphia and the New York State Society of CPA's, among others, on the artistic, tax-planning and philanthropic needs of collectors. Michael's innovative inheritance planning strategies have been featured in Trusts and Estates magazine and he has been quoted in articles in the *Wall Street Journal*, *Forbes* and *Worth* magazines. He is a frequent guest on the PBS show

"Wealth and Wisdom," the author of the book *Life is Short, Art is Long— Maximizing Estate Planning Strategies for Collectors of Art, Antiques and Collectibles* as well as the author of regular monthly columns published in *Art of the Times and Antiques & Fine Arts* magazines.

Suzy Peterfriend-Ross, partner at Briddge Art Strategies Ltd., is a specialist who works with financial institutions in dealing with multi-generational planning for the affluent. She has acted as an advisor to trust companies and financial institutions to develop communication between their wealth management platform and family offices—including Marsh McLennan, Bankers Trust and Synovus Family Asset Management, which she helped grow into a multi-billion multi-service holding company.

Currently, Suzy constructs training programs and business development models to help businesses create their own family office departments and cater their services to the affluent, especially when dealing with art assets and philanthropy. She is the co-author of *Mommy, Are We Rich?*, a monthly columnist for *Art of the Times* magazine, author of extensive articles, and a frequent speaker at professional conferences.

Marketing Your Expertise through Seminars

By Ron Finklestein

A good seminar can be worth a fortune to the people who attend.

But, as any good presenter knows, the investment in money, including travel expenses, is considerable—so considerable value must be given in return to the attendees.

I have attended and conducted hundreds of seminars, and I've noticed only a small number of attendees derive anywhere close to the benefit of what is possible.

I've seen attendees from all over the world who are exposed to some powerful and life-changing tools, techniques, and information from real experts. Yet few derive even a small fraction of value from the golden tips being offered by the speakers.

As both a presenter and attendee, I see this situation as a terrible waste. A good seminar can help bring your personal and business success to a whole new level, both for the presenter and the attendees.

Creating a Great Seminar

Creating a great a seminar is not as easy as it first may appear. The presenters must be sure to present their credentials in the best possible light without misrepresenting or misleading those credentials and accomplishments. As a presenter, if you don't walk the talk, the value of what is taught is questionable.

To avoid wasting your time and money, as well as the attendee's money, present what you know and know what you present. Seminars are great ways to allow people to see you in action and the attendees can self-select into what you teach and potentially become great clients.

Don't think of your seminar attendees as customers. Think of them as clients. A customer is transaction-driven. I sell a product and the customer buys a product. There is no value provided other than buying a product. I am not interested in having customers. I believe I have a moral obligation to provide the best possible information to conference attendees while creating long-term relationships at the same time. Having clients implies a moral obligation to their welfare.

As a presenter, make it easy to allow attendees to get the most out of the seminar or conference. Send them pre-work if that makes sense. Give them homework.

Be sure to supply conference or seminar evaluations. You want to know what works and what doesn't. You must always have the best interest of your audience in mind.

Be sure to put testimonials from past attendees on your web site. Make sure they are real. You can obtain testimonials by asking people who attended past seminars what they feel they got from the seminar and using comments from the conference evaluations.

Preparation before the Seminar

As a presenter, I want to know that my message is getting through and the attendees are receiving significant value from the material. They deserve the very best you have to offer every time you speak.

To the presenter: practice, practice, practice! I have seen too many presenters wing it – and, believe me, you can tell. That is not fair to your audience. Have quality handouts and be clear in presenting your material. I find Toastmasters to be a great place to practice small segments of the talk that may be difficult for others to understand. The feedback you receive is invaluable. It is better to practice with a friendly audience that understands you are practicing then practice in front of a live audience who may not be as forgiving.

The attendees than can make a good presenter great and a great presenter even greater. Before arriving at the seminar I would suggest you do the following:
• Write down some specific seminar goals.

- Search out some solid actionable ideas that will improve your business and yourself.

- Network. Introduce yourself to as many attendees and speakers as you can. Pass out your business card and request them from others.

- If the seminar or conference is long enough to have breaks, sit in a different seat after each break. You can meet some great associates and make life-long friends by networking.

- Take good notes. Keep a separate sheet with ideas you plan to implement after the event. Before you leave the event, narrow the number down to no more than five. Writing them down helps you remember them and reinforces the learning you expected to receive at the event.

- Ask questions both during the Q&A sessions as well as during the breaks. Don't limit your questions to just the speakers. Ask your fellow attendees questions as well. It will help you create dialogue with people you don't know, and sometimes you hear a different perspective that makes a confusing concept easier to understand. It is also a good opportunity to begin creating relationships with fellow attendees.

- If it is a longer program with multiple speakers, choose and focus on just one to three presenters whose work you'd like to further study and implement.

- Buy the books and/or recordings of those you choose for home study after the event. It will reinforce what you learn.

- When you return home, take action immediately. Don't delay. Studies have shown that the longer you wait, the higher you likelihood of doing anything at all is reduced.

- Purchase the CDs or DVDs of the seminar you just attended if they are offered. Review them as soon as possible. You will be amazed that while you thought you heard 100 percent of the information, you probably got no more than 40 percent or so. You'll feel like you are listening to a whole new seminar!

To both the presenters and the attendees: be sure to follow up with the people you meet at these events. This follow-up can be the difference between success and failure. A well-chosen seminar is a great learning opportunity. But you can dramatically increase the value by using the ideas you learned and following up with the people you meet.

When I first started conducting seminars, my biggest surprise was that most successful entrepreneurs in attendance are the very best students. They come with a clear goal in mind and they are looking for that big idea that can totally change their businesses and their lives.

On the other end of the spectrum are the people who take no notes, and within a few days have forgotten most of what was presented. No one can retain but a small fraction of what is heard just once.

I consider myself a perpetual student of business and of life. When I'm speaking at a seminar, if my schedule allows, I attend each and every session. And often I discover new ideas and brand new ways of looking at things.

A seminar can be one of life's best experiences and learning opportunities. My advice is to attend as many as you possibly can. We cannot know all there is to know and many times we forget what we know.

As a presenter, understand there are people in the audience who are more knowledgeable than you. That's okay. Also understand that you are considered the expert and you need to provide value. Value to me is providing information they can use, both in business and in life, to make significant changes to help them along their path to more success.

Don't take that responsibility lightly.

Ronald Finklestein, President of AKRIS, LLC, is a small business success expert, business coach, consultant, speaker, author, and trainer,

and has published two books, *Celebrating Success! Fourteen Ways to a Successful Company* and *The Platinum Rule to Small Business Mastery*. He contributed to *101 Great Ways to Improve Your Life*. Finklestein founded the Business Leadership Association, LLC and co-founded Celebrating Success! NEO Business Conference. Finklestein is available for coaching and consulting and for speaking engagements, workshops, and seminars. You can contact him at info@yourbusinesscoach.net or reach him at (330) 990-0788. Sign up for his newsletter at http://www.yourbusinesscoach.net.

Drive Traffic to Your Business with a Party!

By Deborah Chaddock Brown

Everyone loves a party—especially your customers. Consider opening your doors for a one-day special event.

Have you ever been to a bad party?

Probably not. Why is that? Well, when you go to a party, the hardest thing you have to do is chose an outfit and pick up a gift for the hostess. Even if the food is bad—you didn't have to prepare it. If the décor is not to your liking—you didn't have to clean it. If the people weren't your favorites—you probably won't see them again. And unless your date goes home with someone else, chances are the worst party is still better to attend than to give.

On the other hand, you may have given a party that didn't meet your expectations; people that you didn't like showed up, people you liked didn't, or maybe no one came at all.

There are so many more details to giving a party than attending one, and the better the details are handled, the more successful the party.

Now think about your business.

Have you ever had an event that was less than successful? Perhaps your employees weren't engaged, your vendor showed up late, the advertisement didn't run in the paper, or the whole town went to the local high school football game instead of your event.

Planning an event to drive traffic is an extremely effective way to reach potential customers in your market. However, if you don't have a handle on the details, it could fall flat.

Throw a party—spread the word—and people will come.

During the majority of the 1990s, I was a Regional Franchise Manager for

Pearle Vision, a retail optical chain, where I managed over 50 optical stores owned by 30 different franchise owners in the New England area.

One such location decided to host a Customer Appreciation Day with the goal of driving customers into their store. There wasn't a model to go by, so everything they did was done for the first time. Some of it worked and some didn't. The bottom line? A successful one-day event.

I learned about this event and spent time asking questions and learning what went well and what they would do differently next time.

I wrote down the details in my workbook, *It's a Party, Planning a Successful Retail Sales Event*, in which I walk through the planning process, offer tips for success, and discuss a few things to be cautious of for a successful event. Your event will only be as successful as the effort and energy you and your team put forth.

How do you measure success? It isn't just the ringing of your cash register, although that is a beautiful sound.

A successful event is one that:
• Drives traffic
• Brings new people to your store
• Educates your customers about the products you carry
• Builds relationships with vendors and local businesses
• Creates an excitement and an awareness of your business in the community.

Nine Elements of Planning and Executing a Successful Event:

1. **Determine the purpose of the event**: Before you begin planning an event, you first need to determine the objectives. Is it to celebrate a Grand Opening? To make people aware of your location? To clear out inventory at year-end? To create a local buzz?

2. **Select an offer**: When planning a retail event, the first thing you'll need is a "hook" or an incentive that will bring people to your store. Your first consideration should be: What will appeal to the customer? What offer will

inspire your customers to change their plans and come to your store during your event?

3. **Select a date**: I recommend selecting a date at least eight weeks in advance, to give you enough time to plan. Think of the last big event you planned (maybe it was a wedding). Think of the months you spent planning so that the special day went off without a hitch. Give the same care and attention to your business event to ensure its success. Also, make sure to choose a day of the week when you will benefit from the most traffic.

4. **Obtain Employee's Buy-In**: Take your employees on as partners. Let them know that a successful retail event can mean more business in the future. Consider a one-day employee incentive program for your event. Although you may already offer commissions or bonuses, for this one day, consider something additional to give them a reason to get excited.

5. **Vendors**: As mentioned before, an important component to a special event or party is having something special that will entice customers to come in. Consider having vendors participate. Look at your inventory and select one or two vendors that you would like to highlight. Take them on as partners. If your event is successful, they will be as well. Let them know your plans and see how they can help.

6. **Marketing Plan**: A clear, detailed marketing plan is essential to having a successful event. Marketing a retail event should be simple, focused, and inexpensive. Luckily, there are many ways to do this. Concentrate on a three-mile radius to begin to get the word out. Communicate with the other businesses within your area, mall, or strip center. Talk to the other store managers, and get permission to put up a flyer/poster in their break room. They may even agree to put flyers in their customers' bags the week of the sale. Start to line up simple ways to get the word out with area businesses about a month in advance. For those willing to put flyers in their customers' bags, you might consider offering a special discount to the manager or the entire staff. Another way to promote your event is to utilize the technique of viral marketing—put the word out on your website and send a special email announcement to your subscribers.

7. Food: Who ever heard of a party without food? I would recommend simple fare that includes cookies or brownies—something small and easy to pick up without the mess of a cake or cupcakes or the need for plates and utensils.

8. Planning Calendar: It is essential to plan the tasks out on a calendar so that you stay focused and remember all the numerous details that go into an event, such as: sending out postcards to existing customers, writing a press release, confirming attendance with your vendor, and ordering additional inventory.

9. Follow-up: In the week after the event you will want to debrief with your staff and vendor(s). Ask what they thought went well and what could have been done differently, and take notes so you can remember next year (you think you'll remember, but you won't). Concentrate especially on the following questions: Did you achieve your goals? Was it a success? Will you do it again?

Planning and executing a successful event can be challenging, but the opportunity to build brand awareness in your community, drive new customers to your door, and grow sales is rewarding and worth the effort.

Deborah Chaddock Brown is the owner of AllWrite Ink, a corporate writing enterprise focused on providing solution-oriented content that enhances her customer's brand message. She writes Word People ReadSM. For more information or to order It's a Party, Planning Successful Retail Events, the complete guide to planning successful events, which includes a planning calendar, marketing tips, budget, and a CD with sample marketing materials, visit www.allwriteink.com.

Exhibiting at Business Expos and Trade Shows

By Paige Stover Hague, Esq.

I am not trained as a salesperson, nor have I really ever held the job title "sales rep." I am a small business owner who, in addition to all the other hats I wear, happens to be the only salesperson at my company. I discovered way back in my corporate life that I had a real natural talent for sales and that I was very comfortable in a face-to-face setting talking about the features and benefits of my product and service offerings. But the critical lesson I learned, back when I was a law book publisher, was that I could *really* sell if I could "show and tell," demonstrate, or somehow get the prospect physically involved with the product. The company I own now is a service provider that helps clients produce products and tangible things, so getting our products into the prospect's hands remains a huge piece of my selling strategy.

The other thing I know about myself and my company is that when prospects are contemplating retaining us, they are making the buying decision based on their assessment of me personally—my knowledge, my energy, my honesty and fortitude, my ability to meaningfully partner with them and listen to their concerns, my insight and judgment, my communication skills, my good spirit and probably lots of other things. Now, I am pretty good on the phone, but it's so much easier for me to convey in person the qualities and attributes that make a buying decision easy for the prospect.

These two factors caused me to invest in exhibit opportunities at business expos and trade shows very early in the history of our company. As the years have gone by, and I have gotten better and better at this, exhibiting has become the largest dollar expenditure in our marketing budget. But it has been well worth the cost.

When we first started our company we had not established ourselves as a national business and were just looking to develop customers in the New England area. I joined several local business networking organizations and became very active, volunteering for all kinds of committees and working my way into leadership positions. Most of these organizations sponsored, or were in some way part of, a business expo event. Although I had done many national trade shows in my legal publishing career, I had never done anything like this on my own.

First, I had to develop a concept for an exhibit. I had no meaningful budget (I only had a handful of clients when I started down this path), but I speculated that this would be an effective way to market our company. I took out my already well-worn credit card and purchased the largest tabletop display made. It came with a nifty carrying case and I had a choice of colors for the display background.

It arrived a week or so later, and I took it out of the box with much anticipation... and it was the ugliest thing I had ever seen. It was covered with a gray fabric that worked with Velcro so that you could attach things to it. The concept was fine, but the execution was not acceptable to me—I'm in the corporate image business, after all.

It occurred to me that I could cover the whole thing with fabric attached on the reverse side with upholstery tacks. I then realized that if I bought enough fabric to also cover the table the display would be sitting on I could get a unified effect that would significantly enhance the professionalism of the exhibit. I bought a heavy upholstery-grade fabric because I wanted it to drape well and not wrinkle. At this point I had spent about $300 (I am still using this same tabletop display and the same fabric six years later).

Next, I had to create the signage that I would attach with Velcro to the now covered three-panel display board. For the first panel, I created one sign with a bulleted list of our services in very large print that could easily be read from 12 feet away. The middle panel was just the name of our company, our tagline and the URL at the bottom, and the third panel was a testimonial and a graphic. It was colorful and eye-catching but extremely simple. These signs were about $80 a piece and the Velcro was maybe $10.

On the table, I placed samples of work we had done for clients, my laptop so I could pull up digital files of our work, a loose-leaf binder with more samples, my business cards, and a six-panel brochure we had printed for the occasion, which cost between $200 and $300. I was careful to place the table at the rear of our 10 x 10 exhibit space so as not to create a barrier between me and the booth visitor. I did not have a promotional product, nor did I have candy. I did have a dish where people could leave their card to sign up for our complimentary newsletter.

I do not believe in shouting things at people as they walk through the corridors or trying to put a copy of my brochure in their hand as they meander aimlessly by. I want to give my brochures to qualified prospects. I will stand (or occasionally sit) and flash a smile at everyone who will make eye contact with me. If I can read the person's nametag I will try to use his or her name in a greeting or make a comment about a heavy bag or anything else I can think of. If I can get them to stop I will ask them where they are from or what they do, trying to get them to talk a little about themselves before I say anything about what I do. They always ask.

When I describe my company in a tradeshow environment, I talk in an inverted pyramid. I do this so that if I get stopped at any point in the proceedings, I have spoken a complete thought. I start with a very broad-brush description of what my company does, and then drill down into additional levels of detail. After each level of drill-down I ask the prospect an open-ended question about what they do. This enables me to customize where I go in my next, more specific layer, hopefully honing in on a particular want or need of the prospect. As I'm talking, I am constantly referencing all of the sample work on the table. I hold it in my hands and refer to it hoping that they will take it into their hands and begin a closer inspection. If I can get them to take it, I stop talking. They will always ask a question. Now they are engaged.

Once my prospect is engaged, my goal is to get the person's card or contact info and verbally confirm that I will call later in the week and set up a time to continue the conversation. In my field, trade shows are a prospecting event rather than a sales event. It would be most unusual for me to close a sale at a tradeshow, and consequently, I don't even try. My goal is simply to build enough of a relationship with the prospect that I can move them to the next level in the sales process.

As the years have gone by, my company has evolved into a national business rather than a regional one. It just so happened that as we grew, our clients were increasingly situated in a specific industry rather than a particular geography. For other people, it may turn out to be the opposite, with a geographical niche rather than an industrial niche. My principle marketing strategy now is through national trade associations. In response to this, I shifted my networking activity over to a national organization for my industry, first becoming involved in the local chapter and then working my way up to the national level. All along the way I was exhibiting—first at the local New England meetings, and then I jumped on the train and went down to New York. Evidently people liked me, and I was asked to speak at the New Jersey chapter (I said I would be glad to but I would also like to exhibit). I even went all the way out to the Los Angeles chapter, and now I go to their three-day education event every year.

It took me three whole years at regional shows until I eventually summoned the courage to exhibit at the big national meeting. Now I exhibit at virtually every meeting this organization holds. I also sponsor receptions and general sessions—I stuff my brochures into every bag attendees receive at registration. Eighty percent of my client base is affiliated with this organization, and because of this steady growth I have upgraded my exhibit booth. Now I have a large pull-down sign and two tables of sample material forming an "L" in one corner. It's the Cadillac of booths. I still use my tabletop display and I still flash my toothy smile and use all the same people strategies that I learned at my very first expos.

The biggest difference is that almost everybody knows me. Now, when I go to the national meeting, my booth is full of my clients, colleagues, and friends, and I have even become good buddies with several other vendors who also exhibit through this association. All of these people refer prospects to my booth. But exhibiting has become so much more than simply prospecting. My booth is now a meeting place—a place to sit and have cup of coffee, a place to leave your bag while you grab lunch, a place to rendezvous with a colleague, a place to meet new people, a place to share ideas, and most of all, a place to have a good laugh with me. Exhibiting has made me part of the "club"—a real insider in the organization—and you better believe I benefit from that status.

Paige Stover Hague, Esq. is the owner of several Boston-based communications companies that provides strategic planning, public relations, marketing and business development services to professional services firms, small businesses, speakers and authors.

She is brought in by CEOs and owner managers throughout the United States to consult and conduct programs and retreats that launch or further company-wide initiatives that affect the way employees and stakeholders think about every aspect of their business. The reach of her presentations touches financial operations, human capital allocations, product development and employee engagement. She also presents continuing education programs for lawyers, accountants and financial advisors on art succession planning. She is co-author of *Life is Short, Art is Long— Maximizing Estate Planning Strategies for Collectors of Art, Antiques and Collectibles* (Wealth Management Press 2007).

Stover Hague is a graduate of Duke University and Nova Southeastern University Law School and a member of the Florida and Massachusetts bars.

Sales
By Ron Finklestein

I was talking with a business associate about how to grow a business. My associate made a comment that there are only two things that really matter in any business: marketing and innovation.

My associate grouped sales into his version of marketing, because without marketing there can be no sales. Without innovation there can be no products worthy of others' attention.

Innovation is taking your products and services and creating and promoting them in such a way that makes them unique in your industry. This can be as simple as understanding the difference between a client and a customer and creating a marketing and sales process that implements this approach.

Marketing is the lead generation side of the business, and sales generate the revenue. Sales involve taking the leads generated by marketing and moving people from suspects (someone who might use our products) to a prospect (someone who has a defined need, budget, and timeframe) to a client (someone who has purchased from us).

In many respects, the sales process breaks down because there's a disconnect between sales and marketing. In this section, you will learn how to create a message that aligns sales and marketing and allows you to define your competitive advantage. The real key here is focus. You cannot be all things to all people, so pick your focus, define your competitive advantage, create your value proposition, and align your sales and marketing strategy around your value proposition. This allows everyone in the company to speak the same language. When everyone is on the same page, you will see your business grow. After all, the only true measure of success is revenue.

Pass the Baton Smoothly
The Full Engagement Approach to Winning the Race
By Kurt A. Minson

So often, the flavor of the month for business success falls under the heading of fresh management strategies, new outsourcing tactics, cost cutting, or revolutionary production quality procedures. Even though we all know that "nothing happens until somebody sells something", too seldom does the sales and marketing process get the attention it requires to remain current. The idea of realigning company resources, focusing attitudes and building an infrastructure that will bind them to business promotions rarely comes into vogue with the usual pundits and business experts. Well-known economist and business writer Peter Drucker made it plain when he said that only two things make money for business, "innovation and marketing". The rise of the global marketplace and an ever more fractured landscape in U.S. marketing, makes a reevaluation of this arena vital.

For our purposes, the word "client" will be used instead of the more common reference "customer." We make this important distinction for the same reason we will talk about engagement more often than sales. A customer, states our friendly neighborhood *Webster's New World Dictionary*, is "a person who buys, especially one who buys from, or patronizes an establishment regularly." A client, on the other hand, is defined by the same source as "one leaning on another (for protection), a person dependent on another, as for protection or patronage; a person or company for whom a lawyer, accountant, advertising agency, etc. is acting." The client definition implies a higher level of trust and commitment, which is also reflected in the idea of an engagement versus a simple sale.

Webster's calls an engagement "a promise; pledge, a promise of marriage; betrothal, an arrangement to go somewhere, do something, meet someone, etc. or an appointment." You get the idea. A sale, on the other hand is "the act of selling; exchange of property of any kind, or of services, for an agreed sum of money or other valuable consideration; opportunity to sell or be sold; market; the act of offering goods to the highest bidder." The strength of engagement flows from its central focus word; *promise*. This contrasts with the lower value, commodity seasoned flavor associated most with sales (think of that plaid used car guy) which has little or none of the smooth, crisp finish or intrinsic worth attached to the engagement concept. Many companies outside of the professional services landscape, which includes law, medicine and accounting, still use the lesser sales term. This occurs even when very high-ticket products like homes, boats, cars, tailored clothing, telecommunications, and fine jewelry are confronted with a more fractured marketplace, tougher penetration dynamics, and a Hurricane Katrina of ad clutter. This is a landscape that screams for the closer relations, stronger cross sales, and deeper referral opportunities engendered by deeper, more significant engagements with clients.

The client-engagement versus customer-sales split has never been clearer than when one considers the widely held notion that the sales cycle somehow takes place in a straight line. You know what I mean. 1) Marketing makes a big play into the universe of prospects through an ad or PR campaign. 2) Sales reps grab the leads generated and proceed to pitch products or services (hopefully) face-to-face to a decision-maker or someone else of consequence to get the deal. 3) A customer service rep or department works to field challenges and smooth rough spots in the relationship to ensure that the business deal stays closed while creating a favorable customer impression. Then it's all over, until the next order, sales call, or product introduction picks up the baton and attempts to carry it forward. The reality is that all three of these steps—marketing, sales and customer service actually perform better when expressed as outcomes rather than processes. We'll call these outcomes exposure, engagement, and the experience of the client. What is hidden in plain sight, is the fact that even though most business people look at these elements as distinct and separate from one another—combined, they exist to create the group of outcomes that matter most…more engagements, revenues, and profits for the entire organization. The decoder ring required, top-secret thing is that these three elements and an additional one, the extension of engagement, are really integrated stages of a single, larger race. When well executed, we can call that race the *Full Engagement.*

Every four years one of the major events on the world stage comes in the form of the Olympics. The summer games bring both gymnastics and more obscure sports like judo, fencing, and (gasp) synchronized swimming into the international consciousness. The biggest attraction for many folks, including myself, is track and field. The events are widely varied, with wiry distance runners stretching endurance with practiced strides and bulky giants hurling the hammer, javelin, and discus unthinkable distances. For our purposes a tight comparison can be made between the dynamics of the Full Engagement and the teamwork involved in the various relays.

In most companies, marketing-exposure, sales-engagement, and customer service-client experience functions are handled by separate and distinct groups with different views, agendas, and success criteria. This traditional structure creates a series of straight-line, but mostly disconnected sprints. Marketing does its research and crafts its message, often in a sales vacuum that doesn't have a good feel for the things that are working best for reps in the field. The sales force may push forward in its activity with a message that it did not create and materials that may or may not provide the traction required to be effective once in their hands. Customer Service is arguably more important than the other two, because of its role in solidifying the sales relationship for the long term when challenges arise. Unfortunately, reps in this area have little, if any, strategic impact earlier in the engagement process.

These smaller, individualized races usually do not reinforce each other to enhance the overall engagement process or its success. In this linear format, the potential actually exists for multiple sales races of very different, non-compatible types to be running at the same time within the same business. Just consider the fallout from the ill-fated introduction and uber-flop of "New Coke" or Sony's Beta video system when they were brought to market with the wrong kind of market research and engagement execution when and where it counted most. This type of misguided process and final outcome wastes valuable resources and energy and disrupts the firm's ability to focus and leverage its central concept(s) consistently; essentially dropping that precious Prime Idea for Engagement "baton" to the cinders or ignoring it completely. What owners, officers, and managers must realize is that the engagement process actually is a race—for clients, the market-share they represent, and the revenues/profits they generate. The company that taps effectively into the market mind early, consistently, with a Prime Idea and potent message, can position itself to be competitive. In addition, it must be seen that in its most successful form, the sales-engagement cycle is not a group of linear races at all. Rather, it is a longer, non-linear, multi-runner competition, run with a great deal of crucial interaction between the elements. In the real world, this means that more than one person or group within the company carries the responsibility of constructively moving the sales process forward, but does so within the context of a team format. Returning to our marketing as race analogy, the Full Engagement can be best viewed as a relay with four distinct, but interrelated, legs. Those legs or stages are the "Four E's" of exposure, engagement, experience, and extension.

1. Leg One – Exposure is generated through non-face-to-face marketing of various types, from advertising and Public Relations, to events, books, and Internet. All efforts are made at this stage to differentiate company offerings in order to get ahead of the competition and establish a lead in the mind of the market. This sets the table for leg two. This lead is best built on the power of a strong Prime Idea that the engaging company can "own" in the market mind. Consider the penetration of the BMW message. As the "Ultimate Driving Machine" the only thing that BMW cares about is driving home (pun intended) the beauty, majesty, and thrill of driving. Luxury, technology, fuel mileage or competitive price are not mentioned for their own sake.

This singular focus, which must be carried through the entire engagement process, like the proverbial relay baton, provides the energy this firm needed to become preeminent in its segment. While a number of good and great companies have put sufficient effort into this early part of the exposure stage, energy must also be put in place to conscientiously align these exposure efforts with sales-engagement and customer service-client experience feedback. These links work to extend the engagement energy generated into the larger corporate culture to feed and impact results. This process takes the idea and practice of engagement beyond those directly involved in the cycle, allowing the excitement and power of the race to be injected into other parts of the business. The company will maintain the integrity and cohesion of its Prime Idea and gain the power to enhance promotional effectiveness by leveraging information from real world clients and their engagement outcomes.

2. Leg Two – Engagement conversations are initiated, developed, accelerated, and hopefully closed once engagement personnel receive leads/traffic and the "baton" from the exposure created in leg one. These reps must "explode" the focus of the company Prime Idea in a cultural manner that clarifies how their product or service will apply and fit well with a specific client in multiple ways. This vision must also jibe with the abilities and style of the rep in play. Energy must be expended in the engagement stage to take the race lead provided by leg one exposure and either expand on that lead or sustain it for the next stage. This translates into a closed profitable deal with the client being open to additional engagement activity in the future, either with more or better goods purchased. The Men's Warehouse, founded less than 30 years ago, has become the consolidating force in the men's tailored clothing segment by having company founder and chairman George Zimmer point at prospects from the TV screen and guarantee that clients "will like the way they look" in all the company's marketing. Training their "wardrobe consultants" to stack multiple, complete looks with shirt, tie, belt, and pocket silk for each suit or sport coat purchased, and offering tuxedo rentals and using actual employees in their ads, ensures that this promise sticks from exposure to engagement and beyond.

Outside these somewhat traditional roles, runners in the engagement stage must also consistently align their efforts with exposure, customer service-client experience, and larger corporate perspectives through a natural extension of the engagement. This allows folks in the engagement stage to gather crucial client data and capitalize on the penetration established in leg one, while avoiding pitfalls that will be identified by service reps at the next stage. Once again, this coordination of ideas and efforts within the cycle allows the baton to be passed without incident to further promote the company's Prime Idea. A smooth transition also enables the company to be more efficient in face-to-face opportunities, while expanding cross-engagement options and building promotional potency by using outcome data derived from real world interactions.

3. Leg Three – The Experience the client has with a business or its products and services can make or break that company's perceptual value in the market mind. A great experience will grab the baton and add tangible value by reinforcing previous and ongoing engagement activities and opening the door to fresh opportunities. Customer Service Reps must capture the energy of their stage two counterparts and, whether ahead or behind in the race against the competition, they must kick in to solidify a lead or "blow-up" to make up lost ground. A fine example of "positive" client experience deployment leading to preeminence is the Starbucks phenomenon. Many of us can remember a diner or corner café serving a cup of Joe back in the day for 55-75 cents. But the trendy, up-to-the-moment Starbucks experience has made an ultra-grande-triple-low-fat-super-caramel- Peruvian-yak-latte...extra foam, at $75 and change, palatable for many consumers. This power in the market mind has enabled that coffee retailer to expand their market dominance all over the U.S. The question must be asked though, is the java that much better or is the cachet of being seen in such a cool spot and carrying an emblazoned cup to prove your unquestioned hipness on the street, worth the additional yen that must be slapped down to partake?

To be successful in the experience stage, one must also consider the related, often stickier, issue resolution side of the experience coin. When there is a challenge with a transaction, the provider must be able to resolve it in a manner that the client finds not just equitable, but compelling. This can not only save the day within a present engagement, but also set the stage for expanded relations, greater engagement velocity, and enhanced profits later. Witness the resurrection of Audi. In the early and mid 1980's, the "unintended acceleration phenomenon" all but killed that German car presence in the U.S. This was despite the fact that the weird "I pushed the brakes, but the car sped up" malady was never conclusively reproduced under controlled conditions. Fast forward to November 2006. Audi's technical and ergonomic improvements in response to unintended acceleration bolstered their U.S. sales to a point 5.4% improved over 2005. The 16.4% increase in November U.S. sales alone has put the company on pace to set a sales record for their American division, while GM and Ford continue to bleed red ink. Stage three activities must weave exceptional client experience outcomes fully into the fabric of the company's exposure, engagement, and extension formats. More than any other of the Full Engagement elements, this leg has the responsibility of ensuring final client satisfaction and continued engagement. Leg 4 personnel must be empowered to make great outcomes for clients a reality.

4. Leg Four – The Extension of the engagement beyond the sales force to all other cultural levels of your organization will support the power all previous and ongoing engagement activities. Very much like the anchor of a relay team, this leg must kick it into high gear to close on competition that may be running ahead or slam the door on any team trying to play catch-up. Your Prime Idea must be well articulated vertically, from the CEO to the cashiers and back up the corporate ladder again. Individuals, small groups, and the entire company must be touched in a fashion that recognizes that acquiring more clients, expanding the business relationship with each client to produce more engagements, and growing the size/value of each individual engagement are the only three real ways to grow any business. Everyone in your company has an engagement responsibility that must be embraced in order to solidify the position of the business as a market leader. Wal-Mart, with its cultural designs on reducing their prices, seemingly by any means necessary and on all levels of the organization, is the textbook example of leg four thinking in full effect.

Instead of having marketing, sales, and customer service operate individually in their own silos within a business, it is prudent to align these resources in such a way as to create a Full Engagement platform as described above. Such a combination of exposure, engagement, client experience, and extension of engagement activity, when well-coordinated and well-run, will take clients through the process more smoothly and with better profit outcomes. Before one race is complete, this structure will also empower the organization to flow its clients into a new cycle to up the ante and opportunity for more frequent or larger engagements and deeper referrals.

When a company is successful in bringing all four of the Full Engagement stages to bear with a strong emphasis on smooth and integrated transitions at each point of contact, the result is an energized engagement culture. Such a culture must also be maintained through strategic recruitment, balanced hiring practices over time and incentives to all employees to generate the increased engagement velocity and needed momentum in the market mind that will pay the best dividends. These outcomes, when realized, are ultimately worth their weight in gold, platinum or the precious metal of your choice. Starting with first touch at exposure, through the engagement proper, into the experience cycle where the relationship is crystallized and with corporate extension, where entire organizations get fully engaged, past, present and future business is explored, captured, and leveraged to great effect. Simply thinking differently and reframing your process as an engagement cycle instead of a sales sprint can fuel substantial growth for your enterprise, now and into the future.

Kurt A. Minson, Chief Engagement Officer of The M Group Consultants is the originator of the "Full Engagement" and "Prime Idea for Engagement" concepts. He has an extensive social science background, with degrees in psychology, sociology, philosophy and economics, as well as concentrations in French, German and the classics. He brings a deep insight into human thought, behavior, motivations and decision making into the process of marketing, sales and customer service. Since 1994 his firm has integrated a cultural backbone into the exposure, engagement and client experience work that they do for professional service firms and other businesses in the Midwest. In addition to the conventional weapons of the trade; advertising, design, events, PR and web, Minson uses personality profiles, appreciative inquiry, structured interviews and other tools to tap the cultural essence of client organizations. These investigations uncover the "diamonds in the rough" that can be developed into Prime Ideas and provide the roadmap that allows his firm to effectively deploy engagement and experience training. Minson's other service offerings include image and wardrobe, personal promotions, ideation, diversity, franchise development, branding-positioning and recruitment for engagement. All of these elements are focused on building performance cultures that understand how to take what they have to acquire, expand relations with and keep more clients to build revenues and profits.

For more information, please visit www.mgroupconsultants.com or call 330.762.4441.

Stop Selling in the Pit
What's Your Competitive Advantage?
By Dr. Tony Alessandra

As I've traveled around the country over the past several years working with companies and their salespeople, I've been amazed to find that they do not know, and cannot articulate, their competitive advantage! How can companies and their salespeople expect prospects and customers to give their time and attention if they do not understand, clearly and concisely, what that company can do for them that no one else can do? That's what I call selling in the pit.

Companies and salespeople who don't understand their competitive advantage are all in a deep pit saying things like, "Our product is better quality," or, "Our service is better," or, "I'm my company's competitive advantage." Even if the salesperson is the company's competitive advantage, they won't convince their customers just by saying so because many of their competitors will be saying the exact same thing! That's selling in the pit! To get out of the pit, salespeople have to *define* quality. They have to show the prospect what outstanding service looks like and *how their service differs from the competition.*

In a moment, I'll show you how to determine your competitive advantage, but first let's talk about how you can demonstrate your competitive advantage from the very first moment you are introduced. Suppose someone walks up to you at a business conference, introduces herself, and asks you what you do for a living. *Exactly* what would you say?

Did you have any trouble? Did you stumble? Do you know what sets you apart from your competitors? If this was hard for you, you're not alone. If you were to ask the average car, computer, or caviar salesperson what they do for a living, they'll probably say, "I sell cars, computers, or caviar." But what does every other car, computer, or caviar salesperson say? Exactly the same thing!

So what *should* salespeople who understand their competitive advantage say? How about this for the car salesperson? "My name is Mike and I work with Competitive Motors. I've found that there is a lot of confusion in the automotive market today because there have been over 150 new models introduced in just the past three years. I've developed a computer book that profiles everything the buyer wants in a car and, in less than five minutes, identifies the models most likely to fit their needs."

Your Statement of Competitive Advantage

Mike has given his prospect a *statement of competitive advantage*. It has four components:
- Your name
- Your company
- A statement about a problem in your market
- How you and your product solve that problem

The statement of competitive advantage is a maximum 30-second statement of what differentiates you in the marketplace.

Here's another example. "My name is Marlene and I work with a company called 'The Prescription for Doctors.' Physicians today are being pressured by insurers, employers, and patients to cut health care costs. Yet overhead costs for physicians are constantly rising. We provide a service that allows the physician to spend more time with patients and cut overhead costs at the same time, resulting in better quality care at a lower cost. It's just what the doctor ordered!"

Here's one last example. "My name is Beth. It's nice to meet you. I'm with a company called 'The Greatest Advertising Agency in the World.' I've discovered that almost every successful product has either been the first entry in its category or it has been able to create a new category in the mind of its customers. What we do is help companies who are launching new products or having trouble with old ones ensure that their product is positioned to win!"
That really does set you apart from the competition. And it makes you sound like a polished expert right from the start. But how do you determine exactly what your competitive advantage is? The best way to determine your competitive advantage is to break down the components of your product or service into four distinct categories: competitive uniqueness, competitive advantages, competitive parities, and competitive disadvantages. Let's look at each one individually.

Competitive uniqueness: "What can I do for my customers that no one else can do? What can I offer that no one else can offer?"

Competitive advantages: "What can I do for my customer that my competitor can also do, but I can do it better and I can prove it?"

Competitive parity: "Objectively speaking, my competitors and I are the same here—no real differentiation."

Competitive disadvantages: When you honestly answer the question: "Where does the competition have an advantage over me?"

You may want to do your analysis by market segment, by competitor, by product, or include all of them, but knowing your competitive position will quickly get you out of the pit and on your customer's wavelength.

An example of **competitive uniqueness** exists if a pharmaceutical company receives FDA approval to sell a new drug. Since no one else has the drug, this company now has a competitive uniqueness with this drug.

An example of a **competitive advantage** might be where two companies market the same drug, but one is a large well-known company and the other is a small relatively unknown company. Even though both are selling essentially the same product, the larger company has an advantage because it's well known and people ask for the drug by its company name because of its wide name recognition. If no real competitive advantage exists in your product, try to focus on your company reputation, your excellent service, your responsiveness, and reliability or any other factors than can positively differentiate you from your competition.

Next let's look at **competitive parity**—what things are the same between the competition and us? That is, what do you have that is exactly like what the competition has but is still important to the customer? Birth control pills are a good example. Several ethical drug companies make different formulations, but all with similar records for preventing pregnancy. This is competitive parity.

And finally, **competitive disadvantages**—what specific disadvantages do your product or service possess? That is, what does the competition do better than you do? Your drug may have more side effects than the competitor's. That's a competitive disadvantage.

In the examples I've just given, we were talking about the whole product as being unique or the same. But what do you do if you have a product where some features may be unique, some may be advantages, some may be the same, and some may be disadvantages?

Say, for example, that you are selling a fax machine that uses plain paper—that's *parity*, because others do too. But maybe yours is the only one that will interface with phone, computer, or car telephone—that's *uniqueness*. Yours also has the highest resolution available, that's an *advantage*, 300-number memory, another *advantage*, but it will not do broadcasting and polling, that's a *disadvantage*.

Here's an example in a service business. Federal Express™ will get a package delivered overnight, but so will other companies. That's *parity*. But FedEx has a provable better track record, an *advantage*, and they can tell you in real time, exactly where your package is, that's a *uniqueness* (Of course, in the rapidly changing world of service businesses, some of these benefits may have changed from advantage to parity, or vice versa, by the time you read this).

I can't stress enough the importance of doing this analysis and knowing your competitive advantage. By doing this analysis you'll be in a position to help your customers distinguish between you and your competition. Once they see your uniqueness and advantages, it will be easier for them to make a decision in your favor. In order to discover your competitive advantage, you may have to do some intelligence gathering:
- talk to your customers
- talk to other salespeople
- watch the local newspapers
- attend tradeshows
- talk to your customers' suppliers
- build a file of your competitor's marketing and product information

- do a debriefing when you lose a customer to a competitor
- use a clipping service to gather information on competitors or on major prospects
- obtain annual and quarterly reports of your competitors and prospective customers
- watch the market trends in your industry and in your customers' industries
- become the expert on your product or service and how it can help your customers

Avoiding Price Focus

How many times have you been in a selling situation where the customer's sole focus was on price? Anytime your customers can't tell the difference between your product or service and your competitor's, they will buy on price. You must differentiate your company, your product, your quality, your service, and yourself if you want the customer to stop focusing on price and start seeing you as a partner and not just as a supplier. You've got to show customers how you are different.

I'm sure you can see now why it's so important to know what you have to offer that's unique or different. But you may be wondering what you'll do with that information once you have it. How will you get the information across to the customer?

You're going to use this information in every step of the sale. Your entire sales effort will be built around your competitive strengths. When you are targeting your market, you'll be looking for those clients whose needs are most likely to match your uniqueness and advantages. When you contact clients, you'll open the conversation by letting them know what you can do for them that no one else can do. During the information-gathering phase, you'll be asking questions that will uncover customer needs in the areas where you have uniqueness and advantages. When you are collaborating with your customer on options and solutions, you'll keep your customer focused on your uniqueness and advantages and show your customers how they match their needs. During the commitment phase, you'll be summarizing all of the competitive advantages that your product has to offer, and during the assuring satisfaction phase, you'll be measuring how well your uniqueness and advantages are serving your customer.

Let's summarize the two powerful strategies I've talked about that will give you **The Competitive Advantage**. First, know your competitive advantages and uniqueness, and second, be able to articulate them clearly to your prospective customers in thirty seconds or less. This is your powerful opening to your targeted prospects—that all-important first impression that sets you apart from your competition and clearly establishes your competitive advantage in the eyes of your customers.

Dr. Tony Alessandra helps companies achieve market dominance through specific strategies designed to outmarket, outsell, and outservice the competition. Tony has a street-wise, college-smart perspective on business. He earned his Ph.D. in Marketing from Georgia State University in 1976. Dr. Alessandra is president of AssessmentBusinessCenter.com, a company that offers online 360° assessments; Chairman of BrainX.com, a company that created the first Online Learning Mastery System™; and is the founding partner of PlatinumRuleGroup.com, a company that provides corporate training and consulting based on *The Platinum Rule*®.

Dr. Alessandra is a widely-published author with 15 books translated into 17 foreign languages. Dr. Alessandra's television program, "People I.Q." is currently aired on the DISH Satellite Network and on TSTN – The Success Training Network. Recognized by *Meetings & Conventions Magazine* as "one of America's most electrifying speakers," Dr. Alessandra was inducted into the Speakers Hall of Fame in 1985. For more information, please visit www.Alessandra.com.

Get Out of Your Chair
and Identify the Pain and Survival Issues

By Timothy A. Dimoff

In the business community, we just can't stop talking about how those over-inflated dot-coms failed. Now we are going out of our way to change business names to not reflect anything close to a dot-com name. But, did the business community learn anything new that previous generations hadn't already experienced and perfected into basic business practices from the dot-com bust? Most business minds would argue that the dot-com era did bring about some unique business lessons, but we now have gone back into what I call the "survival" mode. Basically, the boom is over and if you want to survive, let alone grow in business, you need to evaluate both your internal and external processes.

If you follow the national trends that are taking place you will clearly see that employee layoffs or cautious hiring is taking place at most companies, big and small. Labor will always be a company's biggest overhead and when times are tough, labor is the first to be trimmed. What does this mean? The answer is simply that "job security" is no longer a guarantee for anyone who cannot make a consistent contribution to the company bottom line. Additionally, it means that internal restructuring must take place. An example of this is cross-training employees so they can step in to handle a variety of jobs when people are on vacation, sick, or during peak demand time for your products or services.

Unique methods of business restructuring are taking place in response to companies surviving. Examples of this are breaking a service or product down into segments and sub-contracting parts of the production or the service out to other respected and reliable businesses. You will see that a number of "Strategic Business Alliances" are being formed locally, nationally, and internationally.

So, how do you gain an edge in the "battlefield of sales and marketing" when presenting your company's services and/or products? It all comes down to your focus. And what exactly should that focus be? I have found—based on numerous years of experience, research, and discussion with clients¬ — that it *all* comes down to two words: "pain" and "survival."

Every new company and current client you meet will want or need your services and/or products to solve their two most pressing issues — pain and survival. You must first stop their pain. New customers and current clients want you to either solve their immediate pain or keep new pain from entering their organization. Secondly, you need to help them survive. Every company worries constantly about survival. If you can assist a new company or keep a current client from going under (due to any of a variety of reasons - litigation, product quality, production issues, employee issues, hiring issues, training, etc.) you will have their attention, and gain or keep their business.

So the big question is how do you figure out what a potential company or current company's pain/survival issues are? I have found several different methods of ferreting these out. The first method is research. By that I mean read, read, and read more. Read newspapers, especially the business section, and see what the trends in business are. You can get so many ideas as to what the pain/survival issues are by exploring other industries, new technologies, competing companies, and what products are being developed or expanded. Behind each one of these aspects is a reason and behind that reason is the pain or survival issue.

In addition to newspapers, you need to read business and trade magazines, which are loaded with articles that bring issues to the forefront. You'll find an unlimited amount of specific and valuable information for you to better understand your specific industry.

The second area that can help you obtain information on the pain/survival issues for your prospective and current clients is simple and very effective. Just ask the potential or current client what their pain/survival issues are and if your company could assist them by making their business environment much better. I have found that these companies have no problem at all in explaining their needs and are very receptive to our questions and solutions.

The last area that can help you obtain information on the pain/survival issues for your new and current clients is summed up in one word: listen. Many times potential and current clients talk about their pain/survival issues in general conversation. Often they will bring up issues when we are working with them that could be an entry point for the discussion of new services, but we just don't listen. Why? We are too busy doing something else, or thinking of something else, and a great opportunity just passes us by. I firmly believe that most small business owners pass up far too much potential new business from both new and current clients just because we do not pay attention on a regular basis. How many times has a current or potential client of yours purchased a new product or service that you could have provided? You sit there saying, "why didn't we think of that?" or, "why didn't they ask us to do it?" Whose fault do you really think it is?

At a recent training seminar I provided for a national company, I was asked a specific question: What is the one thing our company can do during these rough times that will make the biggest impact on our survival. The answer? *Remove all the chairs from your business office.*

The reason for my response was simple. Companies are in "Business Pain." If you want to survive and grow you need to discover what your current or potential clients' "pain" and "survival" issues are at this current moment. You must be able to get them to share their pain/survival issues, provide a solution to the pain/survival, provide a fair price for this solution, and then actually deliver the solution. But the most important thing to remember is that you must *get out of your chair* to do this. You must physically get in front of your current and potential new customers and focus on these very important aspects of pain and survival.

My consulting firm realizes today that survival and pain must be part of our overall business plan and vision for our company, our current clients, and our future clients.

If your company does not embrace the knowledge and action plan to discover the "pain/survival" in your business world and act accordingly then, "survival" is not in your company's immediate business future.

Remember, you can't do it at your office and you can't do it effectively on the phone so don't forget…get rid of your chairs at work and speak to your audience directly!

Timothy A. Dimoff, President and Founder of SACS Consulting, is a nationally recognized author, speaker, trainer, and registered expert. Dimoff is an author of six national books and numerous nationally copyrighted training programs. He has been featured on CNN, Dateline, NBC, the *Wall Street Journal*, the *New York Times*, the *Los Angeles Times*, the *Chicago Tribune*, the *Washington Post* and several other national media formats. Additionally, he is a member of the National Speaker Association (NSA) and is often sought after for keynote and professional presentations. You can contact Dimoff at SACS at 1-888-722-7937, by email, TADimoff@ sacsconsulting.com, at SACS Consulting, www.sacsconsulting.com, or on his speaker website at www.TimothyDimoff.com.

Enthusiasm + A Quality Product = Buzz
A Prescription for Growth
By Ron McDaniel

People in the marketing trade can tell you that buzz is a large part of what makes our industry thrive. Buzz is a complex idea, and its dynamic can change depending on the circumstances. There are many factors that go into making a buzz-worthy product, and many different techniques you can apply to ensure that your resources are consistent with the type of buzz you're looking for. In this article, I will address the various forms of buzz with regard to how they're formed and what purpose they serve.

In order to create buzz individually, you must have a high level of excitement and enthusiasm for what you are buzzing about. I cannot stress enough how important it is to be able to sustain your efforts in stirring up the interest of others. The result of your efforts will be people spreading positive word-of-mouth about your business or product. If there is no excitement, it will be difficult to convince yourself, let alone others, that what you are doing is worthwhile.

Of course, there are other ways to generate buzz. It's sometimes possible to create a product so good, so different, that it generates its own buzz and sales. It is also possible to do something so newsworthy that you get a lot of buzz from the media. But these are not things you just decide on one day and they magically happen. They take a lot of work and some level of luck.

For the purpose of this article, I will assume you have a high level of enthusiasm for your business or product. As long as you have this I'll be able to show you how the unique qualities of what you are buzzing about will influence every feature of your buzz campaign.

Dull Product or Bad Quality

The first analysis is the situation where you have very high enthusiasm, but a product that does not excite people. Your excitement makes them take a look, but very few people buy. Even fewer tell someone else about it. This is very frustrating for the buzz creator because he is sustaining his excitement when no one else buys into it. One of three things is happening in this case:

1. The product is not the right product
2. The product is of very poor quality
3. The product is very boring and/or a commodity

If the product falls into number one or number two, you have to improve the product or move on.

I see number three all the time with professional service providers. Insurance agents, Lawyers, Accountants, Financial Planners—they all have services that many different people are selling. Standing out here is not so much about the product as it is developing your personal brand to the point that people will come to you for whatever you are selling.

Difficult Product but Good Product
The "difficult but good" product is one that you can sell to people very easily, but your customers and advocates have trouble selling it via word of mouth after that. Thus, you do not get any scale or residual effect on the buzz effort. Businesses that try to do too many things for too many people will have trouble in this area.

Quality of the product may not be the problem here. The quality of your message and your product packaging probably is.

If this seems to be the problem with your buzz effort, consider the following. First, simplify your offering. Explain it in a way that the average customer will easily comprehend. If you get them to understand the broad benefits of the product, they'll always find ways to talk about it.

Next, even after simplification, your product is still probably more difficult to understand than the average product, so devise a strategy to educate your customers, employees, and prospects in a quick and regular way.

Blockbuster Product
This is the kind of buzz that says the quality of your product is great and

your benefits are easy to understand. It also says your product easily creates enthusiasm in others.

If your buzz effort falls into this category, you may have big problems. Are you going to be able to handle orders and questions that are running out of control? Is your quality good now but will plummet as you get busier? People always say to me, "That is a good problem to have..." but they do not realize that the incredible high will be followed by an incredible low if you are not prepared to deliver on your promise.

If you are hoping for blockbuster buzz, have a plan for scaling your company. If you get busy and your quality suffers, your buzz will be short-lived.

Steady Buzz

What does a good buzz marketing job look like? If you are dealing with a big company that can easily scale and maintain quality, the blockbuster scenario is the best. For a small to mid-sized company, the steady buzz will win the race. This is a realistic model for most businesses. If you have good quality and an easy to understand product with clear benefits, a good percentage of the people you talk to will talk about you, and in turn, a good percentage of people that you have never met will talk about you. Enthusiasm will not be sustained in most cases very far out, but in some cases it will be sustained because the quality of the product gets talked about, even if it is not the next big thing.

This version of buzz may not seem exciting, but it represents double-digit annual growth while maintaining high quality and excellent customer service. This is a goal that should cost you very little to achieve if you already have a quality product. Simply increase enthusiasm and get more people to start talking about you via everyday channels on a regular basis.

Quality and sustainable enthusiasm are the two biggest elements for creating buzz and growing your company. By strategically making more people enthusiastic and maintaining or improving your quality, you will experience positive growth.

Ron McDaniel is a long-time entrepreneur, technology specialist, Internet marketer, buzz marketer, and word-of-mouth marketing specialist. He is also a teacher, professional speaker, and author. His mission is to get the world talking about his clients. His book, *Buzzoodle Buzz Marketing - 57 Word of Mouth Marketing Challenges*, shows how to create buzz for yourself and your organization in just a few minutes a day and is available for purchase on Amazon.com. McDaniel is available for speaking, training and limited buzz consulting. Please visit www.buzzoodle.com for more information.

First Build the Relationship, and Then Deliver the Value

By Daniel Waintrup

It was panic time. I was really starting to get a little worried. I had been working for almost six months at a my new sales job at a nationally-recognized financial services firm and had yet to find one legitimate client.

For the life of me I couldn't understand why. My new company had given me hundreds of hours of sales training and I was certain that I was following the "script" perfectly. "Cold-calling" people I didn't know or had never met was certainly not my idea of a good time, but my sales manager assured me that I was doing a good job and that it wasn't a matter of "if" but "when."

Personally, I couldn't understand why the high-net worth individuals who were my target market weren't impressed with my knowledge of the financial markets and my company's impressive array of hedge funds.

I was having trouble sleeping at night and asked my wife, "Don't you think I'm a little young to be developing an ulcer?" After months of heartache, headaches, countless hang-ups, and failed cold calls, I had an epiphany. It came after a conversation with an individual whom I finally had reached after many attempts, who changed the course of my sales career forever with these simple words: "Why would I ever give you a million dollars to invest? I don't even know you!"

These words jolted me. How could I have been so stupid? This individual got me to realize that I was never going "close the deal" with anyone unless I could find a way to establish a relationship with him or her first. He got me to understand that there was little chance of ever making a sale by calling people who didn't know or care about me in some way. This man forced me to realize that I had to find something that I had in common with the people I was pursuing. I had to find something of value that I could give these potential clients that would make them want to like me, trust me, and ultimately, help me.

In my case, that "something of value" that I could give the wealthy individuals I was pursuing was my ability on a tennis court. As a former collegiate and highly-ranked player, as well as someone who had taught tennis to thousands of individuals of all ages and levels of ability, there were few things I couldn't do between the white lines. I had experience playing and teaching at virtually every level of the game. I had been out of tennis for over ten years, but I quickly realized that, as the former pro at one of New England's wealthiest and most prestigious country clubs, I already had a built-in reservoir of high-net worth individuals with whom I had relationships at some point in the past. I just needed to reconnect with them—by getting back on a tennis court.

A typical conversation between me and this potential "client" on the court is indicative of how important it is to have something in common, something you both like and something you both can share together before attempting to transition it to something more.

"Wow that was a great workout, Dan, thanks for the tip on my forehand, it really helped. You still don't miss many balls, do you?"

"Yeah, I'm still hitting well and am in pretty good shape...But I'll tell you, it wasn't easy when I was playing and teaching 50 hours of tennis a week as a pro. I was fortunate to be able to go back to school and get my MBA...."

"What are you doing now?"

"Actually, I'm working in sales for an investment firm out of New York...It's been great..."

"Really? How's the company doing this year?"

"We're having a good year. I'd could send you some information if you'd like..."

"Sure... I'd love to see it. I'm always looking for new investment opportunities..."

"I'll get our latest performance figures out tomorrow."

"Are you around next week to hit a few?"
"Sure! I'll give you a call…"

My first successes for the investment firm that I worked for were with these wealthy individuals with whom I had had relationships in the past, relationships that I was able to transition to another level. After exhausting this supply, I've been able to find and identify a new base of high-net worth "clients" who play or love the game, or have some charitable connection to it, and build a relationship with them by giving them something they value and enjoy: my skill as a tennis player and teacher.

The publication of my first book, *It's Not My Fault—or— Can a Rabbi's Son Find Happiness as a Tennis Pro?* (a humorous memoir based on my life as both a teaching pro and a rabbi's son), has added to my ability to attract and build relationships with high-net worth, tennis-loving individuals. Interestingly enough, the marketing and promotion of the book on radio and TV has given me the chance to meet, network, and develop friendships with potential clients who may or may not have any connection to the game.

For instance, I had this interesting conversation at a recent charity event, with a very important CEO.

"Oh, I love Alan Alda's recent memoir…have you read it?"
"No, but I hear it's really funny."
"I'll bet it's not as funny as my book…"
"You wrote a book? What's it about…?"

Daniel Waintrup, a.k.a. "the Rabbi's Son," is a former tennis teaching pro at one of New England's most exclusive country clubs. He was a nationally ranked player at Temple University, a ranked New England Men's Singles player in the 1980's and 90's, and the 2005 Men's Singles Champion at the Palm Beach Country Club. A featured media personality and professional speaker, Waintrup provides humorous commentary on the topics of tennis, business, networking, self-promotion, and the art of winning—both in life and on the court. In between speaking, writing, and providing tennis analysis on sports talk programs, he is presently working

on the screen adaptation of his book, *Its Not My Fault - Can A Rabbi's Son Find Happiness as a Tennis Pro?* **For more information, please visit www. DanWaintrup.com.**

Eat What You Kill
How to Conduct a Self-Promotional Conversation
That Triggers Your Sales Process
By Paige Stover Hague, Esq.

A lot of people think self-promotion is a bad word.

As children, we are taught that talking about our accomplishments is boastful and egotistical. "I am really good at algebra"—bad, bad. "I am the best saxophone player in the band"—you can't say that. "Nobody in the county can outrun me in the 440-yard dash"—you mustn't do that.

Then you grow up and you discover that your livelihood depends on your ability to self-market. All of us who are small business owners share a common reality—we eat what we kill.

But there are those among us who give self-promotion a bad name. I'm sure you can recall a boorish, overly aggressive salesperson who relentlessly pressed himself or his product on you in a way that only made you want to run away as quickly as possible. This obnoxious behavior is not self-promotion. This is something else masquerading as a sales technique that we hope is rapidly becoming extinct.

There are some flamboyant personalities who can get away with a "hail fellow, well met" style and do it in a way that is authentic, endearing, funny, and memorable. Their style becomes a signature attribute of their brand. Most of us, however, need to find a less "in your face" way of communicating who we are, what we do, and what our unique value proposition is.

Self-promotion is frequently dubbed an art. I think this description is accurate; like art, self-promotion is such a tricky thing to do well. It walks a very fine line between offensive and off-putting, and persuasive and influential. Finding the balance is indeed the art and the challenge. When done well, however, it can make a career, launch a business, and shatter sales records.

I define self-promotion as talking about yourself in a way that makes the listener want to know more. I believe self-promotion is one of the most important skills you can acquire—and it may be the single most determining factor in small business success.

As small business owners, we are also subject matter experts. In addition to having responsibility for client acquisition, we are the lawyer, the financial advisor, the insurance producer, the head hunter, or the psychotherapist.

So our challenge is this—how do we turn our subject matter expertise into a stream of revenue that can put food on the table? Okay, so we need marketing materials and a website and a business card. But the fact is that none of those things are of any use to us if we don't have a reader or a listener. After all, you have to have someone to give your business card to.

Some small business owners get so wrapped up in these self-marketing "toys" that they forget the initial step that actually triggers the sales process: the relationships you need to build and conversations you need to have in order to get the sales process started. These are self-promotional conversations, personal interactions that enable the business development process to begin. The operative concept is to build a personal relationship with a new contact so that he or she will take your phone call tomorrow or reply to your email, and you can begin the process of converting this person from suspect to prospect to client.

My premise here is that no one is interested in your products and/or services until he or she is first interested in you. So how do you build the relationship? Trouble is, you have about 12 seconds to make enough of an impression so that your prospective client wants to continue the conversation. The bottom line: Use your time wisely.

We have all heard over and over that first impressions are everything. Given that you have only 12 seconds, what are your tools?
• your personal image, how you look
• your eye contact
• your hand shake

- your smile
- your confidence factor
- your words

What you do in these first 12 seconds defines your personal brand. Your brand is what people say about you when you are not in the room. You have two choices – you can be in control of what people say about you when you are not in the room or you can let the chips fall where they may.

If you accept the premise that people are not interested in your products and services until they are interested in you, then it naturally follows that you are the brand. What you are selling is you; your products and services are just the tangibles. What you are actually selling is your unique expertise, perspective, experience, system, approach, language, analytical tools, understanding of the rules, and your special way of looking at and presenting whatever content or expertise you are offering. Whether you are selling informational products (such as books, speeches, training tools, CDs, or DVDs) or you are a service professional (such as a realtor, accountant, hair cutter, web designer, consultant, or coach), you are the product.

Previously, I suggested self-promotion was how to talk about yourself in a way that makes the listener want to know more. Let's add some meat to those bones: self-promotion is the *ability to consistently communicate the value you bring to a situation by talking about who you are and what you do in a way that causes the listener to both affirm and buy-in to your effectiveness on the spot.* Breaking this down into its component parts, self-promotion is:

- *The ability to consistently...*
  This means over and over, every time. You have to have these words and phrases perfected. They have to roll off your tongue like the wisdom of the ages. You must plan, script, and rehearse these statements.

- *Communicate...*
  It has come to my attention that there is a general lack of understanding among the business community that communication has two components – a transmitter and a receiver. You have to send a message and the other person

has to be able to receive and, most importantly, understand it. But here's the rub: It's your job as the transmitter to make sure that you are speaking a language that the receiver understands. You can transmit a perfect message in flawless Russian. But it just so happens I do not speak Russian, so your transmission is not received by me. I may smile and nod and go through other socially-acceptable reinforcement mechanisms, but I have no clue what you just said to me. So the burden is on you as the transmitter to make sure that I am receiving your communication. Do not speak "loan to value ratios" with me if I live in a world where my primary concern is the color of your parachute. That does not mean I do not need accounting services; it just means you need to say things to me like "your clients will feel so much more connected to your work if they have an upfront understanding of some of the considerations, blah, blah blah....."

- *The value you bring to a situation...*
There are people who make their living entirely by teaching others how to state their unique selling (or I prefer to say value) proposition, or your USP. If you haven't figured out what yours is, you need to go to a marketing seminar immediately. This is the critical attribute that distinguishes what you do and how you do it from the other 1,100 players in your space. Here is my USP: *I show people how to turn expertise into revenue.* You need to able to state yours as clearly and concisely as I state mine.

- *By talking about who you are and what you do...*
I am assuming for the purposes of this article that you really are a subject matter expert. When you are having a self-promotional conversation, you need to get on the table some of your credentials and your track record. Do you have advanced academic degrees, have you written a book, do you have articles published, have you been quoted in the newspaper? Slip these into the conversation. Then segue into your track record. The best way to communicate the positive results you have achieved for your clients is to tell stories. People relate to anecdotal information; stories can foster an emotional connection between listener and storyteller.

- *In a way that causes the listener to both affirm and buy-in to your effectiveness...*
How do you know a listener is affirming you and your words? The person

may nod yes or send you some other nonverbal, body language signal that he or she is with you. I often call this the "touchback." You need to touch the person you are speaking to in some meaningful way—I'm not talking about physical touching, although some people do that well (like Bill Clinton)—so that the listener will touchback. I am talking about making the emotional connection; your listener needs to **feel**, as opposed to **think**, what you are suggesting is a good idea. The person needs to have a visceral, gut reaction to you. Look for the telltale signs of buy-in, such as asking questions and requesting more details.

- *On the spot...*
  No need for deliberation, no need to go home and think it over—you captured the listener right there in the moment. The best indication is if he or she says to you, "I want to talk to you further. I'd like to show you what I have done," or other words to that effect.

The talented self-promoter acquires the status of solution provider in one magical moment. In an entrepreneurial situation, this may cause the listener to identify him or herself as a prospect for your product or service. Once you have built the relationship based on some shared values or experiences, you must advance it so that you are zeroing in on your goal of being recognized as the solution provider. To advance the relationship, you need to:

1. Listen actively.

2. Be safe and comfortable.

3. Be interesting and likable.

4. Make the other person feel like he or she is the most fascinating person in the room.

5. Find intersections between what the other person is telling you about him or herself and your products and services—in other words, connect the dots.

If you can master these skills, you will be able to move an acquaintance, whether it's by phone or face-to-face, from stranger to prospect in a single conversation. As small business people, we are in the position of having to find the client and deliver the services. Balancing these two functions in a profitable way is what differentiates the small businesses that survive from the other 90 percent that disappear within the first year. Expediting the client acquisition process is a key strategy in this juggling act. Mastering the fine art of self-promotion is an indispensable tool that will make a world of difference. In this situation, it really is all about you, baby!

Paige Stover Hague, Esq. is the owner of several Boston-based communications companies that provide strategic planning, public relations, marketing, and business development services to professional services firms, small businesses, speakers, and authors. She is brought in by CEOs and owner/managers throughout the United States to consult and conduct programs and retreats that launch or further company-wide initiatives that affect the way employees and stakeholders think about every aspect of their business. The reach of her presentations touches financial operations, human capital allocations, product development, and employee engagement. She also presents continuing education programs for lawyers, accountants, and financial advisors on art succession planning. She is co-author of *Life is Short, Art is Long– Maximizing Estate Planning Strategies for Collectors of Art, Antiques and Collectibles* (Wealth Management Press 2007).

Stover Hague is a graduate of Duke University and Nova Southeastern University Law School and a member of the Florida and Massachusetts bars. For more information, please visit www.IctusInitiave.com.

Leveraging Influential Connections

By Daniel Waintrup

I am in the financial services business and my role is to generate qualified leads for investment managers. Our company works with high net worth individuals and my job is to identify people whom I suspect have an appropriate nest egg of investable assets and then build a relationship that might lead to moving some money to our company. I pursue these people in two ways: I try to meet them directly using networking strategies, and I also try to identify people who have influential connections who, in turn, are able to introduce me to the kind of people I can turn into prospects. My goal is to meet people who socialize or work with the rich and famous and build a relationship with them so that they bring me into their circle, making introductions that I can leverage for business purposes. Sometimes these people are prominent CEOs and leaders in the business community, sometimes they are people who are active in social, charitable, and cultural affairs, and sometimes they are genuine celebrities.

One thing I learned very early by working with people in this socio-economic demographic is that nothing meaningful is going to happen until you have earned their trust and they perceive that you are a "stand-up" guy with total integrity who will not jeopardize or abuse their contacts in any way. One little misstep can have significant consequences. It takes a little time to build this level of trust and to get these "influencers" to open up their Rolodex and social calendar for you. But once they do, referrals start rolling in, and business prospecting takes on more of a social dynamic than the rigors of old fashioned cold-calling, which I truly don't think even works in this socio-economic group. They do business in a closed community of trusted professionals who have proven themselves by working with other members of their social network. You can only break in by being "sponsored" by somebody else in the network.

So, how do you meet someone who has the right connections and is influential enough to help you in your business or career? Step one is to identify the person who has access to the people you want to meet.

As a former collegiate tennis player and teaching professional, I decided John McEnroe was someone I should try to meet. Throughout his illustrious career on the men's professional tour, I had always admired McEnroe for the virtuosity and dynamic nature of his game. His confrontational behavior, frequent on-court outbursts, and fiery personality only made him more appealing and intriguing to me. As he has made the transition from one of the greatest players in the history of men's tennis to arguably one of the most knowledgeable and charismatic tennis commentators on TV today, my respect for him has only grown. I firmly believed that if I could somehow meet John, if I could find a way to network with an individual with his level of influence and contacts, it would open up an enormous world of the kind of people I needed to know.

I also realized that if I was fortunate enough to meet John McEnroe, I would have to quickly find a way to establish some kind of rapport with him. I'd have to get him to connect with me, like me, or remember me so that I could lay the foundation for advancing the relationship in hopes that he might consider putting in a good word for me with the right people.

But before I could make those connections, I needed to actually meet McEnroe. When I was worrying over the best strategy to do so, my mother said to me, "One step at a time, bubby, one step at a time. First get your foot in the door, and then...."

"But I need a plan, Mom! How in the world am I going to meet a celebrity like him?" I lamented.

My mother thought for a moment, "I'm certain someone famous like John McEnroe has a favorite charity or fundraising event he likes to attend every year. Do some research....wasn't it you who taught me how to use Google?"

My mother is a smart woman. I did some investigative work and found out that, indeed, there were certain charities that "Johnny Mac" supported. One that he recently became involved with was called Tenacity. Based out of my hometown in Boston, Massachusetts, the organization was helping thousands of inner city kids improve their literacy skills through a curriculum that involved reading and tennis instruction. Tenacity was hosting their annual fundraising event in a few months and organizing a pro-am round-robin for anyone who wanted to play and contribute to this good cause. Mr. McEnroe was going to be involved.

Here was my opportunity. I would attend the event and see if I could meet him. And I took it one step further. I called up the organization and told them, "I think what you're doing is terrific, and I have no problem writing a check to play in your tennis event, but it would be great if the tournament director could give me one round with John."

Tenacity agreed and it seemed like I had come up with the perfect plan. I'd be able to hit a few balls with him, get to talk to the man a little and, hopefully, make an impression.

I have to admit I didn't sleep very well the night before the event! John was one of my idols; would I be so nervous playing with him that I would swing and miss the ball completely? Would I do something dumb that would not make a good impression?

The day of the event finally came and as I waited on court for John to arrive I was excited. This was my big opportunity and I had my little speech all ready to go.

"I've devised the perfect plan," I thought to myself.

As I hit a few practice serves, the tournament director came over to give me the bad news: Mr. McEnroe had been unexpectedly delayed in New York, and would be unable to play in the tournament.

While I was initially stunned and depressed, I knew I couldn't dwell on this setback. I was still going to playing doubles with tennis legends like Mats Wilander (former French Open Champion), and Pat Cash (former Wimbledon Champion), and I wanted to enjoy the opportunity to play with these tennis greats.

Beyond that, I also knew that to be successful in marketing and sales, and in meeting influential people, you always have to have a plan B.

And I had one.

In the previous research I had done on "Johnny Mac," I had discovered that he was going to be in town the following month to sign copies of his best selling autobiography, *You Cannot Be Serious.*

Knowing I was going to have another opportunity to meet him, I devised another plan. I would buy a copy of his book and get in line like everyone else. Unfortunately, time would not be on my side. I would have no more than 60 seconds to make a connection with him. Certainly, it wasn't the best case scenario but one that I would have to deal with. Of course, I did have one unique thing going for me that I hoped would be something John would remember me for: like him, I was also an author, recently publishing my own autobiography (although my editor has told me countless times that it's actually a "humorous memoir"), *It's Not My Fault, or Can a Rabbi's Son Find Happiness as a Tennis Pro?*

I would find out soon if that was enough. As I approached the table where he was signing autographs, I quickly pulled out a copy of his book and slid it in front of him. He seemed bored out of his mind. I wondered how many of these book signings he did every year. But I was running out of time. He had finished signing my book. It was time to make my move.

"John, it's been so great watching you play over the years. I must admit, however, I think I enjoy your TV commentary at Wimbledon and the U.S. Open even more."

"Thanks a lot. I appreciate it," he said, growing a little more animated.

"I'm such a big fan, I wanted to give you something—maybe a few laughs—a copy of my book."

I slid it on the table in front of him and waited for his response. My worries were misconceived. John looked at the book placed down on the table in front of him. He studied the cover photo of me kneeling in a synagogue next to my father, dressed in full rabbinical garb, and laughed.

"Great! Good luck with the book, man."

"Yeah, thanks. I've been promoting it all over the country, done a lot of radio and T.V. It's been fun."

"Hey, give me a call sometime. I know a lot of people." He smiled and winked.

"Thanks, John. I'll do that."

The other strategy that has worked for me in my effort to meet influential people is to serve on Boards of Directors of charitable organizations. This process usually begins with support of the organization, and that means both financial support (writing checks) and volunteerism. One of the great things about this country is that if you are willing to put on a tuxedo and buy two tickets to an organization's annual fundraising gala, you have just gotten yourself into a prime networking environment with a whole roomful of movers and shakers in your community. Now, you need the skills to work the room once you're there; but buying the gala tickets completely eliminates the cold-calling problem.

You can have an even greater impact if you are willing to buy an entire table at the gala. If you buy a table, the chairperson of the event will, at some point in the evening, come over to you and introduce himself and thank you for your support. All you have to do is leverage the moment. The other benefit of buying a table is that it's a great way to entertain key employees, indispensable vendors, new client prospects, and important strategic partners.

Once you buy the gala tickets, you are on the mailing list. You will probably get the organization's newsletter and you will want to use this to look for opportunities to volunteer. In my case, it generally makes sense to help with the tennis and golf events, but I have worked on other initiatives as well. If writing or graphic design is your forte, sign up to help with the newsletter. If you're good with numbers, volunteer to work with the Treasurer. You need to join a committee that will allow you to get to know the other volunteers and, more importantly, show them that you are organized, resourceful, a good team player, committed to the cause and that you will do whatever needs to get done. If you become a superstar volunteer, trust me, within a year you will be invited to join the board.

I don't think people generally understand the incredible power of volunteerism. It allows you to showcase your special talents, demonstrate your leadership capability and increase your visibility with the power players in an organization very quickly. The most dramatic example of volunteerism that I am aware of is Madeleine Albright. Her first paid job in politics was in the White House. Prior to that time, she was simply a volunteer—including her entire tenure in Senator Ed Muskie's presidential campaign. All of her political connections were the direct result of relationships she made while serving on the Board of Directors at her children's private school in suburban Washington D.C. She met some very influential people serving on that board and she was able to leverage those connections. Soon, more connections grew out of the initial relationships, all the way to becoming Secretary of State. Madeleine is clearly a pro.

Maybe I am just lazy, but I would rather do things the easy way. It just does not make any sense to me to try to cold-call people and sell myself on the phone in a market demographic where this approach has an extremely low probability of success. I find it a lot easier to schmooze my way into a meaningful conversation with someone in a social setting and break the ice over cocktails or a game of tennis.

Daniel Waintrup, a.k.a. "the Rabbi's Son," is a former tennis teaching pro at one of New England's most exclusive country clubs. He was a nationally ranked player at Temple University, a ranked New England Men's Singles player in the 1980's and 90's, and the 2005 Men's Singles Champion at the Palm Beach Country Club. A featured media personality and professional speaker, Waintrup provides humorous commentary on the topics of tennis, business, networking, self-promotion, and the art of winning—both in life and on the court. In between speaking, writing, and providing tennis analysis on sports talk programs, he is presently working on the screen adaptation of his book, Its Not My Fault - *Can A Rabbi's Son Find Happiness as a Tennis Pro?* For more information, please visit www. DanWaintrup.com.

Chapter 7

Developing a Sales Process
Two Systems That Work
By Ron Finklestein

You've read dozens of great ways to generate quality leads to grow your business. Hopefully you have already started to implement many of the marketing strategies and tactics in this book and you are beginning to see seeing results. Now what do you do? How do you convert the leads from your marketing actions into revenue? The purpose of this chapter is to help you understand and create a similar process to close the sale as you created to generate interest in your product or service.

Your pipeline is filling up but you are not closing as much business as you expected. There is a reason for this. Inexperienced business owners and non-professional sales people don't understand the sales process and how to quickly qualify and disqualify potential customers. Qualifying means there is a need for your product or service and the prospect agrees there is a need, that they have buying authority to make a purchasing decision, and that they have the budget to spend on your product or service.

In this article I am going to talk about how to move this process very quickly. This is *"The Platinum Rule®."* The Platinum Rule allows you to "treat others the way they want to be treated" by identifying their behavioral style, thereby increasing your personal sales effectiveness and closing more business.

Before we get into the details of this system, I want you to document your sales process. If you don't have one, you need to create one. Ask yourself how you put prospects into your selling pipeline. What tactics in this book did you use and how did you implement them to create and fill your pipeline? Once you understand this, you have solved half the challenge. When you find what works, create measurable, repeatable, and predictable processes so you do not have to go through this process every year. Find what works for you and stick with it.

Creating measurable, repeatable, and predictable processes applies to the sales process as well. Your goal is to develop a sales process that gets you to "Yes" much more often and to "No" much more quickly. How do you do that? There are three steps to this process.

First, it is critical that you gain agreement on the agenda. You are there to help them make a buying decision and they need to understand and agree that you are there for that purpose. If this obstacle is not addressed, anything after this point is going to be a problem. This can be accomplished, during the opening of the sales call, by saying, "We are here today to... and at the end of our discussion, together we will determine if there is a next step and what that next step is. Are you okay with that?" This sets the tone and texture of the meeting as requiring some form of action at the end. This action can be "No, I am not interested" or, "Yes, let's move forward."

Second, both you and your prospect must agree on how the product or service will solve this need. Agreeing there is a need addresses the intellectual side of the sales presentation. The emotional side investigates the impact of the need (or what I refer to as pain).

Let's use insurance as an example. Your prospect is looking to buy insurance for a specific reason: lower insurance premiums, gain initial protection or better protection. Those are intellectual reasons. To better understand the pain (prospects reasons for making a change) you might ask second level questions such as, "What would happen if you did not find a better price?" or, "Why is it important to have this protection now?" or, "What would happen if you continue without protection?" These questions get the prospect emotionally involved in the buying process. You are helping them understand the impact of not making a decision—the real reasons for buying. Once you understand the real reasons for buying, you tailor the rest of your presentation to address these needs. "If I can give you the same protection for a lower price, what would you do with the extra money?" We help them to understand what would happen with the money they save.

The third aspect of the sales process is the decision making process. After you and the prospect have gained agreement on the purpose of the meeting and the pain has been identified and investigated, you are now in the position to do what any good sales representative does—help the prospect make a buying decision.

The decision process is a natural byproduct of creating a good selling process. Many times during the decision process, the prospect will put obstacles or objections in front of you. Objections are questions or concerns that have not been answered during the sales presentation. Objections are a very good thing because this is the prospect giving you permission to ask further questions to gain clarity to move the buying process forward. Many times there is no asking for the order. If done right, the prospect will ask you for the next step. Naturally the next step is to sign the order.

Creating a sales process using The Platinum Rule is very powerful. Dr. Tony Alessandra describes The Platinum Rule like this:

We have all heard of the Golden Rule—and many people aspire to live by it. The Golden Rule is not a panacea. Think about it: "Do unto others as you would have them do unto you." The Golden Rule implies the basic assumption that other people would like to be treated the way that you would like to be treated.

The alternative to the Golden Rule is the Platinum Rule: "Treat others the way they want to be treated." The Platinum Rule accommodates the feelings of others. The focus of relationships shifts from "this is what I want, so I'll give everyone the same thing" to "let me first understand what they want and then I'll give it to them."

The Platinum Rule defines four behaviors styles: Director, Socializer, Relater, and Thinker. Each style has certain behavior characteristics and these characteristics are observable. The personality of every single person can fit within one of these four broad categories. While on a day-to-day basis we might move closer to one style or another, every person has one general category that dominates his or her personality. As we observe people's behaviors, we can adapt our behavior to allow us to treat the other person the way they want to be treated to maintain rapport and effectiveness in our relationships. This leads to developing more sales faster.

The Platinum Rule teaches:
• Why people do what they do. .

- What they need in order to do their best.
- About the strengths and weaknesses of their personal style.

The power of using The Platinum Rule is that it is easy to learn and easy to use. It has a 30-year track record and is being used by companies all over the world. Companies use The Platinum Rule in sales, marketing, customer service, business strategy, and process improvement, to name a few, to improve the effectiveness of the entire organization.

Because of its history and track record, The Platinum Rule provides concrete actions and steps you can implement to become more effective in dealing with suspects, prospects, and customers.

What makes it so simple is that it is structured around three specific observable behaviors:

- **The Verbal**: the actual words they use – the content.

- **The Vocal**: the way they say the words – inflection, intonation, and emphasis.

- **The Visual**: the way they subconsciously communicate their intentions through body language, facial expressions, and gestures.

Through the simple act of listening and watching what they say and how they say it, you can quickly and easily understand their behavior style and how they want to be treated. Your ability to adapt your behavior and meet them where they are is where theory and action meet.

The goal of The Platinum Rule is personal chemistry and productive relationships that results in more sales, faster. You don't have to change your personality. You simply have to understand what drives people and recognize the options you have when dealing with them.

Everyone possesses the qualities of each style to various degrees and everyone has a dominant style. The key to using The Platinum Rule is in understanding what a person's dominant behavioral style is and treating him/her appropriately.

Here is a very basic breakdown of the behavior styles defined by The Platinum Rule: Directors are driven by two governing needs: to control and achieve. They are goal-oriented go-getters who are most comfortable when they are in charge of people and situations.

Socializers are friendly and enthusiastic and like to be where the action is. They thrive on admiration, acknowledgment, and compliments. They are idea-people who excel at getting others excited about their vision.

Thinkers are analytical, persistent, systematic people who enjoy problem-solving. They are detail-oriented, which makes them more concerned with content than style. Thinkers are task-oriented people who enjoy perfecting processes and working toward tangible results.

Relaters are warm and nurturing individuals. They are the most people-oriented of the four styles. Relaters are excellent listeners, devoted friends, and loyal employees. They are good planners, persistent workers, and good with follow-through.

How can you apply this knowledge to grow your business? When you identify the behavioral styles of your clients and prospects, you will know how to sell to them by treating them the way they want to be treated. Let me give you some examples:

Directors are goal-oriented. When selling to Directors, the best approach is to give them the headline first, focusing on results. Since they like to be in control, let them give you permission to tell the rest of your story (if they like the headline).

Socializers like to have fun and they will sell themselves if you can get them excited about your products and services. Your message should focus on the outcomes they will experience, the fun they will have, and the recognition they will receive for being visionary enough to implement your solution.

Thinkers don't like to be wrong, so you need to be prepared when selling to a thinker. They want to know that your facts and figures are correct. They will want to know the details behind the methodology and how the results were documented. Don't press a Thinker for a decision. They will decide when they are ready. Build credibility by doing what you said you were going to do.

Relaters want to know that you care for them. Relaters are concerned about the impact that the change will have on the team (family.) Spend time building a relationship.

The power of The Platinum Rule is that it is easy to learn and implement—but in order to experience great success, it does take some practice.
To Your Success!

Ronald Finklestein, President of AKRIS, LLC, The Small Business Success Expert, business coach, consultant, speaker, author, and trainer, has published two books: *Celebrating Success! Fourteen Ways to a Successful Company and The Platinum Rule to Small Business Mastery.* **His articles have been published by entrepreneur.com, thestreet.com, and msnbc.com. He has been interviewed The Training and Success Network (TSTN), been profiled in The Akron Beacon Journal and quoted in a variety of newspaper articles. He also co founded the Celebrating Success! conference. Finklestein is available for coaching and consulting and for speaking engagements, workshops, and seminars. You can contact him at info@yourbusinesscoach.net or (330) 990–0788. Sign up for his newsletter at http://www.yourbusinesscoach.net.**

The Platinum Rule® is a registered trademark of Dr. Tony Alessandra. Used with permission. For more information on The Platinum Rule, see http://www.alessandra.com/products/prrsproducts.asp

About Ron Finklestein

"Small Business Success Expert" "Entrepreneur." "Passionate" "Leader." "Motivator." "Get Results." "Team Builder." This is how business leaders and clients describe Ron.

After a successful consulting career, Ron has spent the past 6 years building his business AKRIS LLC and helping entrepreneurs and business owners build their businesses by helping them solve the tough problems that hold them back. Ron is called The Small Business Success Expert by his clients because of his passion for their success and his knowledge of business. Ron is passionate about making a difference in people's lives by helping them to achieve their business and personal goals and dreams.

Ron has experience in working with businesses across a wide range of industries and on every aspect of a business, from information technology to marketing, leadership to sales, allowing him to offer practical and proven ideas and strategies to improve any business. Ron knows and understands that all successful people exhibit seven behaviors and he has build products to help implement these behaviors in businesses of all sizes. Because of the depth of breadth of Ron's experience, he can quickly and decisively see and identify business and personal challenges, identify innovative solutions and create opportunities out of most any problem.

Ron is well known in the business community for his leadership abilities, creativity, innovation and energy. He co-created a business conference in Northeast Ohio called Celebrating Success! NEO Business Conference (www.neobusinessconference.org). For the last several years, this conference showcased over 60 successful businesses and allowed each business the opportunity to share what they did to be successful (with an emphasis on lessons learned).

Ron has an established reputation for building strong relationships and using those relationships to help others enhance their own personal and professional success. Ron is a frequent speaker and presenter on various business topics including *Building Businesses, Leadership, The Platinum Rule®, Attitudes and Behaviors of Success, Sales and Marketing, Entrepreneurship, Business Strategies and Business Mastery.* Ron is involved with numerous business, non-profit organizations and initiatives as part of his personal commitment to personal and professional growth and the growth of his clients.

Ron has owned his business since 2002, AKRIS LLC. AKRIS LLC focused on helping grow and improve small businesses:

- Twenty-five years of Fortune 1000 consulting experience

- Author of Celebrating Success! 14 Ways to Create a Successful Company (www.yourbusinesscoach.net). This is a study of small businesses and what they do to be successful.

- Ron is also coauthor of The Platinum Rule for Small Business Mastery (www.celebrating-success.com) with Dr. Tony Alessandra and Scott Zimmerman. This book helps business owners understand how to get the best from employees in your organization.

- Owner of AKRIS LLC, which provided business coaching and consulting services to business owners and entrepreneurs to help them build a better business.

- Executive Director of Business Leadership Association, a nonprofit that raises money for leadership training.

- Creator of The AKRIS Business Mastery Advisory Board (www.businessmasterynow.com). This board allows business owners to learn from, grow and prosper by understanding that multiple minds are more effective in making effective decisions than any single mind.

Currently, Ron resides in Akron, Ohio where he is President of AKRIS LLC. He spends his time consulting, coaching small business owners to greater success, writing and speaking about how to implement success strategies in business.

Over the years Ron has spoken to or for business groups, chambers of commerce, community groups, associations, in-house training programs, continuing education programs, seminars, lunch and learns, workshops, etc. Participants and attendees have described Ron as "energizing", "enthusiastic", "fun", "engaging", "motivational", "thoughtful", "informative", "inspiring", "effective", and "motivating." If you are interested in learning how Ron can help you in your business or to have Ron speak to your business, team, organization, association or group, contact him at (330) 990-0788 or ron@akris.net.